flying saucers rock 'n' roll

REFIGURING AMERICAN MUSIC A series edited by Ronald Radano and Josh Kun
Charles McGovern, contributing editor

Flying Saucers Rock 'n' Roll

conversations with
Unjustly Obscure Rock 'n' Soul Eccentrics

Jake Austen, editor

Duke University Press
Durham + London 2011

Printed in the United States of America

on acid-free paper ∞

Designed by Jennifer Hill

Typeset in Chaparral Pro by Tseng Information Systems, Inc.

Library of Congress Cataloging-in-Publication Data

appear on the last printed page of this book.

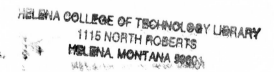

To Maiya and Noble,

who thrived and blossomed

perhaps despite,

but likely because,

their lullabies and

nursery rhymes were

"Signifying Monkey,"

"Wooly Bully,"

and "Male Stripper."

Contents

You find ways to identify friends before they're friends. Now there are phone apps for it and breathalyzers, but you used to have to do it by observation. It wasn't difficult, because even when you're a kid the important things stick out like flags.

I met Chris in art class. He had a stupid grin and spent most of his time making bongs and cock-and-balls out of clay. He had a stupid nickname for every person and item in his life, and sometimes used "carny" talk so teachers and parents wouldn't understand him. I went to his house one time and he pulled a giant green bong out from under his bed and torched it up. He had a rubber hose rigged up so he could blow the smoke out the window even in the winter and his folks wouldn't smell it.

Jon used to hang out with a girl I knew who threw frequent keggers. I met him at the spot one day, and he said he was going to hike up the mountain to the reservoir and hang out. We got to talking about how the city's water supply was readily accessible up there, under a big rubber membrane you could jump on like a trampoline. I had occasionally fantasized about putting a couple of hits of acid in there, just to see what happened. Out of nowhere Jon said, "You could put some acid in there . . ." That's how I knew Jon was okay.

I saw this kid at the guitar shop in a homemade

T-shirt with spray paint stencil letters, and I was pretty sure he was okay. Turns out he played guitar and drew comics and basically everything that makes a guy okay. His name was Randy, and the first thing he asked me was "Have you heard the Sex Pistols?"

When I was a little kid if I saw another kid with a copy of *Mad* magazine or a Rat Fink sticker I knew I could talk to him. In junior high, it would have been *Fangoria*; in high school *National Lampoon*; and in college *Slash*, *No Mag*, or *Coolest Retard*. Nobody at my college read any of those, though, so I spent a lot of time in the city. In town I saw a lot of people and I could usually tell. I could tell when somebody was one of us.

Look through any issue of *Roctober*, and you can tell it's one of us. *Roctober* has a way of cutting through the crap and getting right to what makes you take an interest in a something. We love awesome bands and crazy culture icons, each with a singular mania, and we love that *Roctober* is ready to articulate them for us. Bands with primate members, masked bands, bands of all little people, bands from space or wrapped in aluminum foil; bands of sock puppets, drag queens, naive artists, junk prophets, voodoo priests, and trannies with ineffectual makeup. . . . Whether inspired, depraved, obsessed, or moronic, *Roctober* lets them each shine their unique light on us, giving them patient attention and enough time to make their cases. Not looking for excuses to dismiss the easily dismissed, but rather looking for reasons to take them at face value. *Roctober* likes all the things you like, and for all the same reasons.

Roctober has a homemade shirt, a stupid grin, and a bong under the bed. *Roctober* wonders aloud if it could get the whole city tripping balls. *Roctober* is one of us.

STEVE ALBINI
Chicago, Illinois
April 10, 2010

Acknowledgments

It would be impossible to name all the people, publications, and musicians that have helped and inspired us over the years. Though we've certainly missed more than we are remembering, the contributors to this book would like to acknowledge the following for their assistance in assembling the pieces included in this collection:

Jessica Abel, Bob Abrahamian, Jennifer Alexander, Pedro Bell, donnie l. betts, Maggie Brown, Chris Butler, Paul Crayton, Robert Dayton, Derek Erdman, Art Fein, Gary Pig Gold, John Greenfield, Dave Hoekstra, Barbara Holt, Anthony Illarde, Lux Interior, Steve Krakow, Kelly Kuvo, Michael Lazarus, Miriam Linna, Joe Losurdo, Jason Lutes, Mario, William McCurtin, Annabel Merinuk, Thora Merinuk, Billy Miller, Phil Milstein, Sergio Mims, Jason Mitchell, James Moore, Eric Nix, Chuck Nolan, John Porcellino, Bob Pruter, Quintron and Pussycat, Noah Schaeffer, Marcus Shaffer, Paul Slifer, Dan Springer, Rob Syers, Yuval Taylor, Nick Tosches, Claude Trenier, Milt Trenier, Skip Trenier, Alex Wald, Jason Walker, Martin Willis, Ken Wissoker, Tommie Wix, Rick Wojcik, Ken Wong, Caroline Shirley Woodward, Harry Young, and the spaceboys of Zolar X.

And our deep gratitude goes out to anyone who has contributed to, or read, *Roctober* over the last two decades.

Hi Yo, Silver!

Although I welcome clichés in silent films, country lyrics, and *Archie* comics, I'm no fan of them in real life. When musicians or professors I know become entangled with, respectively, heroin or an undergrad, I don't pass judgment about their morality, professionalism, or weak wills, but rather I feel embarrassed about their unoriginality. By this standard, I should have been pretty ill at ease when I found myself in a rundown hospital on the Southside of Chicago, seated at the deathbed of a wizened old bluesman, choking out his final wishes in rural dialect.

Several factors, however, redeemed me from stereotypicality. The singer was not imparting rough-hewn wisdom to make me a better man, not trying to guide me toward the crossroads where the mystic secrets of the blues would be revealed. He wasn't sacrificing himself for my Caucasian redemption, and he didn't anoint me with coolness by sharing his essential "soul." Cool was not a commodity that the Black Lone Ranger, who was instructing me about which mask he wanted to wear at his funeral, had to share. When he rode the number 28 bus in his powder-blue Lone Ranger outfit, plastic guns by his side, a ragged, hand-sewn mask covering his face, urban teens laughed at him. Even in his element—blues clubs such as the Checkerboard Lounge, in which he'd become a fixture over the decades—the Ranger was begrudgingly allotted only five minutes a night on stage with the band, singing one of the three Muddy Waters songs in his repertoire, receiving modest applause and no pay.

But despite being an outsider even among marginalized groups, the Black Lone Ranger had earned a place in Chicago blues history. Sadly, that place seemed to be a dark corner, solely consisting of faded memories made murkier by Old Style beer and Newport smoke; an oral history asterisk to tales of headliners and icons. And it was in regard to this fate of obscurity that the Ranger offered me something significant: a sense of purpose.

For the better part of the last twenty years, I've been able to gather a group of amateur music historians to document scores of forgotten figures, using the most meager of media outlets: do-it-yourself zines, community radio, and public access television. While we haven't been Alan Lomaxes or Harry Smiths (our documentations don't redefine music history), we've avoided the music magazine traps of letting publicists and advertisers determine editorial content. Although *Roctober* will never be blessed with the budgets or circulation of the mainstream periodicals, it will never be cursed with oppressive word counts or demographic limitations. And even if we've never wielded enough power to put much money in the pockets of our interviewees (or in ours, for that matter), we take satisfaction in the fact that Google no longer mocks them with a smug "Your search did not match any documents."

The author with Black Lone Ranger.

I started publishing *Roctober* magazine when I was a student at the Rhode Island School of Design in 1992, if you can use the terms *publishing* and *magazine* to refer to a messy clump of stapled Xeroxes ornamented with crayon marks. I had been making photocopied comics, joke books, and newsletters since grammar school, but my inspiration for *Roctober* came less from having printers' ink in my veins than from having a typewritten interview in my backpack and no place to publish it. Weeks earlier the six-foot-seven Sleepy LaBeef, a rockabilly behemoth, had played at Chan's Egg-roll and Jazz, a massive Chinese restaurant in Woonsocket, Rhode Island. Motivated by a call for submissions from some punk rock locals for their proposed zine, some friends and I decided to go to the show and interview Mr. LaBeef. I had enjoyed the singer's resonating baritone several times in Chicago bars, and his down-home charisma, 1950s rockabilly credentials, and thousand-song repertoire held the promise of an amazing backstory.

Roctober number 1 (1992). Cover art: Michael Lazarus.

By pre-Internet standards, I had pretty good research resources: Brown's Ivy League archive at my disposal and access to a network of obsessive record and magazine collectors. But I was surprised to discover that there was little in-formation to be found on a man I considered a legend. It was dis-appointing, but simultaneously exciting; while it was wrong that history had ignored Sleepy, we were in a position to correct that injustice.

The interview went well. But the zine we originally did it for—as went many of the best-laid plans of people who rocked tattoos and piercings before you could get them in malls—never happened. Not wanting to let our work go unseen, and realizing that the best resource I had as an art school kid was a deep pool of talented peers, I asked my classmates to contribute comics, essays, illustrations, and origami designs as side dishes to the LaBeef main course. Thus, the first issue of *Roctober* was born.

Since then we've published almost fifty issues, most with color covers, averaging around 100 pages. Circulation ebbs and flows (peaking around 5,000, but usually settling at around half that) depending on the health of record stores, independent distributors, and the influence of reviewers. But we've always had a hearty base of fervent subscribers, and have never been at a loss for profoundly gifted (unpaid) contributors. We've featured work by some of the best underground cartoonists (including Jessica Abel, Chris Ware, and Ivan Brunetti, who let us publish his surprisingly unrepulsive audition samples for the *Nancy* newspaper strip); over 25,000 borderline-worthless record reviews (a not untypical example: our assessment of the band Orso read simply, "Bore-so."); exhaustive examinations of theoretical genres (like "robot rock"); and an ongoing exploration of everything Sammy Davis Jr. ever sang, said, or did. But the heart of the magazine has always been the lengthy conversations with lost, ignored, or forgotten artists. *Time Out* or *Spin* might ask a writer to boil down an interview to a word-count of 2,000, 700, or fewer words. If a *Roctober* conversation yields 20,000 worthwhile words, then that uncondensed epic is seeing print!

The mighty Black Lone Ranger was not the perfect *Roctober* interview (his piece is not included in this collection). This is in part because myth and mystery were so important to him (his tall tales outnumbered truths), but also because his low-key career did not have an epic arc that reveals itself in a lengthy, relaxed conversation. We've had some of our best luck with folks whose work might be familiar, but whose biography is unknown (like Sam the Sham of "Wooly Bully" fame); with figures once embraced by the press, but abandoned so long ago they deserve reexamination (David Allan Coe); or with stellar talents like Billy Lee Riley who traveled in the shadows of legends, never getting the big break themselves. But often our best interviews come from the true fringes. A band such as Zolar X may have expected mainstream success, but their quirks, ridiculous antics, and bizarre lyrics understandably never got them beyond their small core audiences. And sometimes the most interesting subjects have been genuine unknowns, like Guy Chookoorian, whose success came in a genre so peripheral (Armenian American novelty parody records), it nearly qualifies as ether.

To deliver these interviews, *Roctober*'s brilliant group of contributors work countless hours on articles that require them to be researchers, private investigators, interrogators, psychologists, and in some cases, prison chaplains. In addition to a shared desire to bring these stories to light, each writer brings along his (or, in rare cases, her) own motivations. Gentleman John Battles values the relationships he builds with his heroes. One could say he collects semifamous friends the way he collects rare records and monster movie memorabilia. But a more accurate assessment is that he offers profound loyalty to people used to being screwed over. Before his recent career revival Roky Erickson, garage rock legend and electroshock therapy victim, spent decades with only a handful of people he could trust, and he counted Battles among those few.

Though I suspect his record collection rivals Battles's, Ken Burke is more a proselytizer than a procurer; spreading the rockabilly gospel is his sacred mission. A fine musician himself, Burke's tireless work tracking down the genre's heroes, villains, and scrubs are acts of religious fervor undertaken with the precision and dedication of an illuminated manuscript transcription.

Other *Roctober* writers are driven by more personal but no less profound motivations. James Porter grew up in Pill Hill, a middle-class African American neighborhood on Chicago's South Side, where many working musicians make their homes. His consumption of pop culture involved great intensity (every music-themed article, TV show, and radio broadcast meticulously catalogued and cross-referenced in his photographic memory and scrapbooks) and broad diversity (inspired by his father, a Chicago cop with a love for country and western). Today, when James engages a veteran musician in deep conversation, he is not so much delighting in nostalgia but rather filling in the puzzle pieces of his own youth, figuring out what made him the only kid in his schools in the seventies whose tastes extended back to the fifties, across oceans, and beyond color lines rarely crossed in notoriously segregated Chicago.

Conversely, Jonathan Poletti is as interested in scattering his puzzle pieces as putting them in place. Unlike Gentleman John, he seems just as satisfied if his intense research and journalistic doggedness creates for him enemies rather than friends of his subjects. Mr. Poletti makes innumerable phone calls, maintains thorny correspondences, and tracks down obscure, unpopular texts in pursuit of profiles that ultimately seem to be less about their subjects and more about exploring and deconstructing his own, often ugly, notions of personal, gender, and sexual politics. Ultimately, I expect Jonathan will someday publish a collection of his studies of Zolar X, Jobriath, Lenny Bruce, Wendy Carlos, and the rest of his obsessions, which will collectively read as one of the most jarring, vivid autobiographies ever published.

My ulterior motives are a bit more selfish than those of my colleagues on righteous journeys of gallant service or redemptive introspection. I've never been a particularly sensitive soul when it comes to rock 'n' roll consumption, foregoing the poets and balladeers for the more intense and absurd corners of noisemaking. Not long after launching the magazine, I realized that my greatest reward for tracking down howling R&B shouters, ridiculous gay disco art freaks, and bizarre garage rock eccentrics is that their untold histories and far-out philosophies are usually as wildly pleasurable as their music. To a degree I may be helping these artists tell their tales as a significant service to art and history. But mainly I do it because I *really* dig being entertained. Having Sugar Pie DeSanto share stories of warding off James Brown's advances felt like watching an awesome 3-D movie. Being eye to eye with Oscar Brown Jr. as he critiqued the U.S. government with language that bordered on sedition was positively thrilling. And hearing Paul Zone vividly describe the Fast's stage show, in which breakfast cereal and number-2 pencils were substituted for pyrotechnics, made me experience the kind of pure, honest laughter that comes too rarely in adult life.

Roctober launched at a good time to start a zine. Our notoriously messy layout has always embraced the literal cut-and-paste aesthetics of classic zines, but working in the desktop publishing, cheap Xeroxing, and computer-scanning era has its advantages over the purple-fingered mimeograph period, or the days of sticky Smith Corona typewriter keys. In the early '90s, with some help from Seth Freidman's righteous revival of the *Factsheet 5* zine guide, there was an explosion of thousands of small-press publications, predecessors to today's millions of blogs and specialty websites. High school kids, music geeks, and shut-ins the world over became accustomed to mailing off an envelope stuffed with a few well-concealed dollars and waiting a wildly variable period of time to get an off-the-grid, quirky publication in return. It didn't hurt that zinedom's main cheerleader, the DIY-centric punk rock scene, was going through an uncomfortable, but lucrative, mainstreaming. At one point during the Green Day–led pop punk boom, *Maximumrocknroll*, the not-for-profit "punk bible," was making so much money that they randomly sent checks for a few hundred dollars to *Roctober* and, I assume, dozens of other zines.

Although *Roctober* was on the surface slicker and more professional-looking than many of its Kinko's-born brethren, several things made it clear that we had more in common with a ninth-grade-girl's-diary zine than with an ultrahip indie rock mag, or MTV-friendly music glossy. The most important of these has always been our refusal to recognize demographic boundaries. We pride ourselves on our ludicrously expansive definition of rock 'n' roll, that includes, but is not limited to, R&B, metal, punk, rap, doo-wop, disco, noise, one-man band music, gospel, jazz, glam, country, big band, and any vaguely rhythmic audio produced by monkeys, little people, or professional baseball players. In addition to this, we strive to stand out by having an approach that is more populist than hipster-ism usually allows. Instead of making readers feel stupid for not knowing about some obscure performer, our writers share their enthusiasm for their subjects in such an infectious way that it holds the interest of those who have yet to, and may never, hear the artist's music. Each interview's introduction is meant to offer welcoming information to the innocently ignorant and artful affirmations to the intimately informed. Readers respond because our kooky subjects are respectfully presented, without a hint of ironic distance, as genius auteurs rather than sideshow spectacles. Never buying into "so-bad-it's-good," the unwritten *Roctober* manifesto makes it clear that any art that isn't boring is high quality. Certainly everything bombastic or colorful is not great; loud, melodramatic music can be unoriginal or insincere enough to elicit yawns despite thunderous volume and lightning-like flash. But genuinely strange, unprecedented, joyfully out-of-kilter work is almost never dull.

We often receive mail stating that *Roctober* is the music magazine for people who thought they were totally over music magazines. And when we are reviewed a frequent theme is that there is something revolutionary about making readers interested in music they didn't think they cared about. This is typified by an excerpt from a *New Disorder* webzine review: "*(Roctober's)* not all punk, or even a little bit punk, but the magazine as a whole couldn't be more punk."

People frequently ask me if *Roctober* will transition to a web-only publication at some point. Obviously, given the current economics of both the music and print industries, this

Roctober number 41 (2005). Cover art: Derek Erdman.

seems like it would make sense, yet our work would not be possible in cyber-zine form. Our virtuoso contributors are willing to toil over articles and interviews without pay in large part for the unique reward of physically holding the work in their hands. Likewise, I would not put in the hours without the prospect of being able to fantasize that I am walking in the footsteps of iconic print magazine editors like *Mad*'s William M. Gaines, *Famous Monsters of Filmland*'s Forry Ackerman, or *Maximumrocknroll*'s Tim Yohannan. I love magazines, and would like to think *Roctober* is an offspring of not only the punk zines I dug in the eighties and the goofier rock magazines I loved from the seventies like *Creem* and *Rock Scene*, but also of the fabled mimeographed sci-fi fanzines that preceded their rock 'n' roll successors. I grew up in awe of the voluminously researched articles in the *New Yorker*, the abstract haikus that were the regional rankings in Wrestling fan mags, the sublime balance between Civil Rights Movement coverage and bikini cheesecake shots in Chicago's own *Jet*, and the glorious absurdity of teenybopper rags, such as *16*, Britain's *Smash Hits*, and Cynthia Horner's *Right On!* (which championed Prince before any other publication). I was blessed to grow up in Chicago, a city that not only had a great public library, with dusty boxes of '60s hippie newspapers and '70s punk magazines in their periodical archives, but also had stores like Larry's, Bob's Newsstand, and Shake, Rattle & Read that made ancient monthlies accessible.

In my mind *Roctober* is as much a publication that honors the history of magazines as the history of rock 'n' roll. Our logo pays homage to *Right On!* We've had tribute covers of *TV Guide*, *Highlights*, and *Famous Monsters*. We published a "swipe" issue, consisting of articles reprinted from legendary, out-of-print music magazines like *Punk, Bomp*, and (my all-time favorite) *Kicks*, supplemented by new interviews with the defunct publications' creators. We've even published a *Mad Magazine* tribute issue so extensive that it led to one of my proudest moments in publishing: receiving a cease-and-desist letter on glorious Alfred E. Neuman stationery. Public Radio often brags of "Driveway Moments," broadcasts so intriguing that listeners remain in parked cars, glued to their radios long after reaching their destinations. *Roctober* is proud of our similar achievements: "Faux Constipation Moments," where our lengthy articles so fascinate a reader that he or she sits on the toilet long after their business is done. As long as there are toilet tanks, twelve-hour between-gig tour van rides, and slow days working retail at record stores, *Roctober* will proudly continue to be a "pulp and staple" publication.

Roctober has given me many gifts over the years, and it's hard to isolate the highlights of the experiences it has allowed me to enjoy. The pieces included in this collection spotlight some of those moments (look for the delightful pornography-fueled event following the David Allan Coe interview), but there are myriad others. On the basis of one seminegative clause in a glowing review of his memoir, Eddie Shaw, the brilliant, self-critical bassist of '60s garage punk band the monks invited me, a stranger, to be the only nonband and nonfamily attendee at the monks' reunion weekend in the Minnesota backwoods. Slack jawed, I enjoyed bonfires, storytelling, and jam sessions with my all-time favorite "lost" band. A visit to the Chicago suburbs to get photos for an article about Jack and Elaine Mulqueen, a couple that hosted a local children's dance show in the '60s, inspired my wife and me to start *Chic-A-Go-Go*, a cult-favorite cable access dance show that we have happily churned out for over 700 consecutive weekly episodes. And spending time sitting in a Skokie deli eating kreplach with Milt Trenier, the jump blues legend who married his way into Chicago suburban Jewishness, was one of the most pleasant afternoons I've ever spent. Simply put, despite having made less money than a nonunion janitor and having put in a lot of ninety-eight-hour workweeks, *Roctober* has given me a profoundly satisfying life. I truly dig sharing the stories, music, and energy of some of the hippest square pegs in music history.

Not long after his bedside directives, the Black Lone Ranger rode off into the sunset. His brother (who was wearing a turban encrusted with costume jewelry when we met) and his sister (who did not dress like a character from a cliffhanger movie serial) were happy to receive the instructions from their mysterious sibling, and the Ranger's funeral was held according to his wishes. Standing over the casket at Taylor's Funeral Home and gazing at the masked man's earthly shell (in full costumed glory, of course), I realized that the Black Lone Ranger had actually offered me more than an opportunity to document his existence. The way he spent years in the shadows of blues clubs waiting for a few minutes of action demonstrated the patience and optimism that define the lengthy careers of never-say-die *Roctober* artists such as the Good Rats, Oscar Brown Jr., and Zolar X. In each case they refused to succumb to negativity, conventional wisdom, and, in some cases, reality. The lesson these icons of obstinacy offer is to never quit, even when you probably should. These days, this kind of quixotic stubbornness can come in handy for anyone committed to print media. It's especially inspirational if you publish a low-circulation zine focusing on cult figures so obscure that they barely have cults.

Although a nice slice of the local blues community came out to the Ranger's service, the Windy City did not pause and hold its breath at his passing the way we did when Studs Terkel, Walter Payton, Harold Washington, or Harry Carey died. In fact, his death was hardly noted save for one poignant obituary in the *Chicago Sun-Times* that respectfully honored most of the Ranger's fanciful mythmaking as fact. I was tremendously pleased to see a much-maligned man championed in mainstream print, and not only because it gave him the dignity he deserved. It also jogged the memories of thousands of clubgoers and Chicago Blues Fest attendees who had seen him in their periphery, and it introduced him to countless others. Most importantly, it helped inscribe his story in recorded history, echoing our magazine's goal of letting the world know that though they may be obscure, odd, and off the beaten track, people like the Black Lone Ranger are real, and their existence is worth noting.

Fortunately for that masked man's legacy there was a *Sun-Times* staffer who knew, and cared, about the Black Lone Ranger's story. That writer was a *Roctober* subscriber.

Oscar Brown Jr.

Oscar Brown Jr. did it all. Though he thought of himself as a songwriter, Columbia Records and a few enthusiastic jazz fans convinced him he was a vocalist. He was a playwright, a poet, an activist, and when called upon he could don the hat of political candidate (including a quixotic run for Congress), TV host (*Jazz Scene U.S.A.*), radio performer (appearing as a teen on

Photo courtesy donnie l. betts.

Studs Terkel's *Secret City*), curator (at Chicago's DuSable Museum of African American History), and actor (including a memorable role in Larry
Cohen's 1996 blaxploitation revamp *Original Gangstas*). Around 1948, as
radio host of *Negro Newsfront*, he earned the billing "America's First Negro
Newscaster." Some see him as a forerunner to socially conscious black
singer-songwriters like Gil Scott-Heron or Meshell Ndegeocello; others
consider him a genuine revolutionary, a man so radical even the Commu-
nists wouldn't take him. As he is a deity in Chicago's black arts community,
it feels blasphemous to worship at just one of Brown's temples, but nonetheless, I'm compelled to highlight his awesome achievements as a lyricist.
His collaboration with Max Roach on 1960's *We Insist: Freedom Now Suite*
was an ambitious, thrilling Civil Rights–themed project. Notable covers of
his compositions include versions of "The Snake" by Al Wilson and Johnny
Rivers, "Brown Baby" by Mahalia Jackson and Lena Horne, and "Dat Dere"
by Rickie Lee Jones and Mel Torme. But like many poets schooled in oral
traditions, his words had the most impact when they came out of his
mouth. His comical dissection of street swagger in "But I Was Cool," his
evocation of a street vendor's cries in "Watermelon Man," and the chilling

rhythmic re-creation of a slave auction in "Bid 'Em In" were masterpieces when performed by their composer.

In our conversation, from early 1996, Mr. Brown tells his amazing story, and demonstrates the rebellious nature that kept him on the fringes despite his tremendous gifts:

Oscar Brown Jr.: I'm a Chicagoan; I grew up in the Chicago public schools, went to Englewood High School and finished there in 1943. I went to about five or six colleges, but I'm still a freshman—I never did quite make it in the university world. However, I did get involved in performing, first in radio as an actor, and I became a newscaster, and finally I became an entertainer, as I am now—that is, a singer, actor, and performer in various media. I had a program called *Negro Newsfront* and it was on for about five or six years from 1947, the latter part of '47, thru about 1952. It was on several stations *(laughs)* 'cause I used to get kicked off the air all the time for being really controversial. I started out on WJJD, which was a station that was sunup to sundown, so my starting time would change during the year, because I was early morning. Then they said they didn't have any more time for me, and I asked my listeners to send in cards and letters so I could try and get a new sponsor. I got so many cards and letters I just took a whole bushel basket full of 'em over to the Parker House sausage company and told Mr. Parker to pick a card—any card . . . read these cards. He became my sponsor, and then the Baldwin Ice Cream Co. was one of my sponsors—these were all little black businesses around. The main sponsor, however, was my father's business, the Midway Television Institute, which was a school that taught refrigeration and radio and television to veterans. Anyway, that's what that newscast was about. It went from WJJD to WGES, which was Al Benson's station, and there it had a big audience because that was a very well-listened-to station, and after that, I had big problems with them. They kicked me off the air, and I went over to WHFC, and I hung in there for a year or so doing both news and DJ work. That was kinda my early beginning.

James Porter: *How did you get kicked off of WGES—a black music station—doing a black-oriented talk show?*

Oscar Brown Jr.: Well, I was very outspoken. I used to have editorial comments that would get me in hot water at the station. I left that and went into the labor movement. I became a program coordinator for the United Packing House Workers of America, that was the organization that represented the people who work in the stockyards. In those days, Chicago was known as the "Hog Butcher of the World," by Carl Sandburg's poetic standards. It was a very exciting job; there were 20,000 people in the district that I was representing, and my job was to conduct programs for women's rights, political actions, civil rights, farm labor relations—the cows and pigs all came from the farms, and so we wanted the workers and the farmers to understand some of their common problems because we felt that the owners, the bosses of the packing houses, tried to pit the farmers against the workers, and tell them, "We can't pay good prices for your cattle because the workers want so much," and then they'd tell the workers the opposite—"We can't pay you any higher wages because the farmers are demanding too much." So, my job was then to go down to these little county fairs and put up an exhibit to try to befriend the farmers. So it was really an interesting job; I did that for about five or six years, and then I got killed in a political war, in the union. I went to work for my dad in the real estate business—he had a business at 4649 Cottage Grove Avenue by this time. He'd moved from the Television Institute into this private real estate business, and I went to work up there. But, I wasn't very successful as a real estate person; I was trying to write a show called *Kicks and Co.* I was writing songs and I was trying to get various singers to become interested in my songs. This would be in the middle fifties into the late fifties. I guess I should back up a little bit because in the latter part of the '40s, as I got to be twenty-one, I became very interested in politics. I joined the Communist Party, for one thing, and I ran for political office—I ran for the state legislature on the Progressive Party ticket in 1948—I lost—and I ran for Congress as a Republican in 1952, at which time I also lost. I wasn't a Republican, but it was so difficult to get on the ballot as an independent that we decided, my young crew and I, that we would try and get on the ballot on the Republican Party ticket just so we could raise issues 'cause we wanted to fight the Democrats. We were really young zealots, and that went on till I got booted out of the Communist party when I was thirty years old, about 1956. It was one of those situations where, "you can't fire me, I quit!" *(laughs)* We fell out on the race question. I was just too black to be red! *(laughs)* They called me a "Negro nationalist," which meant that I was very interested in the problems that befell black people, and I saw things from that perspective, which was kinda natural, 'cause that's where I was. During that period, around 1955, in order to keep me from running for office anymore, I got drafted. I was twenty-eight years old by this time, but they put me in the Army and then kicked me out for being a Communist. McCarthy was doin' his number—I was scared to death; on the way down to Arkansas to be in the Army, I just knew I was gonna go to the stockade! However, I didn't . . . the Supreme Court reversed it, 'cause it was totally unethical for them to force me in and then kick me out, 'cause I didn't wanna come in the first place! And I'd taken the Fifth Amendment and all. But anyway, all of that stuff sorta faded as I was in the Army; I got to singin' in the service clubs with a fella from Chicago named Al Coletta. He and I called ourselves the Two-Tones.

And that was your intro to showbiz?

Well, I was always interested in being in a show—I was always a ham. I mean even when I was workin' for the union, if some errand carried me to a place where there was a stage I'd find myself wanderin' across the stage. . . . I think the thing that got me goin' was songwritin.' I had been writin' songs as a hobby when I was a teenager, then I kinda got serious about it. I copy-righted some of 'em, and I was thinkin' about gettin' 'em published. But finally, when my first son was born, I wrote a lullaby called "Brown Baby," and I liked that so much that I tried to get it to Harry Belafonte and I began to write more songs. I really started writin' songs just to keep from goin' crazy in the Army.

So Harry Belafonte recorded "Brown Baby?"

No, no, no, Harry Belafonte didn't do shit. *(laughs)* No, but he encouraged me a lot because I saw him as an example, as sort of a role model, as some-body I wanted to be like. I mean, we were the same age, but he had gone into show business, he had made a hit record, he made movies, he was goin' into production, he had his own office—this was what I really aspired to be.

Somewhere down the line you wrote a song for a group called the Delegates, on Vee Jay, with Dee Clark called "The Convention." . . .

That happened sorta at that time I was writing songs, tryin' to get singers to do 'em. I wasn't tryin' too much to be a singer myself, although I had per-formed in the Army. But when I got out of the Army, I started writin' more songs, and I got fired from my job in the union. I went to work with my father in the real estate business, ostensibly—I really wasn't doin' much real estate business. I had a license to sell real estate, but I didn't sell one building—mostly I was upstairs, writin' songs, and by this time, I had a loft, it was my office, and I had gotten into the idea that I wanted to be a playwright, as well as a songwriter, and so the best way to do that would be to write a musical. So I started with my own musical called *Kicks and Co.*

When was this?
This would have been about . . . 1957.

It appears to me that you were down with the whole theater and jazz scenes. How did you sidetrack into rock and roll with the Delegates?
Vivian Carter — Vivian was the Vee, and her husband Jimmy was the Jay — so they had this company. Vivian was on the radio while I was on the radio, so I knew them. And when I started writin' songs, it was just a question of getting songs written. I wasn't particularly — at that time, it wasn't the way it is now . . . you have rock and roll and crossover and rhythm and blues and all these little differentiations with names . . . the pop, and the easy listening . . .

It was all one world, huh?
Yeah, it was music! *(laughs)* so yeah, there was rock and roll, of course — it had just come in . . .

But it wasn't separated . . .
Well, not . . . it wasn't divided — rock and roll was all of it! White people weren't even in it yet! *(laughs)* When they got into it, *they* became rock and roll and we were now rhythm and blues! But this is something that's done in boardrooms and in sales meetings. This has nothin' to do with what the creative artists are doin' in the clubs or in the rehearsal halls or anything else. Show business is two worlds, and the names which we're talkin' about usually come from the business side. *(laughs)*

And "The Convention" was kind of a novelty thing, where you were spoofin' the acts of the day?
With that particular piece, I was makin' a spoof . . . they were attacking rock and roll, that is the established businesses, because rock and roll messed 'em up! Up until rock and roll came along, they had the "Hit Parade," and the music was generally played on the radio that was popular was the music that was show tunes, and out of the movies, and out of a sort of white milieu. All of a sudden, it started gettin,' you know, Little Richard! *(laughs)*

"A-WOP-BOP-A-LU-BOP-A-WOP-BOP-BOP!"
Yeah! Whoa! And the whole thing began to change! *(Starts imitating Richard's piano style)* "Ding-ding-ding-ding. . . ." *(both laugh)* It all just changed! And,

BMI came in, the Broadcast Music Incorporated. All the music prior to that had been ASCAP music and that was show tunes and stuff. BMI started playing this black music and that began to take over. After a while, they started squeezin' the Hit Parade out—Snooky Lanson and all that stuff! *(laughs)*

No more Patti Page!
Well, Patti, I think she hung in there for a while! But all of that was kinda bein' eased out . . . or had to adapt and had to start singin' that stuff. Then, of course, in '63 here came the Beatles, and this was the first time, a situation where white guys could sound like black guys . . . and prove that they weren't. *(laughs)* They were all for that—"oh, wow!" When Elvis Presley came along, same kinda thing. But always, up to that time, the music had been pretty much . . .

Grouped together.
So, the way I got in with Vee Jay was simply because I knew Vivian and Jimmy, and I was tryin' to break into the music business and there they were. I even tried to form my own record company, Creation Records.

Anything ever come out?
Yeah, we put out a record, I forgot what the name was . . .

Was it by you?
Yeah, it was by me . . . recorded down here at Universal Studios, I paid for it, had a distributor . . . but I didn't know beans about it, you know; I didn't have the

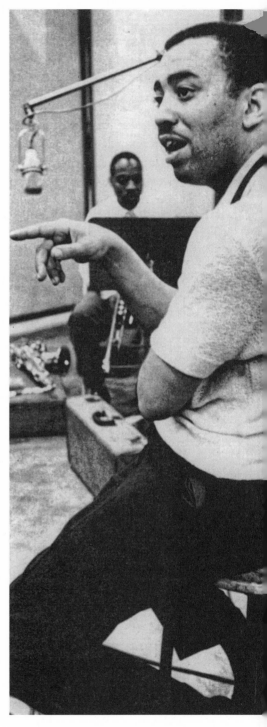

money and you can't just do it like that, you know? So I blew maybe three, four thousand dollars of somebody else's money.

You still have copies after all this time?
Heck naw.

Do you have copies of most of your records?
I don't have copies of any of 'em. I don't have anything to play 'em on. I don't carry that kind of stuff around. I got to be such a gypsy, after while, that it was much more profitable to travel light, for personal and political reasons, all kinds of stuff.

You told me you envisioned yourself as a writer. How did you make the transition to singer?
Well, nobody was singin' what I was writin' *(laughs)*, so that was how that happened! When I was writing songs and I was trying to get people to sing my songs, and I was writing a musical by this time, *Kicks and Co.*, then *A Raisin in the Sun* came to town. Lorraine *(Hansberry, the playwright)*, her family lived across the street from where I lived. Anyhow, I went over to her house and sang some of my songs to her and read this play. Her husband, Bob Nemiroff, was a songwriter; he was also in the music publishing business, with a man called Phil Rose, who produced *Raisin*. So I started sending my songs to Bob Demarol in NYC, for them to kick around to try to get singers to record 'em. He carried it to Columbia Records and Al Ham was interested in my performance, so they contacted me with a contract to become a singer. So I sent 'em that contract with a note saying it looked like a clever circumvention of the Thirteenth Amendment to me and I wasn't into being a singer anyway, and what were they gonna do with me as a writer. Mitch Miller saw that and said, "Who needs him?" At the time, Mitch was head of Columbia's A&R. A year passed and Al called me again. I signed; they never rewrote the contract, but it did launch me into a singing career.

So the first LP was Sin and Soul?
Correct.

There's all these quotes from famous people plastered on the front cover. You had to have been getting around by this time.
By that time, I had written a play, I'd gone to New York, I was hooked up with Columbia Records, and then Nemiroff and his partner decided that they would like to produce *Kicks and Co*. I'd written this play in hopes that

Phil Rose was going to produce it. The three of them got into an argument about who was gonna have artistic control and they fought with Phil, and because Bob had been instrumental in my getting a recording contract, he asked me would I let him and his partner be the producer. I agreed to do that. So when I went to New York the first time to record, I had brought this play along. As the first record came out, I was involved in doing backer's auditions to raise money for the play. All this was happening simultaneously. I got my first engagement, which was at the Village Vanguard. That's when I was presented on the *Today* program, because I was a sensation at the Village Vanguard. (Today *show host*) Dave Garroway himself was so personally impressed that he came to see me with his daughter a couple of nights later. He invited me, on the spot, in the club, to come on the *Today* show, and they turned over the whole two hours of the television show to a backer's audition to raise money to do *Kicks and Co.*

That's a hip move.
It was so hip that the New York State Legislature then passed the law to make sure that that never happened again!

It does not pay to be hip!
No, not in your time. *(both laugh)* Posthumous profits *(laughs)*, but nothing happens concurrent with your living. But that did enable us to get enough money to put the show on, and it opened here at McCormick Place—and closed immediately. It probably ran out of money. The budget was $400,000, but by bringing the show here to Chicago, to open, they spent, they gambled, and they thought by being successful in Chicago, they would be able to recoup their initial 400,000 and go into New York sittin' pretty. However, the cost of flying all those people to Chicago and putting them up in hotels, and rehearsing them and finding rehearsal halls and all that depleted the money so that before we opened in Chicago, they were broke. They managed to raise enough dollars to keep on going. The critics in Chicago hated it, except for *The Defender*, who loved it.

Why did the other papers hate it?
Well, one review said it was "pelvic choreography." It was the Twist, but it was before the Twist had broken out! In fact, the Twist didn't break out until like two weeks after *Kicks and Co.*, and I think that's why it broke out, in New York, 'cause it was big in the black community, but those dances didn't necessarily . . .

Cross over.

I think somebody called it "Amateur Night In Dixie!" It was just the general prejudice. So the black press loved it, but the white press didn't understand it and contested it. We went to New York then, and David Merrick, who was a big producer, let us take over one of his stages during the daytime to try and raise money to resurrect it but that was unsuccessful so it died.

So how did those CBS albums do?

After the first two albums, Al Ham got fired and became my manager, but I was sort of a lame duck at Columbia after that. Al Ham had signed me; he loved me — I was one of his projects. Ham was really there to be my champion! He got fired, I didn't have a champion. So, whoever inherited me, I was alright but I wasn't his; he hadn't signed me. Other acts were being signed, and those would be the ones that he would push. So while I was there with Al Ham, everything was red carpet. Once he left, it got more and more back door, and finally I was just out the door. I had just returned from London, England, where I had done a sensational one-man show with terrific reviews, and I came back pissed at the record company, talking to Clive Davis, who was at that time a lawyer for them. I said, "Why don't you let me out of the contract if you're not gonna support me." I couldn't even get the record in the record store next door to the theater and I've had all these hit reviews! "All the greats rolled into one!" "Must see!" "Sammy Davis, move over!" It seemed like a month later, they dropped me from the label.

How many LPs did you do for them? Four?
Four.

And the last one would have been . . . Tells It Like It Is!, right?
Correct. *In A New Mood* was the second one — no, the third one. That was when they were trying to get me to change.

So how did they try to make you change?
I had been doin' "Brown Baby," "Bid 'Em In," *(a proto-rap about a slave auction)* "Signifying Monkey" *(a cleaned-up street toast). (On* New Mood*)* I started doin' "Let My People Go" *(laughs)* . . . I was in the same old mood!

Somewhere down the line, in this time zone, you had Jazz Scene U.S.A.
Yeah, well, Al Ham . . .

You owe him some favors, huh?
Well, I paid him . . . he was my manager at the time. He was looking through the trades and he saw where Steve Allen was lookin' for somebody to host

a series. At that time, I had a gig comin' up in San Francisco at the Hungry i. He arranged for me to go down to L.A. from San Francisco and audition for this show.

Was this a network TV series?
No, it was a syndicated show—no network was thinkin' about jazz at that time. Now we're talkin' back in '61 or '62?

Did you have any say in who the guests were gonna be?
No . . . mostly it was Leonard Feather. No, I didn't have much to say about that. In the first place, I wouldn't have known who to ask anyway *(laughs)* . . . Leonard Feather gave me a "Blindfold Test" *(a still-running column in* Down Beat *magazine where musicians, facing away from the stereo, try to identify and comment on other musicians' records)* and I flunked it! "Who was this?" "How the hell would I know?" I wasn't an aficionado; I was a consumer! I was very pleased with doing that show—it gave me the experience of television, it was still black and white at that time, so that was quite a while ago. I thought it was well done, and it's out now *(on video)*; I saw a couple of episodes about three months ago . . .

How do they hold up to you, after all this time?
Great! There's me, thirty–forty years ago! *(laughs)*

See, that's the thing—we've been taking about how you were too far ahead of your time, but you always had exposure . . . you definitely had friends in high places!
That's in the highest place *(laughs)* . . . somebody *up there* likes me!

There were more conventional black singers than you who couldn't buy that kind of exposure . . . you were doing alright!
I'll tell you another one . . . the *Today* show. With *Kicks and Co.*? You couldn't even imagine a thing like that—that had to be a godsend! Subsequently, whereas the thing with *Jazz Scene U.S.A.* was middle management lookin' out for his artist and seeing an opportunity and following through, but with a show called *From Jump Street*. . . . that was totally serendipitous! *(1980's* From Jump Street *was a thirteen-week PBS series on the history of black music hosted by Brown)* I mean, at the time I had no manager. I had nobody; I was just sorta walkin' along and fell into it! So that has happened to me from time to time. I've also had opportunities disappear; look like they were right there, and all of a sudden it evaporated, and I haven't been able to understand how that is.

I don't know if you've kept track, but a lot of people, like Johnny Rivers, Albert Collins, and whatnot have covered your songs through the years. What's your favorite?
I welcome 'em all.

I singled out Rivers, because he covered a couple of your songs in the '60s . . . did you ever meet him?
He and I started to record . . . he was gonna record me one time, but we had a big fallin' out because I thought he was just really after Jean, my old lady!

Yeah?!

Brown and Jean Pace.

He was pullin' some . . . like we'd go into the studio and I'd *nail one*, a good take . . . and he'd erase it! That kinda shit was goin' down . . . as I say, we were going to record, but I thought that sex got in the way of that. For Jean, that was an *adventure*, being with Jean Pace in the 1960s—wooo! *(laughs)* A walk down Broadway was an adventure!

So how did you hook up with her? I know she's a performer too.
I met her at a party at Redd Foxx's house . . . Redd Foxx and I used to perform together from time to time. He was living in L.A. and performing at Basin Street West and she was dancin' in the chorus line there. He invited me to his party the night of the Cuban Missile Crisis, I remember that, and I was playing in a club there called the Crescendo. After work, I went to this party about two or three blocks away—his joint was there, and there she stood . . . aw, buddy! *(laughs)* And that's how we met. This was during the period when I was coming out there quite frequently to do episodes of *Jazz Scene U.S.A.*, so I was constantly in Los Angeles, performing in Los Angeles as well.

This takes us to the mid-sixties. What were you doing, stagewise?
I was performing in clubs like the Troubadour in Los Angeles . . . I had gone to Las Vegas but they had asked me to leave, quick, because I wasn't attracting gamblers. *(laughs)* I did the Troubadour, the Hootenanny on the West Coast, the Cafe Au Go-Go and some clubs like that in New York. In '65 I met Luiz Henrique, I was just goin' around to clubs, and I had gone to Cafe Au Go-Go, and this young Brazilian man was there playing, and he and I became good friends and started collaborating on some songs.

He would sing songs in Portuguese to me, or he would do something and I would do lyrics, translating them and all that . . . that led to our doing this album together and doing a show called *Joy '66* that next year, which included Jean, and ran for several months here *(in Chicago)* at a club called the Happy Medium. Stagewise, that's what I was doing—*then*. Once I was in Chicago, and stationed there, I began to audition other actors to do another show, so we did a second show called Summer in the City. At the same time, I commissioned Phil Cohran *(founding member of the AACM [As-*sociation for the Advancement of Creative Musicians] *and an early Sun Ra sideman)* to write the music to Paul Laurence Dunbar's poetry, and we sold that to the Chicago Board of Education—toured shows for about a dozen weeks. At the same time, I made contact with the Blackstone Rangers *(Chicago's most storied street gang, later known as the El Rukns)*, and we began talkin' to them about some alternative activity to what they were doin,' which was basically gangbangin' and terrorizing the neighborhood. We were doing Summer in the City. The fact that there was this gang presence was bad for business and that's one of the reasons that I contacted gangs — could we do something for them that would stop them from steppin' on my hustle! I said we'd do a show for 'em, but they said, "Well, we got some talent; can we be in the show?" We wound up doin' a show called *Opportunity, Please Knock*, which really changed my life, basically, because it let me see that there was this enormous talent in the black community. This is where all the dances came from; this is where all the popular music comes from; so I began to really concentrate on that. *Opportunity Please Knock* ran for a little while, with those kids being on the *Smothers Brothers Comedy Hour*.

I always thought it was bizarre that Dick Smothers had to talk about what you were doing during the performance of the song, instead of before.
I don't think he explained what I was doing, because I don't think my name came up in that.

Yeah, it didn't, but I remember him mentioning Opportunity Please Knock.
It is no explanation of *Opportunity Please Knock* without me because there wouldn't have been one. It wasn't something that was just . . . *done*, it had to come out of . . . it was a whole political thing. When I was talkin' to the Blackstone Rangers, we weren't just talkin' show business. We were talkin' *politics*. Why are you guys gangbanging? Why are you fighting the East Side Disciples? So we started talkin' about elections, we started talkin' about the Red Guard in China . . . instead of you guys being the ones who are

terrorizin' the community, when the old lady sees you at the corner, she should know the young warriors are here and she should feel protected and safe. So, we were trying to instill this against the process, against the whole concept of white supremacy that was on them. So, it was more than just a show; it was a political effort. We tried to get the TWO *(The Woodlawn Organization, a community association)* for example, to donate enough money just for us to put ads in the papers 'cause we had a dynamite show — the people were standing, cheering, *in tears* and all after every show. They wouldn't give us a quarter. Now Woodlawn has disappeared. The people who control the money — Rev. Brazier *(Arthur Brazier was a Martin Luther King associate who was pastor at Woodlawn's Apostolic Church of God and president of TWO)* and them — they got big churches and big operations. But the Blackstone Rangers and those young people who dwelt in that area, that looks like a war hit it, and a war *did* hit it. When I went to Brazier, we had the show all organized, and all we needed was they would put some ads in the paper and let the people know what these kids have done, what they can do, let the people come and see it, and we'll pay you back — just lend us the money — this is a hot show! No, they said they couldn't put the money into anything but plumbing and carpentry and bricklaying . . . actually, what we did with the money was we turned it over to Jeff Fort and some of those guys and let them mess with it till they could put 'em in jail for misappropriating' public money. But anybody who knew them would know that they was gonna misappropriate the money . . . I took 'em over to Seaway Bank to try to teach them banking so they would have sound business principles to operate with. "I don't wanna get caught in a crossfire when you start shootin' each other — and I know you will — about chump change, about money I could've been makin' every week if I wasn't foolin' with you! So let's get this organized." I got them together. We used to talk, you know, really hard business. The first weekend, we made 15,000 bucks. A bunch of older gangsters tried to move in on the $15,000.

Did they succeed?
No. Nope. They had opened a bank account and they were sayin' "Where's the money? Where's the money?" Jeff Fort said, "Why didn't you put the money in the name of the Blackstone Rangers?" A half a dozen older guys, who I thought were the OG's of the operation, the Old Gangsters, but they weren't. They were just some cats who were tryin' to make a move on it. One of them *(the older guys)* made the mistake of saying "Well, what differ-

ence does it make what name we put the account in? Blackstone ain't shit." To them, that was like stompin' on the flag in front of a bunch of Marines; that just infuriated the Blackstone Rangers. And the Big Chief, Bull was his name, Gene Harriston, stood up and said, "I'm the Big Chief," pointed to Jeff Fort and said, "That's the Little Chief and these are the main 21" — talkin' about the crowd of young men there, and then he turned to these seven or eight older guys and said, "Who are you motherfuckers? This is Oscar Brown Jr. and the Blackstones' thang." So when I left there, I was Papa Blackstone on the bus goin' back there and I had the account and it looked like we were gonna be able to do great things. Bull and I then went to the *Tribune* the next day, and the *Daily News*, and the *Sun-Times*, and the *Chicago Defender*, and told 'em, "We don't have any money but we have a dynamite show. If you'll just give us some publicity and help us, we can keep going. And they told us that the police didn't want them to say nice things about these gangsters, so they didn't even print the reviews that their own reporters had written about the show. And so we were shut out. And when that happened, the gang then reverted to their gangster stuff . . . I had to get the hell out of there — Jean and I left and went to New York.

From there, you started Joy *again, with Sivuca.*

Let me tell you something else that happened that's quite interesting. After the Blackstone Ranger thing — during it — Dick Hatcher was running for mayor of Gary. He had a big benefit out there — Harry Belafonte was the headliner — and I came out there with half a dozen kids from the Blackstone Rangers. When Hatcher got elected, he hired Jean and me to come to Gary to work with the youth there. He got a $75,000 government grant and put us on the payroll and said, "Find the talent in Gary and start workin' with them." In order to discover the talent we had a contest. All the kids in Gary between thirteen and eighteen or something were invited to be in this contest. The winners of the contest were the Jackson Five!

Just before Motown?

That's how they got to Motown! Motown would never have heard of them, because the kids who finished second were damned good too! The kids who finished third were damned good. Gary was full of talent, but their chances of gettin' that kind of exposure weren't too likely. By the time we did our little show the Jackson Five were on Motown, and they were gone. So, at the end of that year, I was hoping that we could stay there and create a new industry because there was so much talent that instead of it just being Steel Town, it seemed like it could be as much of an entertainment town as Motown was. But the governor didn't have that money for us to continue the program, and in the meanwhile, someone had become interested in a play called *Big Time Buck White*, and asked if I would be interested in directing it, in California. I had seen *Big Time Buck White* while I was in L.A., and I was so impressed with it that I had begun writing some songs about the characters. And so, when I went there, instead of just directing it, I talked him into letting me convert it into a musical, which is what happened. So in 1969, I guess it was, we went to New York and did *Buck White* as a musical. While I was doing that, my friend Luiz Henrique, who had been down in Brazil, had gone home to Brazil after our *Joy '66* experience; he came back with half a dozen songs that he had written and I started writin' lyrics and we started talkin' about bringing Sivuca, whom we knew, into the show. He was, at that time, living in New York—he had been performing with Miriam Makeba.

You got back into recording around this time on Atlantic.
That was a result of a fellow named Joel Dorn being at Atlantic Records . . . he signed me to that label.

You had a single, "The Lone Ranger," based on the old joke where Lone Ranger and Tonto are surrounded by Indians, the Lone Ranger asks, "What are we going to do?," and Tonto says, "What you mean we, white man?" That looked like a hit until it got pulled.
Yeah, it was on the charts with a bullet. I guess the bullet hit something! I understood that in Washington they just came and physically took the record out of the radio stations.

I guess the people who owned the copyright were still around.
You can't copyright a title, and to snatch it for that reason was not . . . true. For example, I had a song called "Watermelon Man" and Mongo Santamaria had a song called "Watermelon Man"—*both of us had songs called "Watermelon Man!"*

Whose came first?
I imagine his did, but I didn't know it. Mine grew out of a childhood experience—*(sings)* "HEY, WATERMELON MAN, get your WATERMELON MAN"—the watermelon man used to sing in the alley. When I was a little kid, I started hearin' that.

Brown with documentarian donnie l. betts. Photo courtesy Mr. betts.

In the early '80s, you had a play called The Great Nitty Gritty, *which had popping and locking before* Flashdance.

During the auditions, they had some pop-lockers, and they had some modern dancers over there auditioning. One gang would be the pop-lock movement, and the other gang would be the modern dance movement, and then sometimes it would coincide. And man, the critics didn't know what they were seein'! That was before Michael Jackson came out with "Thriller" and all that!

I guess, in retrospect, some white critic would say you were ahead of your time. A black writer would say that you were just reflecting what you saw!

When we were doin' *Kicks and Co.*, when we had the dances, we didn't want 'em just doin' Arabesque, we wanted 'em doin' the Twist!, The Hully Gully— we wanted 'em to reflect what we are! And put *that* into a dramatic context. And I studied later, I found out that Scott Joplin had the same aspirations! He wrote ragtime dance, ragtime ballet, and it was his intention to take all the dances that were popular in his time—like the Cakewalk—and put them into a classical context, but that is really . . .

That's what strikes me as weird—when you're black, you're considered culturally deprived. When you're white, you're culturally diverse. The white creator is called diverse and ahead of his or her time.

Oh, I will be after I'm *dead* . . .

But the scary part is, that the white will be immortalized while still alive.

It doesn't hurt so much, from a personal standpoint, because I think I got what I deserved—it's the life I cut out for myself. If you're gonna fight this man . . . I haven't filed federal income tax since 1965, so I just fight 'em. After I saw what happened with the Blackstone Rangers . . . after I realized where I was and the hostility of the whole situation, there's no point in our trying to ingratiate ourselves with these people because we're not . . . *we* didn't come here right. We're not in the situation in the right way. We came as a degraded race and were held that way. Even when we were told we were citizens it was

Brown with daughter Maggie Brown.
Photo courtesy Toya Werner Martin.

Brown with son Oscar Brown III.

not with the freedom that everybody else became citizens. Everybody else who wanted to be a citizen, came, and was naturalized and bought into it. We were just declared citizens by edict, which meant that the slaves had to cast their political lot with the masters!

. . . and so how did you manage to evade paying income tax since '65?
I don't *evade.* . . . evasion is when you try to avoid payin' some tax—my contention is that only United States citizens owe . . . and that's no way for them to have made my family citizens of this! My grandfather was born in 1860 in Hines County, Mississippi; he was not considered a person. In 1865, they decided he was a person, and that person was a member of this political organization and all his descendants would then be likewise, if they remained here. Well . . . that's crap. We're kidnap victims. We were brought here; the country acts like it didn't affront us at all. They act like they owe us no apology and that they bear no blame—that we actually benefited from having been dragged here in chains and having the shit beat out of us. We have been bred to go along with it—we have been bred to be afraid. *(Brown pronounces* afraid *to rhyme with* bred—*afred.)* We don't produce a damn thing for ourselves. We don't produce shoes, food, gasoline, oil—nothin'. We have the talent and ability to turn this around if we only come to the realization of where we are and where we come from.

I used to watch the sitcom Roc *every week, so it was a surprise to see you on that show.*
Well, I was somewhat surprised myself! *(laughs)* I was on there for three episodes . . . I was supposed to be a piano player, but the piano didn't have any sound comin' out of it *(laughs and starts playing air piano)*!

You play anything?
Nope! *(laughs)* I play the laptop computer! *(The* Roc *experience)* was good for money—I bought a car. I don't like that kind of television, personally.

Did more people recognize you?
Whole lot! Lot! I mean, like the next *day*! I was on *Roc* Sunday—Monday, *phew*! That became the most significant gig I'd done in ten years, as far as most people were concerned.

Any thoughts for the future besides writing?
Well, no. . . . I'll be seventy years old on my next birthday, so I'm not looking for the grand tour. I'm not trying to go to any awards benefits, that's for

sure *(laughs)*—I don't feel like being bothered! I find that fame and fortune bring a very low class of people into your life. You meet some slick characters who need money! I'm not a total recluse. I've written some tunes in my head; I'd like to get 'em out. There are some plays I've written; I'd like to see them produced. I'd like to be around—I'd like to be a part of that.

Update

Around the time of this interview Brown released his last solo album, *Then and Now*, which featured new recordings mingled with classics. At the time he had been performing around Chicago with two of his children—jazz vocalist Maggie Brown and Oscar Brown III (known as Bo)—a stand-up bassist who was a major figure in Chicago's performance poetry scene. Brown created a new show for the trio that incorporated many of his best-known songs, titled *Street Cries* (later renamed *Brown in Brownsville*). Bo was killed in a car accident in late 1996. Brown and his daughter continued to perform together, and released a live album in 2002. In 2005 Brown died at the age of seventy-eight from complications from a blood infection. He was on the cusp of renewed interest in his work, as his first poetry collection was published later that year and filmmaker donnie l. betts had just completed his long-in-the-works documentary, *Music Is My Life, Politics My Mistress—The Story of Oscar Brown Jr*. After a successful run on the festival circuit a truncated version of the compelling film was shown on PBS, once again giving Brown the national audience he deserved.

Interview conducted by Jake Austen,
James Porter, and Bosco (1998)

David Allan Coe

Interviewing a weary David Allan Coe in a House
of Blues dressing room illuminated by the blue
light of a soft-core Cinemax porn movie may stand
as the *Roctober* staff's most surreal adventure. The
trio of interviewers was made up of three wor-
shipers who had come to the Church of Coe from
different temples. When James Porter was growing up he only knew Coe from his debut blues LP.

Bosco had originally been drawn to Coe's "Outlaw Country" stance and his amazing songwriting. I became a Coe convert while flipping through a clipping file in a library. Coming across a 1975 photo of the singer I was taken aback to see a hulking, rhinestone-encrusted masked superhero lording over a Nashville honky-tonk. Without hearing a note of music, I knew this man was a true entertainer.

Bosco's opinion is the most popular one. Coe is the *most* outlaw of the Outlaw Country crowd, known as the only one who actually killed people, spent a significant amount of time in prison, and was a prominent motorcycle club member. In fact, legend has it that a journalist saw Coe's Outlaws biker jacket at a Willie Nelson show and named the genre after it. James's opinion of Coe as a blues singer is not one most Coe fans share. Though he won awards and bushels of press overseas for his blues records, they sold relatively poorly, and most know him mainly from the country LPs he released on Columbia. My take on Coe as an entertainer, though, is ultimately what makes him the perfect subject for inclusion in these pages.

David Allan Coe is one of the most diversely talented performers since Sammy Davis Jr., a comparison he himself makes in the last line of his 1978 autobiography, *Just for the Record*. His performances include his straightforward singing, but he also throws in everything from impersonations (his show the night we interviewed him featured his takes on Johnny Cash, George Jones, and, bizarrely, Jello Biafra), to illusions, ventriloquism, and even trained monkeys. A 1977 *Billboard* review of a show at New York's Other End may be that magazine's only live concert summary that described a singer opening his act with twenty minutes of magic, including sawing a girl in half. Similarly, the editor at *Variety* probably factchecked with the writer of a 1988 review that mentioned ducks and doves illusions. Coe has used a chimp named Rocky and a spider monkey named Panuch in his act, as well as trained jungle cats. Coe once said he thought of his ventriloquist dummy, Sandy Hilton, as "a live individual." Clearly Coe is so unusual, individualistic, and bizarre that strong arguments could be made that he could be dubbed a Vaudevillian, a performance artist, or a punk rocker.

Now, the term *punk* is not one you want to use when referring to an excon, but this definition has nothing to do with jail sex, and everything to do with punk's DIY aesthetic that David embodies like few others. Do It Yourself is the way he's always operated, self-releasing his own porno material at a time when he was achieving mainstream success, self-publishing his own books, booking his own shows, and establishing his own distribution networks. In fact, he's tried hard to maintain control by owning as much of his productions and publishing as he can. His latest book, *This Is David Allan Coe*, a scrapbook of cut-and-paste memories, handwritten notes, and two dozen different fonts, looks more like a punk-zine than any actual zine from the last ten years. This book makes you envision DAC *(as many fans refer to him)* late at night at a Kinko's with a copy card, scissors, and Elmer's Glue. Is it any wonder we were excited to see what David had in store for his latest set?

This was actually a pretty high-profile show for Coe. Over the last few years his Chicago appearances have included such odd venues as Ditka's, the sports bar owned by the legendary Bears' coach, a bogus downtown Urban Cowboy bar called Remington's (that paid Coe with a bad check), and a side stage at an outdoor city fest, one that is usually reserved for local lightweights. Wherever he played, though, you could be assured there would be a colorful crowd. Every previous show I'd been to was populated with gruff bikers, redneck types rarely seen in Chicago, and intense freaks of every stripe. So when we got to House of Blues and saw the crowd waiting to get in, it seemed like something was wrong. My first tip-off should have been when I saw avant-garde musician Dave Grubbs and his entourage entering. A gaggle of French journalists, in town to do a story on Grubbs and Tortoise, were in tow, and it seemed that half the staff of his label, Drag City, was in attendance. Of course, it made sense that Coe would have a following among musicians, even of disparate backgrounds. What was *really* surprising was the rest of the crowd.

Though there were a few beards sprinkled throughout, the majority of the crowd was made up of short-haired college boys. Not trendy college radio DJ types, but frat boys with corporate ambitions. And they weren't poseurs; they seemed to know all the words to the songs. I couldn't figure it out, and perhaps it doesn't happen when he plays Billy Bob's in Fort Worth, but in Chicago there has been a huge demographic shift. The place was packed, but looking around the room it seemed like Hootie & the Blowfish was about to take the stage.

The show began not long after they opened the doors. As soon as Coe, traveling with a small band, took the stage, the sparer sound revealed that Coe's voice and health were not in the best shape. Though clearly sick, David put out for the fans. He did songs from all eras, even going back to his debut album, *Penitentiary Blues*, and he did new numbers with new

verses (including a funny commentary about Michael Jackson's lack of racial pride). Musically the searing southern rock guitar and the meaty bass sounded great, but the drummer's electronic kit had a pretty hollow sound in such a big room. It was far from the best Coe show I'd ever seen, but anyone who knows Coe's story is excited to see him any chance they can.

For those who don't know the Coe saga, it's a long, twisted, fascinating one. The information here comes from various sources, but much of it comes from Coe's autobiographies and books. Now it is true that Coe is a storyteller and a braggart—a man who offers contradictions, exaggerations, and absurd boasts. But in my opinion, most of what I'll include here is credible. He's been challenged on some things, but his explanations often pan out, and when you take a good look, his critics' credibility leaves something to be desired. So what if Shelby Singleton says you're "90 percent bullshit"? Singleton released six Orion albums! Now I love Orion (a masked Elvis impersonator whose records were packaged around a book implying that the "King" faked his death and was now performing incognito), but that is grade "A" bullshit. And just the fact that *Rolling Stone* magazine would have a higher opinion of Coe as a musician if he did kill somebody than if he didn't is problematic. But more of that later. Let's start at the beginning.

David Alan (he added an l when he went showbiz) Coe was born September 6, 1939, in Akron, Ohio. His mom came from Pennsylvania Dutch Amish stock, and his dad was a nonpracticing Mormon. Their ancestor Joseph Coe was a founder of the church (though some Mormon historians identify him as part of group that attempted to depose the Prophet of Mormonism, Joseph Smith), and over the years David would embrace and denounce the Mormon religion at different times. While he sang reverently of his grandfather's polygamy, and practiced it at times (he boasted of having seven wives at once, and it's clear that he had more than one woman living with him in a wifely role at several points in his career), he also stated that "the Osmond family is very talented *(but)* are the total opposite of what I am." Donald Mahon Coe, David's father, would eventually have a career as a worker at Goodyear, but right after David was born he joined the army. In 1943 he divorced David's mother, Dorothy, and married Lucille Coburn, who would take the evil stepmother role in years to come. Though David's sister was welcomed into her home, Dorothy was less generous with the Coe boys, and made David's early years difficult.

David's rough childhood saw him practicing cruelty (he hit his brother Ray with a pickax on one occasion), theft, underage smoking, and general troublemaking, and by the age of nine he had already been placed in detention homes, being put in solitary once when he was seven. At nine he was driven to Michigan and placed in the Starr Commonwealth for Boys, surrounded by youth who were real criminals. It was here Coe started playing the harmonica. Before that, his main musical exposure came from the Irish songs his father sang to him. He escaped from the home at one point and went to his natural mother's house, but she turned him in.

In high school he fell in love with a girl named Wanda, stole a car, and ran away with her. After a friend ratted him out, he was sent to Boys Industrial School in Lancaster, Ohio, a tough, segregated institution. Here he got the words "I Died In Prison" tattooed on his back. Coe eventually would cover his body with prison tattoos, including a spider on his penis. When he got out of BIS he was dressing like Marlon Brando in *The Wild One*, and his daily routine would include fighting, stealing cars to cruise through the Burger King parking lot, and gunplay. He was expelled from school and joined the army at sixteen. He spent time in the stockade, but was eventually able to get discharged for being underage. Not, however, before experiencing another discharge, after he collected the clap and his first sexual experience from a prostitute. Not long after leaving the service Coe stole another car, got caught, and was sent to National Training School in Washington, D.C., and then to Chillicothe Reformatory in Mansfield, Ohio. He began writing songs and singing in prison. At one point he was put in the hole and sang harmony with a group of black convicts, who didn't know he was white. He wrote hundreds of songs during his teenage incarceration, some still in his set today, including "Jack Daniels, If You Please." While he was there he claims to have met and played guitar with Charles Manson, though the math doesn't seem to work out on that one, as according to several sources, Manson was paroled from that institution in 1954, when Coe would have been fifteen. Coe would be institutionalized with quite a few prominent prisoners during his many incarcerations, including Russell Clark from John Dillinger's gang, Joe English from the Purple Gang, and Dr. Sam Sheppard, whose story the TV series *The Fugitive* was based upon. Decades later Coe wrote a book, *Psychopath*, based on the mysterious murderer Sheppard said killed his wife.

In 1958 he was eighteen years old and released. He moved in with his grandfather, started dressing like a pimp, joined a gang, and was in perpetual trouble (some real, some trumped up by cops), eventually landing in the Ohio State Reformatory, and the Ohio State Penitentiary for carrying a porno book in his pocket. Once outside again, his musical talents began to be recognized. He signed a contract with Bright Star Promotions, played at the Ohio State Jamboree, and had one of the songs he wrote recorded by a singer named Bobby Boyle. Then he was arrested, "for suspicion," because he had what the police identified as burglary tools (a screwdriver and a tire iron) in his possession, and spent a year in county jail.

When he got out he made some of his first professional appearances as a singer at the Z-Lounge as the Jive Kings featuring Screaming Tee Coe. Figuring his Puritan family background wasn't cool enough, David had faked being Italian for a while, going by the name Tony Angelo Luckarelli. He eventually settled on Tony Coe. He had a girlfriend Eilleen (known for some reason as Humpback Kate) and worked at the GoJo hand cleaner factory when he wasn't singing on the weekends for twenty dollars a night. He also played at a place called Picks Bar under the name Dave Coe and the Wheelings.

In 1963 he was back in trouble and prison, doing his longest, hardest time. Coe wouldn't spend much time away from the Ohio State Pen or the Marion Correctional Institution until he was paroled in 1968. During this period David (or Tony) began performing and singing seriously in prison.

He was in the variety shows (including the big Christmas Pageant, where they would let transvestites perform in drag), and played in various bands, including a hillbilly combo. He met and performed with black musicians during this stretch, including Screamin' Jay Hawkins. He became pretty famous as a singer in prison, "as famous as Elvis was on the outside," he claimed, and that would fuel his confidence in the years to come. This is also where Coe would get into his most *in*famous troubles.

Two incidents David has spoken about that have been challenged in print occurred around this time. One involved a man being killed with a ball-peen hammer in the yard. Coe was one of the suspects and spent time in the physical space that was that institution's Death Row, though not as a man convicted to death, when he was being held for suspicion. He, and journalists, have exaggerated, twisted, and confused this as part of his legend. This is discussed in the following interview. In a separate incident, a black inmate called Bear approached Coe in the shower and demanded oral sex. Coe claims to have killed him with a mop bucket, also addressed in the interview.

When he was released in 1968, he had written over 500 songs. He went to live with a religious family and accepted Jesus. When the mother tried to seduce him, and the father constantly accused him of having sex with the homely daughter, his faith faltered. He left and went to trade school, becoming a certified welder. He sang on the weekends at Club 66 as Tony Coe and the Dynamics, and this is where he first became associated with the Outlaws Motorcycle Club. After getting interested in bikes, Coe had joined a club called the Headhunters. He also ended up marrying a barmaid he hardly knew, Betty Mae Ward. Her mental instability (she hadn't told him she had several children that had been taken away when she was deemed an unfit mother) would haunt him and shape his relationships with women for years to come.

Coe was drinking at the time (and though Coe has had *a lot* of problems over the years, he maintains that he has avoided drinking, drugs, smoking, and even sweets for much of his adult life). This led to some bad decision making. Betty made him give up music, and he took jobs as a welder. They bought a small house, but argued a lot, including a violent incident after she cheated on him. Several separations and lots of drama, including a stint with her in a mental institution, followed. Coe decided to get back into music. A friend in Shelby, Ohio, named Jim Horn had a small record label named Cabut. He recorded and pressed a single, "One Way Ticket to Nashville" b/w "The Prisoner's Release." In 1969, after being released from parole, he headed to Nashville with the record to promote himself.

After arriving he made an arrangement with the Supreme record pressing plant where he would sweep up the shop and they would let him sleep behind the presses. Bob Mooney, who owned Supreme, helped David get his songs around, and Coe spent the next few months doing anything he could to get noticed. He busked on Broadway, sang at a small club called the Wheel, and he teamed up with a singer named Betty Ford. They released a single, "Play All The Sad Songs" b/w "Suffering," on REM, but soon broke up due to complications surrounding Coe still being legally married to Betty number 1. Soon David had his first legitimate break. When visiting his mom in West Virginia, he found himself playing on stage behind Nashville star Hugh X. Lewis. This led to an audition with Audie Ashworth, one he would re-create in concert for years, where he showed he was Nashville material by doing impressions of all the big stars. He got a publishing contract, and when a reporter heard about his dramatic life, he wrote a melodramatic human interest story about the singing ex-con in the newspaper.

The article caught the attention of Shelby Singleton, who owned Plantation and Sun records. Plantation had a huge hit at the time with Jeanie C. Riley's novelty record "Harper Valley PTA." Singleton would put out plenty of gimmicky things over the years, including Orion's LPs and the gay trucker novelty tune "C.B. Savage." Singleton hooked up with Coe, gave him a hundred dollars, lent him a car to go back home and retrieve all the songs he wrote in prison (on scraps of paper), and offered him a contract. Soon Coe's debut, *Penitentiary Blues*, would be released. Though he had experienced a crazy life up to this point, the next few years would be even stranger.

Betty number 1 decided she didn't want a divorce. She moved to Nashville and helped David spend his new money. She got involved in orgies, witchcraft, and drugs. They were growing apart, but stayed together after she got pregnant with their daughter Carla, born July 22, 1970. David's record was released to good reviews. He started using cocaine and touring with rock musicians, including Grand Funk Railroad, and distanced himself from Betty by spending time in Florida when he wasn't on tour. He came back and recorded an artistic, uncommercial follow-up album, *Requiem for a Harlequin*, based on an epic poem he had written in prison. The record did poorly, his label was struggling, and with hopes for success beginning to disappear, so did Betty, who returned to Ohio with the baby while Coe remained in Nashville, trying to clean himself up and get another shot.

The steps he took to make it (on the country circuit, forgoing his blues singer dreams) are legendary. He'd park his touring hearse, with his name painted on it, downtown so the music fans would see his name, and he'd feed the meter all day. He got a hand-me-down sequin Nudie Suit from Mel Tillis and started wearing it everywhere. (Nudie Cohn was the tailor who crafted the famous flashy sequined country outfits.) He began hanging around the Ryman Auditorium, home of the Grand Ole Opry, and intentionally worked up a sweat. When tourists would see him by the back doors, they'd assume he was famous, that he'd just got off stage, and they would ask for his autograph. He also began to develop the persona of the "Mysterious Rhinestone Cowboy," a musical, sequined Lone Ranger in a mask whose music meant more than his identity. He hung around Tootsie's Orchid Lounge, and was in Mysterious Rhinestone Cowboy mode when his photo was shot for the cover of the *New York Times Magazine*. The article was about the new Nashville, and Robert Altman's *Nashville* film, but his cover photo was the most memorable part of the feature.

Despite that star moment, Coe was far from the A-list. The singer (who around this time hooked up with a sixteen-year-old backup singer named Debby; in July of '72 they had a daughter, Shellie S. Stephanie Coe) was releasing piffle like the Nixon novelty record, "How High Is the Watergate, Mamma" b/w "Tricky Dicky, The Only Son of Kung Fu." But while his music career was stalled, his biker career was taking off, as he became involved with a motorcycle club, the Death Angels, who joined the Outlaws national club. When not playing music, he got involved in crime again, pimping women and dealing in stolen motorcycles. He was eventually arrested, let off on a technicality, and then chose music over the Outlaws.

After several hard years in Nashville he was due a break, which came when Kris Kristofferson asked Coe to play a televised benefit. It worked out well, and Coe was invited to tour with the Rhodes Scholar/singer-songwriter. In Austin, Texas, Coe saw a country scene, led by Willie Nelson, where longhairs and freaks were more accepted, and that too bolstered his confidence. By this time several of his songs had been recorded by smaller artists like Billy Joe Spears and David Rogers, but in 1974 Tanya Tucker, a teenage singer who specialized in mature songs, had a monster hit with David's song "Would You Lay with Me in a Field of Stone." David's name was now gold, and Columbia offered him a recording contract. He soon had more money than he'd ever dreamed of. He bought a castle (converted from a castle-themed motel), but he and Debby had to move after hateful neighbors shot his dog.

His Columbia debut, *The Mysterious Rhinestone Cowboy*, was well received. He began touring and played the Palomino in L.A. While there he got a chance to meet Nudie, the tailor, whom David had always admired. Whenever he could afford it he would buy Nudie Suits, and they developed a good relationship. At the time only Porter Waggoner and David were still wearing rhinestones in Nashville. Coe would later commission a suit from Nudie that paid tribute to Porter and Dolly Parton, his favorite female songwriter. After Porter and Dolly broke up, he threw it into the audience where it was torn to shreds. When he got home he learned that Nudie had died that day.

He also went to Austin to hang out, and it was here he met Chet Flippo, who soon wrote a glowing feature about Coe in *Rolling Stone*. It was also around this time that Coe was approached by George Jones's manager, Bill Starnes, who wanted to book a tour for Coe, and offered him a lucrative contract that included a bus. The financing for the bus came from Jimmy Hoffa. Soon Starnes died under mysterious circumstances, and Hoffa disappeared. David kept the bus.

In 1975 his second album, *Once Upon a Rhyme*, was released and it yielded his first hit single, "You Never Even Called Me By My Name." He also played some pretty high-profile shows, including Willie Nelson's Family Picnic. It was around this time that he made a deal that would haunt him for years to come. Channel 13 in Dallas wanted to do a documentary on him. He would return with them to the prison he served in, visit death row, and they would interview his old friends. He agreed, but believed he was going to have some say over the editing. When they got to the prison, L. Block, where he had been put after the yard killing, was closed. They went to his family reunion and talked to his people. David saw them film lots of material he was pleased with. Before the special aired, David was to do a live concert on the station. When he arrived at the station he saw the rough cut of the film. In his opinion, they had edited out everyone who said anything good about him, and left in everyone who called him a liar. Enraged, he punched the director in the face, and then performed a concert that included the first live broadcasts of the phrases "motherfucker" and "suck my dick," and he generally insulted the filmmakers on the air. The documentary aired the next month. *Rolling Stone* then published an article, picked up by papers around the country, about Coe being a fraud. Though it was somewhat evenhanded, several things in the article seemed excessively anti-Coe, including transcripts of a 1974 interview where he used the word *nigger*. Though they had spoken highly of him up to that point, from then on Coe would be belittled in the magazine and their record guide.

Though this may have held him back from crossing over into the mainstream, his career as a country singer remained steady. He released the strong "Long Haired Redneck" in 1976, and though he wasn't having huge hits, Columbia stood by him, and Coe would release one or two albums of new material every year until 1987. He told *Billboard* in 1982 that none of his albums had sold less than a respectable 150,000, and his *Greatest Hits* sold 400,000. His nonprofessional life also became steady (briefly) when David married Debby in 1976, heretofore to be referred to as Deborah Lynn number 1.

Around 1978 he wrote his autobiography, *Just for the Record*, published by *Easy Rider* magazine. He also starred in his first movie, a violent low-budget film called *Buckstone County Prison*. He was also enjoying his biggest commercial triumph as a songwriter, as Johnny Paycheck's version of "Take This Job and Shove It" had recently became a number 1 *Billboard* country single (a 1981 movie based on the song featured Coe in a small role). Coe moved to the Florida Keys, putting up his extended family, including bodyguards, band, family, and, possibly, multiple wives. Though he had referred in his book to having seven wives at some point (probably between his first two legal marriages), he definitely had more than one woman in a wifely role at this point. Melanie "Meme" Broussard, who he'd been with since 1976, is referred to as a wife on several records, bitterly when she left him in 1980, though she returned in '81. He published a together/forever poem about her in '82, though that was when she left him for good. He does not list her as a legal wife in his new book. He is pictured on the cover of *Family Album* with her and Debby. After that record came out Deborah Lynn number 1 told David's parents she was "the happiest she'd ever been in her life." The next day she emptied the bank account, took the child and the dog, and never came back. David from then on made his albums more and more personal and more and more specific in dealing with his depression and problems.

Also in 1978 he had some health problems. His appendix "busted" in Houston, and after emergency surgery he found himself performing in a wheelchair. Musically, he became influenced by his surroundings and began to write songs in a pseudo-Caribbean style similar to that of Jimmy Buffett. Though he admired Buffett, he did not like comparisons, a fact he would address in "Jimmy Buffett Doesn't Live in Key West Anymore," a song on his self-released "biker humor" album *Nothing Sacred*. His Florida paradise life would eventually end when the IRS descended upon him, Willie Nelson–style. He eventually would recover, but his lifestyle took a hard hit.

In 1980, David's divorce from Deborah Lynn number 1 became final. A clue to the conditions in which she left him may be his vitriolic dedication he gives her on his 1981 album *Invictus Means Unconquered*: "I hope you and Billy Tee will be happy in the poverty-stricken life you have to live. And I hope this is the last song that will ever be written about or for you. Get well soon." Next to it is a photo of David cheesing it with his arms around Meme and a woman named Dawn. Meme is touching his crotch. On the professional front, he made his Opry debut that year.

At some point he married Deborah Lynn number 2. They had no children, and were divorced in 1984. I'm suspicious that Deborah and Meme might be the same person, though he does list Deborah's last name as Pardue, while Meme was definitely named Broussard. I suspect Coe might have just made all his wives take the name "Deborah Lynn" (like Ike Turner naming all his women Tina), especially because he thanks a "Debra Lynn III" for helping him get over Meme. Anyhow, the divorce was devastating to Coe, putting his friends on a suicide watch. In the early eighties he also published two more books, a volume of poetry and a self-help book called *Ex-Convict*, a guide to prisoners on how to act in prison and when they get out. In it he explains a mantra that has gotten him through life: "BE A POSITIVE THINKER." That philosophy was about to pay off.

His 1983 album *Castles in the Sky* finally yielded a huge hit, "The Ride," a song about a hitchhiker getting picked up by Hank Williams's ghost. His 1984 *Just Divorced* album would feature his biggest hit ever, "Mona Lisa Lost Her Smile." He declared in *Billboard* that year that he was going to be more commercial. The pop albums that followed elicited strong reactions from his fans, and not all positive. But soon all that would be academic. In the mid-eighties Columbia dropped Johnny Cash. Coe's reaction to this travesty was that he refused to record for them. His management told him he had to wait out his contract, so after 1989 Coe left and began self-releasing records, as well as signing a contract with King to produce low-budget, newly recorded albums of his old hits and covers for the truck-stop market.

Around the time of David's divorce, Jody Lynn Beaham, a beautiful construction worker, moved to Nashville. Perhaps "Jody like a Melody" spoke to her, because she relocated with one mission: meet David Allan Coe. After a brief stalking, they became involved, but David, not trustful of women at the time, left her. Unbeknownst to him, she was pregnant and had his first son, Tyler Mahan. Kris Kristofferson then made David come to an all-star intervention, where they put the baby in his hands, told him it was his, and brought out Jody Lynn. They were married soon, and their partnership brought an incredible domesticity to Coe's life. Two years later they had Tanya Montana, followed by Shyanne Sherrill the next year, and Carson David three years after that. David, who attended his last three children's births (there are amazing photo of Coe in scrubs in his book) became a devoted father. His kids have appeared on numerous album covers and he even had Tyler perform in his show as a cute singing toddler. Jody Lynn toured as David's keyboard player for years, and ran the fan club. They settled in conservative Branson (before the boom) and eventually opened a store there with Willie Nelson. At one point David and Jody even had their own theater in Arkansas, where they would perform primarily magic shows for small but appreciative audiences. If you're a strict Outlaw Coe lover, this would be a low point, as he was cleanshaven, wearing magician's tuxes, and sporting Conway Twitty hair. Though his magic theater was a short-lived venture, he has called it one of the happiest periods in his life.

Coe continued to tour, though, and highlights include the huge Wembley Festival in England, which he played in 1987 and 1990, a tour with Neil Young, Farm Aid, and the Rock and Roll Bash, a big Wrestling event with his good friend Dusty "The American Dream" Rhodes. The cable channel Nashville Network gave him some mainstream exposure around this time. He had appeared on public television before this (the ill-fated documentary, plus an appearance on *Austin City Limits*), but being on Ralph Emery's show *Nashville Now*, and the talk show *Crook and Chase* really positioned him as "regular Nashville" for the first time.

In 1990 he had trouble again. His belongings were seized due to a lawsuit concerning his father (who died in 1986, buried in a Coe tour jacket) breaking a lease Coe had cosigned. Nineteen ninety-one brought some good news as daughter Shelli Stephanie, now a beautiful young woman, reunited with David. He was regularly seeing Carla already, and now he could finally retire the song "Missin' the Kid," which he had written about Shelli in 1983.

Nineteen ninety-six and 1997 were huge years, both positively and negatively, for Coe. He published his bizarre cut-and-paste scrap book, *This Is David Allan Coe*, a hefty 300-plus-page epic. The main impetus for publishing it seems to be his disappointment at not being mentioned at all in George Jones's book. They'd known each other since 1976, and shared a producer, Billy Sherrill, so Coe, who loves to see his name in print (he reprints his press clippings liberally in all his books), probably read Jones's book with anticipation. He also didn't like all the bad things Jones said about other people. In reaction, this book has Coe going out of his way to mention everyone he knows and say nice things about them. This includes people he's put down in the past, including Charley Pride, who he once called an Uncle Tom, but now praises.

However, as he was finishing the book he learned that the IRS had seized his bank account. Jody Lynn kept the books, and thought she had it figured out, but after doing all they could they still owed thousands. By playing at a festival called Outdoor with the Outlaws, with Coe, George Jones, Black Oak Arkansas, Kentucky Headhunters, and Confederate Railroad (an act that started as Coe's backup band), David expected a big payday that would get him out of the hole. Sadly the event was a poorly promoted bust, and only sixty-nine people paid. In debt, and low, soon David was dealt the ultimate blow. His most successful marriage was headed for divorce. David would not be separated from the children, as in earlier divorces, but nonetheless this was the end of the most stable period of his life. He had seen it coming; his *Living on Edge* album, self-released earlier that year, hinted at the troubles.

There was some good news in his life, though. His old label Columbia/Sony, had started an Alternative Country label, Water Dog, and they wanted to sign him. His first new album, 1997's *LIVE: If That Ain't Country*, was released to good reviews, and great sales for a record with no airplay. David embarked on a brutal tour schedule, about 200 a year. He was booked well into 1999 and he was living on the road, conducting his business over the Internet. All four of the kids he had with Jody spent the summer with Coe on the tour. And, as evidenced by the crowd at House of Blues, his touring and new album were paying off with a wider fan base.

As he continues to pick up new fans there are certain issues that many find troubling, notably his views on race and homosexuality. Whether you think Coe is a racist or not depends on your definition (he vehemently defends himself against any charges of racism, and he apparently thinks about the subject a lot). He definitely is candidly race conscious, and has many opinions on racial issues. He has written songs about racial politics, he has lived with black people (in prison and out), and he has insulted the Klan in his songs (though the ambiguity of the lyrics made many think he was pro-Klan). (He elaborates in the interview.) If your definition of "racist" involves concepts of biological superiority, that may not apply to Coe. When he talks about race, he is usually talking about cultural conditions. For example, in *Ex-Convict* he discusses how blacks do time in prison better than whites because they know how to make the best of a bad situation, are used to the conditions this type of environment produces, "don't give a shit about all the things the average Anglo-Saxon holds in esteem," and have better unity. If your definition of a racist involves racial insensitivity, he's profoundly guilty. He uses the word *nigger*, and he thinks that, as a writer, stereotypes are a good tool. But to him, *nigger* certainly isn't a word to use as a threat against blacks or in conspiratorial tones around whites, because he used it conversationally in front of James. And when he declares, "a nigger walked in and said, 'You're gonna suck my dick' . . . I picked up a mop bucket and hit him," I'd venture he killed him less because of the *nigger* part, and more because of the "suck my dick" part.

Speaking of dick sucking, Coe also has lots of theorizing about homosexuals in his book, but for the most part it has to do with prison culture. He even boasts that he's only had two or three homosexual encounters, and that he always took the masculine role. In prison the only homosexuals that are really dangerous, he explains in his books, are undercover ones who are capable of violence rather than being exposed. Coe actually wrote a backhanded Gay Rights song on his raunchy album *Nothing Sacred* called "Fuck Aneta Briant" (the most outrageously misspelled-for-legal-reasons title this side of the *Dukes of Hazzard*–themed "Dazzey Duks"). The song takes the antigay activist to task, with the amazing lyrics "Fuck Anita Bryant / Who the Hell is she / Telling all them faggots / That they can't be free / Throw that bitch in prison / then maybe she'll see / just how much them goddamned homosexuals mean to me / Because they . . . Wash your clothes / clean your cell / help you drain your hose / give you smokes / laugh at jokes / sew up all your clothes / rub your feet / beat your meat / Heaven only knows / What I'd do without those homosexuals / They all read and

Left to right: Porter, Coe, Bosco.

write / Fuck all night / Clean your fingernails / help you dress / play you chess / lay you down some rails / Be your wife / take your life / in a jealous rage / who says we don't need them homosexuals?"

Getting back to the present day, after the show we were escorted up to Coe's dressing room. To describe the scene as surreal would be an understatement. House of Blues, Inc., has an "eclectic" and "down-home" decor, which means that every room looks like a log cabin with every square inch of wall and ceiling painted in bright colors by a pseudo–Howard Finster. The only light in the room comes from a TV in the corner playing soft-core cable porn with the sound off. The large man slumped in the chair in the middle of the room has his back turned to the set, as he relaxes in the silent room. His dark, tinted glasses shade tired eyes, and his beaded beard hides a face that looks weary and sick. His sleeveless shirt displays the bright, fresh tattoos that an artist named Squinch had recently done to cover David's prison ink. We sit down on the couch in front of him as he tells his assistant to try to find him a doctor, and to prepare to possibly cancel tomorrow's show. After brief introductions, we start our tape player, try to keep our eyes off the soft focus shenanigans on the TV monitor, and over the next hour engage in this intimate low-key conversation:

James: *I really liked the fact that you did a couple of songs off of* Penitentiary Blues.
DAC: Thanks.

James: *I came up thinking you were a blues singer, because long before you had the hits with Columbia my father bought* Penitentiary Blues. *Is anyone going to reissue that?*
You know, Columbia records bought that. They bought *Requiem for a Harlequin* and *Penitentiary Blues*. I *tried* to buy it back from 'em a couple of times.

Bosco: *They just shelved them?*
They're just sitting there on it. They don't even know what they got.

James: *I understand that right around the time that* LP *came out, you played New Orleans with Grand Funk Railroad.*
Exactly.

James: *What was the story behind that?*
See I started out with Grand Funk before they were famous, up in Michigan, and there was a guy named Terry Knight who used to have a band, Terry Knight and the Pack. Bob Seger lived about three miles from me on a farm, and there was another band called the Third Power. So, we had an opportunity to play down in New Orleans. At the time I didn't even have a band, because I had just went out on my own and made my first album, made it on my own, playing by myself. The Railroad bought me a little squirrel monkey. I had a diaper on that monkey and had it on a chain and that monkey was walking around on stage while I was playing. . . .

James: *Just you by yourself, and the monkey . . . ?*
Yes. It was a strange situation; I had never experienced anything like that. There was like 10,000 people there. And when I got through playing and came off the stage, there was like a catwalk thing that went over the top of the people's heads and went into where the dressing room was at. As I was walking in there some guy handed me some pills, and I just took 'em, I didn't even know what it was. And it turned out to be mescaline. Later I watched myself actually get up and go to the bathroom, but I actually didn't go anywhere *(laughter)*. And it kind of flipped me out the next day when I found out all the stuff that I had did on this mescaline. So I just never got into the drugs scene because of that one situation. I, being a Virgo, always liked to be in control. That just kind of was a weird situation. And

then when I got out of that show I went to New York City and played a place called Max's Kansas City. I was the first guy from Nashville to play up there, even though I was playing blues as well as country stuff, but mostly blues.

Jake: *How'd you go over?*

Real well. It was funny, *Rolling Stone* said, "David Allan Coe went to New York City to look at the freaks and found the freaks looking at him." I guess I was just as different to them people as they was to me.

Jake: *What happened to the monkey?*

The monkey died, man. My grandmother, she kept him one time when I was on tour and her house caught on fire and the monkey got burned up in the flames.

Jake: *What was his name?*

His name was Panuch.

Jake: *Speaking of monkeys, you did "Monkey David Wine" tonight . . .*

I didn't . . .

Jake: *No, I'm sorry, you did "Death Row," about your last meal, but both are toasts where you make crazy lists similar to Screamin' Jay Hawkins's "Alligator Wine." Were you in prison with Screamin' Jay Hawkins?*

Oh yeah. I was not only in prison with Screamin' Jay Hawkins, but he was in the cell next to me, and we were both in the band—he played saxophone and stuff in the band. And actually a lot of songs that I was writing, Screamin' Jay got out of prison before me, and he kind of did his versions of the songs. You know, I've never seen him since I got out of prison. I don't know how much touring he does. I was in Africa one time and he was there. I always wanted to ask him, hey man why did you do this? Why didn't you just do your own thing? You know, in those days they called me Screamin' Tee. And it was a whole different deal. He was there for biting some girl's nipple off her breast or something. And then when I got out of prison, I met my all-time hero. The first day I was out of prison I went into Sun records and I was talking to Shelby Singleton over there; at the time he had Sun records and he had Plantation records and two or three other things. They had a black label also that was producing different black singers. And there was a promotion man there; I got to talking to him, and he says, "Your music sounds pretty black oriented and black influenced," and I said,

"Well yeah." And he said, "Who's your favorite singer?," and I said, "Hank Ballard." He said, "Hank Ballard?" And I said, "Yeah Hank Ballard and the Midnighters." And he said, "Shit, Hank's right over recording right there in the studio." And I went over and met Hank Ballard. And we got to talking, and he said, "Where are you staying?" I said, "I just got into town, I ain't got a place to stay," and he said, "You wanna stay with me?" And I said yes. I got an apartment with Hank Ballard, and we started writing songs together. I got to talking to Hank about "The Twist," and I said, man you must have a lot of money. And he says, "Oh they bought me a Cadillac," and I said, "You're kidding me? Fucking Cadillac for 6,000 dollars, what the fuck are you talking about?" So we got these lawyers, and went back in, them people up in Cincinnati had that record label King records. It's all kind of really strange because Syd Nathan owned King Records at the time. I record for King records now, but Moe Lytle owns King records — it's a whole different thing. They still got a lot of Hank's stuff in the vault. I went and told Shelby, "Hank ain't nothing but a country boy. I don't know if you ever thought of having a black Country singer?" This is before Charley Pride came along. I took Hank in the studio and cut "Sunday Morning Coming Down," the Kristofferson song, on him. And nobody would play him. And then Otis Williams from Otis Williams and the Charms came down and we did some country things on him, and it never happened. That seemed like an awfully long answer to one question.

James: *Did you produce the Otis Williams country album, with the Midnight Cowboys?*
You've seen it?

James: *Yeah, I didn't know you produced it.*
I didn't produce it; I was just kind of responsible for getting Otis there and getting them interested in it. You know, Stoney Edwards, he did some of my songs, another black country singer, that I think is probably the greatest black country singer in the world, but he never got the recognition. It's kind of like in Nashville they got their token black guy which is Charley Pride, so they don't need another one, you know what I mean.

Jake: *Now a lot people don't know your story . . .*
Do you have my newest book, *This Is David Allan Coe*? Bobby get them *This Is David Allan Coe*. This is almost like my personal photo album; plus it talks about Hank Ballard, it talks about Charles Manson — you know I

taught Charles Manson how to play the guitar. And Jimmy Hoffa bought my first bus for me.

Jake: *Is there anything you want to update or get straight?*
Like what?

Jake: *Obviously one of the things that happened with you in your career is that media changed their tune and the story on you at one point . . .*
Now I can tell you the story about that. There's a guy named Chet Flippo that was involved in *Rolling Stone* magazine, he was married to a woman named Martha Hume, who was involved in *Country Music* magazine. Chet Flippo was a big supporter of the Willie Nelson Family, of which I was a member of. Willie and I were both being managed by Neil Reshen out of New York City. And Neil also managed Miles Davis. Anyway, what happened was, we went back to Channel 13 in Dallas, Texas . . .

Jake: *On KERA?*
Yeah, and what happened there was I said, "Fuck" and "Motherfucker," and I said a few things on TV.

James: *Live broadcast?*
Yeah, live broadcast, so anyway, *(as part of the special we)* went back to the penitentiary there. Well, it's kind of hard to understand. There's a guy named Pete Perini now who was the warden at Marion Correctional Institution but when I was on Death Row in the Ohio State Penitentiary, he was just a captain and he was the . . . if you do something wrong in prison you go in front of a board or a committee, and they sentence you to so many days in the hole, or whatever. What happened was, there was a fight in the yard. And there was a black guy named Kincaid that got killed with a hammer and, uh, they had me and a guy named Hound Dog and a guy named Jimmy Blanton; they had three of us as suspects in this killing, and they put us all on death row, L. Block. In the Ohio State Penitentiary it's kind of a weird situation. You got eight rows of cells like this, and you got so many cells down here on each row. Well the bottom row is death row, and up here is L. Block, which is maximum security. OK, now if death row becomes full, and they put a death row inmate on the second tier, that also becomes death row. Even if there's only one person there, it's still death row. So, they came and said to me, the committee, they said, "We're going to put you on death row, motherfucker, until you confess to this deal here, and we're going to take you into town, and we're going to try you for mur-

der." So they put Jimmy and they put Hound Dog on the L. block section, and they put me down on level two, which was death row. And every day they would, you know, come and question us and try to say who did what and whatever. Well, Jimmy Blanton was already doing two life sentences, and I had known Jimmy Blanton since I was ten years old. We was in several different institutions together. So Jimmy sent a note down to me with one of the trustees and said, "I'm going to take this, I'm going to take this." And, so Jimmy rang his cup and they come and got him, and he just told the warden, look I'm the one that did it; I'm the one that did this. Well they knew obviously what was going on—I mean they're not stupid. They knew that Jimmy was taking the rap because he's already doing life; what the fuck could they do to him anyways, you know what I mean. So, one time when we were sitting around talking at Willie's house, Chet Flippo and Martha are there, and I'm telling this story like I'm talking to you guys. Well two years later *Rolling Stone* called me up and said we want you to tell that story, and I said, "Fuck you, I ain't telling that story. There ain't no statute of limitations on murder, motherfucker." So when this article came out in *Rolling Stone*, Chet obviously got mad because his wife was involved and her ego was involved, so they did this hatchet job and said that I'd never been to prison, that it was all made up by the Shelby Singleton corporation, that I'd never been on death row, and all that stuff. Then this magazine out of Dallas called *Iconoclast* got mad about that and they came to talk to me and they said, "David, we don't want you to confess anything, we just want you to tell us some names so we can say yes this incident really happened." So I told 'em, and they went to Ohio and they got the newspaper article that had the story where the inmate was killed and these three inmates were put on maximum security, and L. Block was death row. And they went to Pete Perini, and Pete Perini now is the warden. Now Pete Perini doesn't want to say, "Yeah I put the motherfucker on death row, yeah beat the motherfucker's brains out trying to get him to confess about a murder." They ain't going to say that. It's just like Sam Sheppard—they make you sign a release before they let you out the joint. So anyway, that deal went down and *Iconoclast*, which is a small magazine, wrote the whole story how they went down there and talked to warden, and Pete Perini says there's no record of David Allan Coe ever having been *convicted* of murder. Well we know that. No one ever said I was convicted of murder. I never said that. All I said was that I was on death row, which I was, physically, on death row.

Jake: *The thing is, before that in* Rolling Stone *you were a genius and all your music was good. After that . . .*

Exactly.

Jake: *If you buy the* Rolling Stone Album Guide *today, all the records are now one-star or two-star records. You went from being a genius to——*

James: *As a matter of fact, when* Penitentiary Blues *came out,* Rolling Stone *recognized it; they mentioned something like, "David Allan Coe is twenty-nine years old and he's got tattoos everywhere, including some places I won't even mention."*

Exactly, and I won Blues Artist of the Year in a magazine called *Blues Unlimited* out of England, and they said I was the greatest white blues artist they ever saw, greatest white blues songwriter, guitar player, you know, long before Stevie Ray Vaughan or any of these fucking guys. I was on tour with B. B. King and Mavis Staples and the Staple Singers and Hank Ballard, and B. B. called me on his bus and he said, "David Allan, I'm going to tell you son, you're the baddest motherfucker that I've ever seen not to be black, but," he said, "Son you're going to starve to death, 'cause nobody wants to hear no white boy sing the blues." And that's when I started hanging around Centennial Park and met Kris Kristofferson, and I went out on the road with Kris, and Kris told me the same thing. We did a show in New Jersey and he said, "I got a guy I want you to meet I found in Chicago, John Prine." He put me and John Prine in a room, and we sat for fuckin' nine hours and just played songs for each other. And I said I can't believe you, and he said I can't believe you either. And then, of course, John introduced me to Steve Goodman *(author of* DAC*'s hit "You Never Even Called Me by My Name")*, and that's how all that happened. But people just forget what country music was like when I went to fucking Nashville. You know, it's amazing . . . Bobby Bare was on TV one night and he said, I just wish they had some kind of category for David Allan Coe because the guy really deserves some kind of recognition. All you longhaired, young motherfuckers with earrings playing country music, you couldn't have did that if this guy didn't take the heat for that shit. He'd get the beer bottles thrown at him and shit. I get the same problem when I get these guys that come up and give me these Ku Klux Klan cards, you know. They want to meet me backstage. And I always piss 'em off, 'cause they go, "Oh man, you don't like niggers." And I go, "I don't like white people." You know.

Jake: *They heard that one line off* Nothing Sacred.
Right, and to me it's humor. You know, "It's hard for you to work a dollar a week / and the Ku Klux Klan is bigger / so why don't you take the sheets off your bed / and let's go hang a nigger." You know I figure you're just a stupid motherfucker if you do that, that's what I'm saying.

Jake: *James's dad ordered that album through the mail.*
Aw jeez . . . *(laughs)*

James: *I got to tell you about this, I used to read* Easy Rider *magazine, and that's where I found out about* Nothing Sacred. *That's where my father found out about it, because he still identified you with* Penitentiary Blues, *and here it was ten years after, and so we ordered that, and then like a year later you sent us a form letter that read like, Dear Customer, since you liked* Nothing Sacred *so much, I'd like you to audition these lyrics to the next record, and there you were with the "nigger" song.*
(laughs) Oh yeah, it is a great fucking song, you got to admit that . . .

James: *I wish I still had the form letter. Oh yeah, that brings me to another thing, I was reading you once put out a record called "Two Tone Brown."*
That's a bad motherfucker, now you'll love that record. I'll tell you the story about it. "Two Tone Brown" is about a black guy who marries a white chick; they call the baby Bright Bright Brown, 'cause he's kind of lighter, and this baby grows up, he marries a white chick and he has a baby and they call him Light Light Brown, and this goes on, they keep marrying trying to cross the color line. Trying to get out of the ghetto, trying to pass for white. They finally get this motherfucker that is *white*, and this motherfucker falls in love with a nigger, and they call that baby Two Tone Brown. Can you picture this: this is generations trying to get this kid to finally pass for white, and they finally get this motherfucker and he falls in love with a black chick. *(laughs)* It's fucking killer, it's a great song. I have never in my whole life had someone ask me about that record except one guy who played on the record, and he played lead guitar for Wayne Newton. And I call him Wrong Change; his name is Dale Sellers. He plays left-handed guitar upside down. I don't know if you know this, but Jimi Hendrix was my first lead guitar player when I first went to Nashville.

James: *Yeah, he was in Nashville for a while.*
A guy came to a show the other night and he said, "Man, I was in Centennial Park when you and Jimi Hendrix and your band was playing there and

they shut the power off on you for saying "Fuck," and they had to take Hendrix to the hospital because he was in the middle of a guitar solo. *(laughs)*

James: *What happened to that funeral hearse that you used to travel around in that had the 45s pasted to the window.*

Shelby had that for a long time. He must have just had it taken off to a junkyard or something.

James: *That was on the back cover of* Penitentiary Blues, *and they have the picture of you with your fly open . . .*

I was skinny then.

Jake: *How often did you wear the mask (*as the Mysterious Rhinestone Cowboy)*?*

I did the mask up to the first Willie Nelson picnic, and I never wore it after that.

Jake: *How long did you wear it? It's on that great photo on the cover of the* New York Times Magazine.

Wasn't that something? Man that was fucking unbelievable; that was a great picture.

Jake: *So how long were you wearing the mask?*

Probably about two years. The statement was, I wanted people to like my music, not like me because I was pretty or the way I comb my hair or whatever. Bringing things up to the modern era, I just think it's amazing that Dimebag Darrell from Pantera came to see me in Fort Worth, Texas, the other night, and he had a whole shopping bag of David Allan Coe stuff that he bought at the souvenir stand, and he gave me their new video, and I watched it. You got to understand, I don't know these guys; I don't know who he is?

Bosco: *You don't know these guys? Cause Phil* (Anselmo of Pantera), *all summer he's wearing your shirt.*
This guy worships me, and he says, "Just tell me you're all right through it all, you're OK, and is there anything you can tell me?" And here I am, I'm fifty-eight years old, and I'm saying to this kid, you got to try to keep your publishing, don't let them get your publishing away from you. If you take every drink everybody offers you, you'll be a fucking alcoholic before you know it. And then I watch this video, and they drink eight fifths of fucking whisky before they go on stage. The kid's telling me, yeah we got a lot of lawsuits against us. And then I see this video where they're trashing these fucking hotel rooms and shit—no wonder you got lawsuits against you motherfucker, goddamn! Now that I know, I'm really impressed that these guys——

Jake: *Well they're musicians, so of course they'd know about you, but I was really surprised by this crowd here tonight. I've never seen at a David Allan Coe show . . .*

James: *Yuppies!*

Bosco: *You're crossing the line!*
We're getting big college now, I mean short hair. I still get a lot of hair and a lot of beards, but not like it used to be. And you see several black people now coming to the concert. Down South you got people coming there. We got on the Internet now, you know. I just got e-mail from a guy, his name is Armstrong—he sent me an e-mail—he's black and his wife is black and they like me and he was trying to explain to his wife about the "If That Ain't Country" song, you know the part "working like a nigger." To me, a songwriter is no different than an artist. You can take colors and mix them and you're painting with colors. When you use stereotypes, you know, you see the picture. When someone says lazy as a Mexican, stingy as a Jew, working like a nigger, wild as an Indian on whiskey . . . you just get a visual, and that's what words are for. And that's why I get mad at the Klan when they come. To me "working like a nigger / for my room and board," for me that's painting a picture; that's what I seen there.

James: *In your book,* Just for the Record, *you say, you're, "looking for a woman that will treat me like a white man."*
(Laughs) You got to understand, the way I was brought up, I probably didn't know . . . I knew I was white, but I didn't identify with white. When I was in

National Training School for Boys in Washington, D.C., there was probably sixty blacks for every white person there. The only white guys that weren't getting fucked in the ass were the ones that could either fight or sing . . . And I was a singing motherfucker. *(laughs)* I was singing my ass off.

James: *What about that band you had in prison?*
It was an all-black band.

Jake: *Anyone else prominent in that band?*
Yeah, there was a trumpet player named Joe Ambossi; he's a big arranger now out in Las Vegas. There were several that were in the prison band that were pretty famous and became pretty famous; there was a saxophone player and he was a black Muslim—Logan Rollins was his name—and he became pretty famous, the most famous to come out of that situation *(Coe has referred to this bandmate elsewhere as Sonny Logan Rollins, so he may be confusing him with Sonny Rollins).*

Bosco: *How'd you hook up with the wrestler Dusty Rhodes in the early '80s doing that music ending to the wrestling match?*
See Dusty Rhodes is a big David Allan Coe fan and I'm a big rasslin' fan. So Dusty came up with the idea of the Great American rasslin' Bash, and we put that deal together . . .

Bosco: *And it goes down in history as the first music/wrestling crossover.*
You'll see Dusty's picture in that book.

Jake: *In* For The Record *you talk about that shower incident. Is that an accurate account?*
Yeah, that was after that deal *(in the yard)* there. A lot of people get those two things confused. A lot of people want to associate the death row thing with the shower incident. That was two totally separate things. I did go to L. Block, which was the same thing, but it wasn't death row at the time I was in the L. Block section. But that was basically the same thing; the guy walks in the shower and told me he was gonna fuck me, and I told him he had the wrong guy. And there was a mop wringer there, like on a bucket, and I just picked it up and hit him with that. But see, that happens every day in prison, and it ain't no big fucking deal to me. I mean there was somebody getting stabbed every day in the penitentiary when I was there.

Jake: *Anything significant over the last few years that wasn't covered in the books?*
Well, I don't know if you know but I just went through a divorce with my

wife, Jody Lynn, after being married for fourteen years. On Thanksgiving Day I was having a rough time dealing with the divorce and I wrote a whole book, and I went back and read it. I'm going to do an audiobook coming out pretty soon about that situation. And I've got another book I've been working on since I was fifteen. I've been studying different religions and different things about . . . this book is going to be called *In Search of Understanding*, and it's about the principles of Jesus Christ that's being taught, and it's a real different thing. It explains that I don't think there's anything such as a bad word, I think words are used to communicate—like colors are used to communicate in paint-

ing—and I don't think there's any such thing as a bad word, (that's) number 1. Number 2, Jesus didn't speak English so he sure didn't make any rules about the English language, and "fuck" is a good word as far as I'm concerned, and sometimes there's no other word that can say what you mean. It gets very in depth about a lot of things, talks about the crucifixion, talks about the Virgin Birth, talks about the basic principles, be fruitful and multiply. And things I believe coming from studying about Mohammed, studying about Buddha, studying about Jesus, studying about all these different messiahs. There's so many people on this earth that doesn't realize that there's a whole earth population out here that doesn't even believe the things that they be-

lieve in. I grew up, my mother was a Pennsylvania Dutch Amish girl and my father was a Mormon, two very strict religious orders. And then when I went to prison you only had two choices—you could either be a Protestant or a Catholic—you couldn't be a Mormon, so I chose to be a Catholic and I learned about that religion. And then I studied the Baptist religion, the Seventh Day Adventist religion, and I studied Buddhism, and I studied Marxism . . . I've got a very extensive library, and I read everything that can be read from the Dead Sea Scrolls to *Holy Blood and the Holy Grail*, which is a very good book—I'd recommend it. I think people should open up their eyes to see that basically religion is something that the minority uses to control the majority, which means that the government uses religion to control the people. They use fear and superstition to control the people. The only ways you can control the people are with your military forces, your police forces, or with their own superstitions and beliefs. So then you have all these secret societies, like the Masons and the Shriners, and all these people that are very male orientated and they're supposed to have all these secrets of life. I talk about all those things. And basically I don't want people teaching that shit to my kids. I want my kids to know about truth. I don't want someone telling my kids about the Easter Bunny. I've never told my kids about Santa Claus. I've never put something in front of them and then took it away and said, "Ah, but it's just a joke, honey." I've never done that to my children and I never would. Because, obviously, if you do that with the Easter Bunny and Santa, when you put Jesus in there, they'll say, "OK, three years from now the old man is going to say this is fucking bullshit, too." I want them to understand the principals.

Jake: *Do you consider yourself a Mormon now?*
Not at all. I don't believe in organized religion. I believe that everybody should have a personal relationship with their spiritual self. Call it God or Jesus or whatever you want to call it. I think everything's within you. You have the power to create, the power to procreate, just like God did. It's all within you, the whole universe, the knowledge of the universe is within you. And you just have to get in touch with yourself. Not bad for a hillbilly, huh? *(laughter)*

Jake: *One thing that can be said about you, it's that just like the boy at school who wears earrings in both ears has got to be a guy who can kick ass, you always used the fact that you were the biggest, baddest, craziest looking guy in the room to actually get away with singing these sensitive . . .*
Exactly!

Jake: *The sensitive ballads outnumber the "asskickers" on your albums at least two to one . . .*
Exactly. Total contradiction.

James: *You had a whole miniseries going with "For Lovers Only."*
See, I wrote "For Lovers Only" as an album. Each verse of the song had a song written about that verse. And it was all to go together. Never happened. You have to get my *Living on the Edge* album so you can understand my concepts. It's basically, I played every instrument, I sang every part, I wrote every song. I play synthesizers, strings, saxophones, whatever the

fuck you hear, I'm doing it. It's on my own label so it didn't get a lot of rec-ognition, but I guarantee you, it is a master-*fucking*-piece.

Jake: *Now that you're hooked up with Sony, what's the plans?*
Sony's gonna be all right. We're getting ready to do a studio album. I'm writing. We sold 60,000 albums *(of* LIVE: If That Ain't Country*)* with no airplay right out of the fucking box.

Jake: *Do you consider yourself an author?*
I consider myself an entertainer. I'm into magic.

James: *And ventriloquism? Whatever happened to the dummy—did you burn him?*
No still got him, Sandy Hilton's his name.

James: *He had a twin, too, right?*
Yeah, Buster Barton. I still got my birds, my doves. I still fuck with them and I do that stuff, you know. I've tried to do some of everything. But I consider myself more of a writer than anything. Whether it's song-writer, or novels, books whatever. I wrote my first fiction novel called *Psychopath*. That's a whole different trip.

David Allan Coe & Rocky the Chimp

James: *Did Anita Bryant ever find out about your tribute to her?*
No, but you know, my wife, we had a big problem with that, 'cause we lived in Branson, and Anita Bryant moved up there to Branson, Missouri.

Jake: *Do you have anything you want to make sure you say here?*
I'll tell you what, I've been doing this a long time and I've been interviewed by a lot of people, but you guys right here, this has been the most interest-ing interview that I've ever done in my life; you are the most knowledge-able people about me that I've ever spoken to.

James: *We're just trying get things right.*

That wasn't the end of our night with David, however. After learning that Bosco has a side job dealing "exotic" movies, David told us how he recently had purchased the Tommy Lee / Pamela Anderson sex video, and was very disappointed. "I bought that motherfucker, and it ain't shit." It then came up that Bosco had procured an . . . unusual video, one that David had been looking for, so we all went down to his car to get it. Though the Coe show had ended an hour before, and a disco party had taken its place in the club, when we ventured outside there were still a handful of frantic Coe enthusiasts waiting to see their hero. Immediately it became clear that these weren't your average fans. A young man pushed a funeral program underneath Coe's beaded beard and blurted out, "David, we played your music at my father's funeral, sign this!" Though sick and weary, Coe signed everything. Then a homely, middle-aged woman started histrionically talking to, or more accurately, talking at the iconic singer.

"David, don't you remember? The sixties!? David, c'mon *Da*-vid." What was most striking was the way she said his name, with a lilt on the first syllable, like she was talking to someone she just spoke to last Thursday. He clearly had no idea who she was despite her continuous repeating of his name. As he apologized and walked with us to the car, she became agitated. Finally in a louder tone she yelled across the parking lot, "David wait, my daughter's here; she's thirty and she might be yours!" The lunacy in her voice was evident, but it was nothing comparable to the banshee howl that followed: "You're walking away from me . . . *again*!"

As we approached the car my mind was reeling. This woman seemed so crazy that she may have made the whole thing up. And if she hadn't, and was just now approaching him thirty years later, she was even nuttier. And why was she just standing still; *she had feet*? Then I realized that all the other fans out there were looking at David and talking to him in a similar way. Perhaps she did have a one-night stand with the Mysterious Rhinestone Cowboy in the Summer of Love, but more likely, much like all these fans, something about his lyrics, his melodies, his persona, his charisma, convinced her that she *really* knew him. Each and every fan out there had been touched by his work, and they all felt they had an intimate, important relationship with him. They all *knew* David Allan Coe.

As we said our good-byes, and the fatigued man made his way back to the club, his fans looked at him with awe and love like he was the Lone Ranger, and had just saved the town. He'd be on a tour bus in an hour, heading to some kind of doctor to get whatever treatment he could get that didn't involve ending the tour. And in the next town, as in every town, there would be people his music had entertained, helped, hypnotized, and maybe even twisted. Some of them he would meet face to face, but most of them he would meet from the stage, singing about his fucked-up life and playing his guitar. And if that ain't country, you can kiss my ass . . .

Update

At a future Chicago tour stop Coe invited James onto his tour bus and told him he was very pleased with the article. There were some inaccuracies he complained, but he could not recall what they were. At yet another visit by the perpetual touring troubadour (tax problems and alimony do not allow the singer to take time off), Coe's manager informed Bosco that his video gift was appreciated. In the decade-plus since our interview Coe has continued to record, releasing two live albums, an audio book called *Whoopsy Daisy*, and a couple of studio albums (not to mention a tsunami of budget truck-stop releases on King/Gusto and numerous collections and reissues). His most prominent CD over the last decade was his collaboration with Pantera's Dimebag Darrell. Their band Cowboys from Hell recorded *Rebel Meets Rebel*, the release of which was delayed after Darrell's onstage murder by a mentally disturbed fan. Other Coe cohorts who have passed on since this interview include his hero

Coe and son.

Hank Ballard, his prison mate Screamin' Jay Hawkins, and his rasslin' pal Dusty Rhodes. In addition to his work with Dimebag Darrell, his profile was also raised when Kid Rock used Coe as his opening act. In a less positive development, Neil Strauss wrote a *New York Times* article taking Coe to task for his offensive underground recordings, leading to Coe having to again defend himself against / rationalize charges of racism. One interesting note is that Coe is often connected with the pro–Ku Klux Klan country singer Johnny Rebel, many people believing that Rebel is a pseudonym Coe used (the mysterious nature of Coe's racially charged, self-released, underground albums contributing to this confusion). Coe has consistently denied any connection to Rebel, and the White Power–friendly davidallancoe .com (a fan site, not the artist's official site) sells Rebel's CDs under the disclaimer "Looking For Johnny Rebel CDs? You Can Find Them Here But DAC Is NOT Johnny Rebel." In more pleasant developments, Coe has been touring and recording with his girlfriend Miss Kim (Kimberly Hastings), has done a voice for the Cartoon Network show *Squidbillies*, and had a role in Toby Keith's 2008 movie *Beer for My Horses*.

Guy Chookoorian

I f you are anything like me, the phrase "The Armenian Mickey Katz" alone is enough to hook you. When I overheard L.A. cable access superhero Art Fein conjure those magic words, it was enough to motivate me to track down the title holder, Guy Chookoorian. In a flash I was just outside Los Angeles, sitting in a Middle Eastern restaurant, sipping thick coffee, and hearing Chookoorian's life story. Like Katz, who did ethnic versions of popular songs by reworking *Billboard* hits as Yiddish comedy, Chookoorian made a national reputation (amongst Armenian record buyers) in the late '40s by recording his first single, "Toore' Patz Dikran," an Armenian translation of "Open the Door, Richard." But that is just one facet of the jewel that is Chookoorian's career. The Kenosha, Wisconsin–born Armenian American moved to Southern California at a young age (Los Angeles has an Armenian American population of approximately 500,000) and followed his showbiz dreams, resulting in a diverse career that spans over half a century. From his days

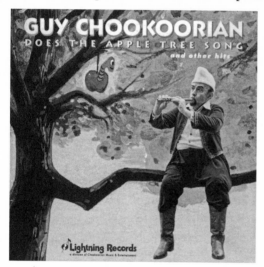

as a teenage cowboy singer on the radio in the 1930s, to his career as an Armenian novelty recording artist in the 1940s and '50s, to his popular Vegas and touring career amidst the belly-dance craze in the 1960s, to his film, TV, and recording career as a swarthy all-purpose ethnic (Armenian, Turkish, Russian, Greek, Italian, Mexican . . . you name it), Chookoorian has had one amazing ride around the fringes of Hollywood. His Tinseltown credits include appearances in *Columbo*, *I Spy*, *General Hospital*, *The Lucy Show*, *Charlie's Angels*, *Ironside*, *Full House*, *Baretta*, *Police Woman*, *The Bold and the Beautiful*, *The Postman Always Rings Twice*, *Masada*, *Lou Grant*, *Barnaby Jones*, and scores more. His Guy Chookoorian Orchestra (featuring a bevy of lovely belly dancers) entertained for three decades around Vegas (at the Flamingo and Aladdin, amongst other places), Hollywood (at Ciro's), and across the U.S. and Canada. His bizarre career has been as unpredictable as the name of the record label he has run for the last forty-five years: Lightning.

Jake Austen: *Tell me about your musical background.*

Guy Chookoorian: As a child, from the time I was very little, I was able to play the harmonica and I used to get up in front of all the Armenian functions and play. This was in Wisconsin and Illinois. I learned to play the oud *(a pear-shaped stringed instrument associated with Middle Eastern music)* watching my dad when he played, and I remember when I was very little, maybe three or four years old, I would sit on the floor and play the oud. Now I thought what I was playing was a song, it might have been nothing, but I was able to play on the bottom string, pick what I thought was a song.

Was your father a professional musician?
No, he was an excellent musician, but he didn't do that for a living. Later my cousin sold us a banjo for four dollars and I used to pick tunes on that, and a friend had a ukulele, so I became familiar with those instruments.

Were you playing traditional Armenian music?
Well, the oud I didn't really start playing until I was older. Some Armenian music, but a lot of the stuff was like "Oh Susanna," what a kid knows. I remember, maybe I was ten or eleven years old I entered a little amateur contest in Waukegan where I played the harmonica; I played "Isle of Capri." There must have been about ten contestants and I came in eleventh. I never really had that much confidence in my musical ability—I'm self-taught, no formal musical training. When I went to the theater on Sundays, in addition to the motion pictures they had vaudeville acts, and the comedians really impressed me and I wanted to be one of those. So when we came to California I used to be at the assemblies in junior high school doing comedy. I had a partner then and we played duets; I played banjo, he played harmonica, and I told jokes. I was about fifteen when another buddy and I went down to a local radio station; we had decided we were good enough to play on the air. So we started working on this local station in Fresno playing Cowboy music and telling jokes at six o'clock every other morning.

So obviously there was no ethnic angle to this act—you were playing cowboy songs . . .
The name of the program was the *Valley Rancher* and we went by the name Gil and Guy, because we were a duet to start. There was another musician they had on the station that played accordion and there was a guitar player, so we became a cowboy band. I started playing ethnic music when we would play for the Armenian picnics and parties.

With the same band?
No, my dad, when he would play for a picnic or a party or a wedding, he would take me along and I would sit in. I would play banjo, playing Armenian music along with the band.

Did you work any comedy into the act when you were on the radio?

We'd play and we'd tell jokes in between, and then the announcer would give the farm report and the weather.

Did you have to get any sponsors?

The thing is, actually, we were not paid so we didn't have to get sponsors.

Did you get work because of your radio show?

We were too young to get jobs; we were in junior high school. But I continued in the Armenian community playing for Armenian functions. I always had this dream, I wanted to be in the entertainment business. Since I was little kid back in Waukegan we would sit on the porch in the summer and all the kids in the neighborhood would gather around, I would be making up stories. I spent more time in the movie theaters than anywhere else. In high school I was in all the assemblies—I was student body president—and we had a hillbilly band: the Fresno Tech Hillbillies. Then I started college, I was working on becoming a doctor—of course it was my mother's idea. I went to college very briefly and then I decided to join the service.

What year was that?

1942, December of '42.

There was a draft, but you weren't drafted?

No, I joined the Air Force. You know, nobody wants to go to war, but all your friends are gone; they are in the service. Every day you are reading something in the paper about one of them being wounded, one of them being killed, and you couldn't stay at home. The streets were almost devoid of civilian traffic and everybody was military, so I joined.

Were you welled up with patriotism?

I wasn't really . . . I could say that I was welled up with patriotism but it was just that we were all going, and I had to be part of it. I didn't hate the Germans and I didn't hate the Japanese. We had some really nice friends who were Japanese in our high school and I couldn't hate them.

Had you ever experienced prejudice as an Armenian American?

In Fresno I didn't experience too much myself, but I knew it was there. I knew people that tried to buy a home in a certain area, and they wouldn't sell it to them.

I ended up in England. I was on a bomber crew; I was a radio operator and gunner. I flew thirty-two missions over Germany and France. Our plane was shot up pretty badly on many occasions. I am believed to be one of the few American airmen to shoot down a German jet-propelled plane, an Me-163. It was never confirmed, but the group I was with, they were under the impression that I had shot it down. I never saw it blow up; I never saw a parachute; all I know is that he was in a spiral going down and the guys are yelling over the intercom, "You got it, Chuck"—my nickname was Chuck— "you got it, Chuck, you got it, Chuck!" I got out of the service in October of '45. I'll tell you something very unique: the roughest mission that I flew was October seventh of 1944 and that's the mission where we lost practically our entire squadron and one year later, October 7, 1945, I was discharged from the service. Ten years later, when my wife and I were expecting our first child, the doctor said the baby will be born on October 7 and, sure enough, October 7, 1955, our son was born. Anyway we were here in L.A. then. In 1946 I worked in a lot of little theaters . . .

You were back in the entertainment industry?
I worked in little theaters; I played for private parties.

Did you have your own band or were you sitting in with other bands?
I would do that—sit in with other bands—but I had my own band.

And what were you called?
Guy Chookoorian Orchestra.

And at that point what kind of music were you playing?
Armenian and American because if we could do double duty we were able to get more work.

Did you have different attire for the different types of music . . .
Tuxedos.

You didn't wear anything "exotic?"
The first time we wore exotic costumes was when we started working clubs and doing a Middle Eastern act in 1958.

In the 1940s were you a full-time musician?
I did odd jobs to support myself. I did everything: I cleaned swimming pools for seven years . . .

Did you have a recording career during this period?
1947 is when I started recording.

Who were you recording for?
My own label, Lightning. I did a 78 rpm record of "Open the Door Richard" translated into Armenian. That was a great gag and it was a great stunt to do on stage. Somebody said, "You know, if there was a record of that I bet it would sell." And it gave me the idea, so that was my first record.

How many did you sell of it?
Several thousand, which was great. For six months I was able to support myself with that one record.

Who do you think was buying your records?
Mainly Armenians.

Where were they sold?
There was a time when I had dealers all over the country. Like two or three in New York, a couple in Rhode Island, Detroit, Chicago, Milwaukee, San Francisco, California.

How did you have enough capitol to start the record company?
The first record cost me the exorbitant cost of $200 to put it out and press 500 copies. Studio cost and everything. I sold those at Armenian picnics. I had asked somebody who had done Armenian records, "How many did you sell?" "Oh, we sold a lot." "How many?" "200." I said, "200, that's nothing to sell," but then I realized, OK I sell 200; it cost me 200 dollars. I can just throw the other 300 away, and I got my money back. Then I started getting orders from Detroit, Chicago. Some guy would write me a letter that says, "Some guy was in our store and they wanted to buy such and such a record; we understand that you are the artist." And they would be ordering hundreds at a time. So I had some pretty good outlets in Detroit, Rhode Island, Fresno and even here.

Were most of your recordings after that first one all novelty cover songs?
Yeah.

What other songs did you cover?
"Smoke, Smoke Smoke That Cigarette" (*"Dzukhe,' Dzukhe,' Dzukhe'"*), "Mule Train" (*"Choriner"*), "I'll Dance at Your Wedding" (*"Harsnikid Bidi Barem"*), "The Ballad of Davy Crockett" (*"Davit Amoo"*), "You Are My Sunshine" (*"Toon Eem Arevs Es"*), "Come On-a My House . . ." (*"Yegoor Eem Doonus"*)

"Come On-a My House" is by Armenian composers, William Saroyan and Ross Bagdasarian (Bagdasarian, a.k.a. David Seville, would later create Alvin and the Chipmunks). Did you know them?
I knew Bagdasarian from Fresno; he used to have a little band around Fresno.

Were you contemporaries?
I was like fourteen, but he was eighteen or nineteen.

Did he play ethnic music?
Not that I know of.

Did he help you at all when you started working in Hollywood?
No. We were friends, I knew Saroyan from "Come On-a My House." Before I would do a song I would ask permission from the publisher, and this was one of the rare cases where the publisher said the composer has to meet you and hear the music before he'll OK it. The next thing I know I went to Saroyan's office in Beverly Hills, and he and his cousin Ross were there and they liked what they heard. At that time I had taken an Armenian song and translated in into English—broken English—and they got a kick out of that. So they thought it could be great if the three of us formed a partnership, started doing things like that. Unfortunately, not long after the two cousins had a falling away and it never happened.

I guess that worked out for Chipmunks fans but not for you. How many records did you put out?
Well, maybe a dozen or so, which later I put on an LP. Also I did comedy records on other labels in the 1960s.

What year did you put the LP out?
1971.

How many did you sell?
Not many, between five hundred and a thousand. It took me fifteen years to get my money back.

Do people collect your records?
Yes.

Have any sold at high collectors' prices?
Not that I know of. In Watertown, Massachusetts, there's an Armenian museum; they have all my records there.

So the late 1940s you started putting out your own records, and you did that until . . .
I'm still doing it *(in the early 2000s Chookoorian put out two CDs collecting his recordings).*

Did you ever record serious Armenian music?
On some of the reverse sides are traditional ethnic songs, but I did orchestral versions, not necessarily ethnic versions.

Did you record for any other label than your own?
In the '60s I did some novelty things, comedy records. I played an Englishman who did tattoos. I did "Clarence of Arabia." I did a parody of Ben Casey—it was called "Ben José"—I did a Mexican accent. I did a few records with Mexican accents.

They sold pretty well?
They became quite well known.

What name were they using for you on the label?
Guy Chookoorian. One of the records, *I Left My Heart in San Francisco,* in a Mexican accent, and the guy that got murdered from *Hogan's Heroes* . . .

Bob Crane?
I got to know him pretty well. At one time he was the highest-paid disc jockey in the United States, and he was constantly playing our version of "I Left My Heart In San Francisco." I called him up to thank him and he said, "Who is this?" And I said, "Guy Chookoorian." He said, "I saw that name on the label; I thought it was a gag." I went down and he interviewed me on the air, and he thought I was pretty funny. He said, "Who's your agent?" I said I didn't have one, and he said, "We'll have to do something about that." He was going to do this play somewhere and there was a part in there he thought I could play, but I had just signed to do the Flamingo and he said, "That's probably better." So that ended that.

So in 1958 when you started doing clubs, was that a major change in your career?
It was in a way, but it was still part time.

What was your act like in '58?
The belly-dance craze caught on, so we started working the local clubs accompanying belly dancers. Anyway the big break came in 1963 when they

The faces of Guy Chookoorian.

needed a Middle Eastern act to work the lounge at the Flamingo Hotel in Las Vegas.

What was the nature of the belly-dance craze? When you did this in clubs was it respectable, or was it considered a little sleazy?
Everybody thought of it as something sleazy. They put it in the same category as stripping, but it wasn't, because at that time there were those who considered that a form of art. They gyrated and all that, but still it was considered a form of art.

What kind of clubs would you perform this act in?
Middle Eastern restaurants and clubs.

Who were the patrons?
It was mixed because there was this interest. There were Americans, but a lot of the ethnics went because it was their music; they identified. In 1963 when we got to the Flamingo in Las Vegas, we were a seven-piece orchestra with seven dancers. We had choreography and stuff like that. When we worked the Flamingo, we were sharing the stage with the Harry James Orchestra, Billy Eckstine, Fats Domino—you get to meet a lot of interesting people. We were there from the end of January, I think, until the end of March, and then we went back again for a short period, in April. Then we came home, and at home we started working in different clubs.

So you were now a full-time professional musician?
That was how I made my living. Near the end of 1963 we went to Las Vegas again to a club called Diamond Jim's Nevada Club, which is now the Golden Nugget. We were there for like five months, came back to Los Angeles and we played Ciro's on the strip, which is now the Comedy Store. In 1964 we first got a call to work on TV. They wanted Greek music for *The Lucy Show*.

Did you appear on camera?
In that particular one we didn't. We were the music, and they had what they called sideline musicians. To date I've been on nearly eighty different television shows and motion pictures, very often on camera, sometimes off camera.

What are some where you are prominently on camera?
Charlie's Angels, a movie called *The Last of the Secret Agents*, one of the *I Spy* episodes.

On the set of *I Spy*. Chookoorian: second from left; Bill Cosby: second from right. Photo courtesy Guy Chookoorian.

You said they wanted Greek music. Were they asking you to do all kinds of ethnic music?
At that time there weren't too many of us around, so whenever somebody would go to the union . . . I was the first oud player to join the union . . . so whenever anybody wanted music . . . I had calls for Indonesian—which I had no idea about—the union would send me because "He's the guy who plays all that strange music."

What were some of the different ethnicities that you would represent?
Armenian, Greek, Arabic, Turkish . . .

Did they ever put dark makeup on you?
Yeah.

Were you comfortable doing the different races and ethnicities?
Yeah. We had to work, and not only that but it's part of our culture; that didn't bother me. In *Masada* the miniseries, we were Jewish musicians; that didn't bother me. Whatever they called for. Sometimes they were confused: they want belly-dance music, and they would ask for Greek music; sometimes they didn't know.

You would just give them what they wanted, I suppose; it wasn't your job to educate them.
In one of the pictures we worked in, the composer had composed some-

thing and it sounded Neapolitan Italian, and the director said, "That's not what I want; I want something Middle Eastern," so I played a Middle Eastern song and they changed it.

You played music in films, but on stage you were also a comedian.
That's what kept us working. See, we would do a show on the road or in the clubs; in between the dancers I would do a comedy routine.

Jokes or little skits?
I would be doing jokes. Ethnic jokes — I would do jokes about the oud, say it was a watermelon on a stick. At one of the clubs I was working in somebody had discarded a cowboy hat and I put that on my head and next thing you know I developed a hillbilly routine. Not the same jokes I used to do on radio, but hillbilly stuff. That's what kept us working, the comedy, and in between shows we'd play conventional dance music so the people could relate.

Like regular pop music?
Yes.

This was during the '60s. Were you playing like Beatles songs, rock 'n' roll, Elvis . . .
Some. "You Got to Change Your Evil Ways"; "Yesterday," the Beatles song; "You're No Good."

Were you still incorporating Armenian versions of pop songs into your act?
Sometimes, when one of the Armenians would ask for it. What I would do is certain songs that they might understand and get a kick out of. What I used to do, my name is Chookoorian, and I used to say, "except on St. Patrick's Day when it's "Chuck O'Ryan." One of my jokes, I'd say, "And now I'm going to do a song from my native land." and I'd start out with Middle Eastern wailing, and I'd ask the audience to join in, and of course they couldn't, and I'd say, "That was terrible, let's do the second verse, and the same thing, and then I'd say, maybe we will have better luck with the third verse, and then we'd do "When Irish Eyes Are Smiling." That became sort of a trademark.

Are you still working clubs?
The last time I did any kind of big club engagement was 1982 in Lake Tahoe. At that time my wife was going through examinations, and when we got to Lake Tahoe the doctor called me and told me my wife had cancer. So I

wanted to get off from the engagement at least for a day to be present when they operated on her. They wouldn't let me go. They said, "Your name is on the marquee; you signed the contract." So they held up the operation until I got home. Luckily they got it in time — she is still alive today. I never went back. I didn't care to go on the road anymore.

That makes sense.
We work around here; we do casuals, one-nighters. The clubs are very bad; they don't pay any money.

What was the last movie or television you did?
Did you see *Fight Club*? It was either that or JAG.

Were you on camera in Fight Club?
Both times. In JAG I was a Russian musician; in *Fight Club* I was a glorified extra.

So you weren't a musician in that movie?
No. They sometimes use me because of my look. I did *I Spy*, and they hired me as a musician, and they kept me on several extra days because the director liked my look — my beard — and he'd stick me in every scene, next to Robert Culp, next to Bill Cosby. It was the look, the beard.

What year did you shave off your goatee?
I did it on several occasions but it grew back, but this time it has been at least a year. Now everyone is wearing the same beard.

You started it! Did you ever do any serious acting?
I would like to have done more serious acting. One film I had a featured part in was an American film made by an Armenian called *Chickpeas*.

Tell me about the Vine Street Irregulars?
The Vine Street Irregulars are these people who used to hang out on Vine Street between Sunset and Hollywood Boulevard, or had their offices there. The music publishing and recording companies were all on Vine Street.

Who is in the group?
There are several guys, you never heard of; Gold Star Records, those guys are a part of it. Herb Jeffries, Gary Owens, Frankie Laine, the Mills Brothers — of course they are gone now, Kay Starr, the list goes on. . . .

What does the group do?
Once a year we have a dinner and honor somebody who was a Vine Street Irregular.

Have you ever been honored?
No. Somebody once said, "How about Guy?" but there are so many people that are so much bigger. I *was* big in my field. One time my band accompanied Donald O'Connor; it was a thrill. We were the only Armenian band that could have done that.

You've had a great career.
I'm satisfied.

Update

In the wake of this interview's publication, and the accompanying segment on our Chicago cable access show, some of Chookoorian's childhood friends in the Midwest were excited to learn he was still alive, and he has since reconnected with the Wisconsin/ Illinois Armenian communities (leading to some nostalgic conversations, and a few

CD sales). Though he is working less these days, Chookoorian occasionally plays functions as a trio with his son and daughter. Chookoorian's son, Arshag, also performs country and bluegrass music as Billy Doohickey, and his band Billy and the Hillbillies were a fixture at Disneyland for many years. In 2009 Time Warner Cable in Los Angeles shuttered the city's public access studios, ending the reign of Art Fein, who had brought Chookoorian to our attention, and who had the musician as a guest several times, including his farewell episode ("He apparently thought I was pretty funny," Chookoorian recalls). Though mortality caused the Vine Street Irregulars roster to dwindle, ending their annual ceremonies, Chookoorian still attends Monday morning meetings of WWII, Korea, and Vietnam veterans at a West Hills Wendy's. The group of pilots, gunners, and other aviation-leaning military men (the gathering is known as Wings over Wendy's) has unofficially made Chookoorian their designated stand-up comic, having him tell a few jokes each week before they clear out before the lunch rush. Tuesday mornings he has breakfast with recording industry veterans (and Art Fein) at Fromin's Deli in Encino. I joined Chookoorian for pancakes one Tuesday and he shared more Armenian Hollywood adventures, including anecdotes about legendary L.A. DJ Art Laboe bringing his octogenarian mother to Ciro's belly-dance shows in the '60s to satisfy her yearning for traditional Armenian music, and memories of playing private parties at the mansion of attorney Robert Kardashian, now best known as the father of the celebutante sisters. He also recalled running into an old friend from the Armenian community while playing oud on a Cher recording session, only to learn that his friend fathered the artist formally known as Cherilyn Sarkisian, and he remembered that his belly dance act at the Flamingo in Vegas was called Cleopatra and the Nymphs of the Nile (Cleopatra was an eighteen-year old Filipina). He also proudly produced a printout of the "Top Ten Requests" from the Armenian Internet radio station www.hyevibes .com, on which "The Apple Tree Song" was number 6, with a bullet.

The Fast

Of all the rock 'n' roll stories (n)ever told, you'd be hard pressed to find one with as many twists, turns, triumphs, and tragedies as the tale of the Zone Brothers. Under the names the Fast, Man 2 Man, Ozone, and a few others, they negotiated the New York underground from the late sixties to the mid-eighties, managing to remain obscure despite talent, breaks, friends in high places, and what for a long time seemed like invincibility. The brothers journeyed from glitter to glam to power pop to punk to new wave to metal to goth to Hi-NRG to just plain gay disco, but it was the music world's labels that kept changing; the family kept their vision of "Pop-ism" pure. If there's one thing that the story of the Zones reeks of it's über-perseverance, a spirit of never giving up . . . even when one perhaps should. But it's also a tale of fraternal bonds, pride to the point of hubris, and finding humor in the face of adversity.

There's a word that Paul, the last surviving Zone brother, often uses to describe the vibe of the brothers' artistic endeavors: "Animated." By this he doesn't mean lively or energetic. Rather, he means that they created an alternate reality where the Zones could be perceived not as people who existed in the three-dimensional, flesh-and-blood world, but rather as *animation*, living cartoons! Brought to life through bizarre costumes, campy, ridiculous lyrics, strangely enchanting pop music, oversized props, sexual ambiguity (and unambiguity!), and a willingness to go *too* far, this surreal Toon Town vision was the truest constant throughout the long, bizarre careers of the Zones.

The saga began in 1953, when the boy who would become Miki Zone was born in Brooklyn to a doting mother and a blue-collar father. Armand (a.k.a. Mandy) was born the following year, and the baby, Paul, two years after that. A sister, who never really got into music, rounded out this good Italian family. Good, but certainly not "normal." The brothers never really developed a relationship with their ex-Marine sergeant father, who was always working two or three jobs, giving Ma Zone more time to spoil her three little men. She supported them in anything they wanted to do. And what they wanted to do was *rock*.

As soon as he reached teenhood, Miki put a band together. "I'd be sitting in school and failing everything because all I would think about is having my own group," Miki explained in a 1980 interview. Miki (guitar) and Mandy (vocals) got some neighborhood kids together and started playing block parties and school dances around '68. They went through a number of names, including Clown Wrasse (named after a striped fish), Cold Power, and For Sale, changing the moniker monthly so they could get hired back at places that were less than satisfied by the band's unique approach. Though it was a time when you *had* to play covers, Miki (always the leader) already was asserting his individuality, by choosing *all the wrong covers*! Instead of Top 40 they kicked out "Tattoo" by the Who, "Jennifer Eccles" by the

Hollies, and "Dedicated Follower of Fashion" by the Kinks. And by 1969 the band already was wearing high-heeled shoes, satin pants, and feather boas.

"This was way before glam. Glam basically didn't come into its own until '72," explains Paul, who as a twelve-year old wasn't yet in the group, but was already fulfilling his role of chief hanger-on-er. "We were never hippies. We were wearing long hair, of course, but more to the style of British bands, the Who, Kinks look. To us that's what rock 'n' roll music was. There was makeup, outrageous clothes; it was very hard for us to find a niche."

That's an understatement. To dress like that would have been a problem anywhere, but in Brooklyn it made the boys particularly unpopular. They weren't dressing oddly to be part of a clique . . . they were genuinely "weird" kids. The only friends they had were involved in music. And at home their father, who (when not working) pretty much kept to himself, had very little to do with his weirdo sons.

Their mom on the other hand completely supported their habits. "She would give us tons of money and buy our clothes, and make things for us." explained Paul, "She completely understood."

That is to say, she understood what was going on through the filter of what her sons were into and the records they had. She knew what was happening, even though it *wasn't* what was happening. The boys went out of their way to get into the most outré music; the first Alice Cooper LP, the first David Bowie album. In 1970 they were inspired by seeing the Stooges at the Electric Circus, with Iggy in silver and a dog collar. When they saw the Alice Cooper band on their first tour, as an opening act at the Fillmore East, people hated their whole show, and hardly clapped. Except for the Zones. This is where the boys were getting fashion tips, from records that they found in bargain bins. Despite what Mom thought, this was hardly what was "happening."

But she kept subsidizing smoke machines, angel wings, and fire extinguishers. Her sons were good boys, no drugs (yet . . . they were notoriously clean for years) and in 1972 Miki and Mandy were still in school, students at Brooklyn College. They lasted about a year before fully devoting their time to the band. Paul never even considered college.

Were they good boys? It depends on your definition. By the time they settled on the name the Fast they were going into the city, buying bottles of wine and hanging out at clubs. "We were noticing things in the paper about other groups like New York Dolls, Wayne County, Queen Elizabeth, Teenage Lust, the Harlots," explains Paul, "These were some of the groups who were there. Forget it! We immediately went as quick as we could to these types of shows, which were held in little ballrooms, little hotels, loft parties."

In addition to Miki and Armand, the band featured drummer Peter Hoffman (a.k.a. Mizz Marrall) and bassist Tommie Mooney (a.k.a. Marshall Moon). Paul was hairstylist, photographer, and gofer. Nobody knew who they were and they couldn't get on bills with other bands, so they rented little ballrooms in hotels, put ads in the *Village Voice* (a couple hundred dollars, courtesy Mom, for a little square) with the promise, "Direct from Wonderland—The Fast." Miki's favorite book was *Alice In Wonderland*, and the show at that point was, in Miki's words "Science Fiction–Acid Rock" with a Lewis Carroll theme.

"People would start to come and see us because everybody was just desperate to see something. Literally there were under ten groups to go see," laments Paul. "We're talking '72, which was a real down point in music. There was literally nothing new coming out that could really grasp you. It just wasn't happening. There wasn't even the Stooges anymore. That at least was our sort of music. Velvet Underground was over. The only thing that was happening was maybe British music, Bowie, T-Rex."

About 50 to 100 people would come to see the Fast, which wasn't bad considering the Dolls were drawing around 150–200 and they were the biggest group on the scene. Paul worked the lights, the door, and played cassettes between the opening band and the Fast. They charged $5, and never had problems with licenses or authorities.

At that point the Fast's stage show was completely over the top, with a smoke machine, elaborate winged, glittering costumes, and heavy theatrical makeup. "KISS would come see us all the time," recalls Paul. "Miki—his stage makeup was one big black heart on one of his eyes, and all clown white makeup, clearly recognizable as Paul Stanley's big star on one eye."

They would enter the stage with a siren blaring (which covered their tuning) and then would burst into originals and humorous covers like "Cabaret" and "My Boy Lollipop." Musically the originals were grounded in power pop, with early Who influences. The group never went through a garage/raw R&B stage, as Miki knew from the outset what his vision was. But despite Miki's mod/pop visions, the band was firmly identifiable as punk due to Armand's vocals—melodramatic wailings in a confident, coarse falsetto that could be so jarring that the band often had more in common with Suicide than Small Faces. Descriptions of the band by fans and the underground press included "The first Renaissance Mod group" and "The Who meet the 1910 Fruitgum Company."

In addition to the costumes and music, what set the Fast apart were stage antics . . . low-budget stage antics! Inspired by Alice Cooper breaking open pillows on stage, with a subsequent explosion of feathers, they would rip open boxes of Cheerios, showering the audience in them. Miki would buy $30 guitars so he could play them for the last number, and then saw them in half. And, of course, they eventually developed the most famous Fast antic . . . the pencil solo!

It all started when they saw in a magazine that there was a shop called Think Big down in the Village that sold giant objects. Soon the Fast's trademark become a seven foot long, bazooka-sized number-2 yellow pencil. Riffing off that prop, Miki developed one of the most absurd rituals in rock 'n' roll history.

Vector, of the late '70s New Jersey band the Lubricunts, the self-described number-1 Fast Fan, recalls the first time he saw the solo: "The pencil guitar solo was a combination juggling act, guitar-hero solo and vaudeville bit. He'd bring out about 100, maybe 150 pencils, and he'd stuff them in his overalls, stuff them in his ears, up his nose, and down his pants. He'd have them under his armpits and between his legs, so he could hardly move. He'd load up the pencils while the drummer played a beat, almost like introducing a magic trick. He's putting on a nice act just loading the pencils, and I'm wondering what he's going to do next. Basically it was a fifteen-minute guitar solo with the pencils used as picks, hammers, and slides. He'd break the pencils out, beat them until they'd break then grab another. He'd use the giant pencil as a violin bow. He'd use the guitar strings and pencils as bow and arrows. All this with his knees together and armpits close to his body until he used enough pencils to free himself of his bondage. It was usually done during 'These Boots Were Made For Walking.' It was a real crowd pleaser."

They pleased crowds at small clubs like Coventry and Kenny's Castaways when they got to play clubs. One venue was out of reach, however. The place to be in that era was Max's Kansas City. It was still in its original incarnation, a trendy artist's haven run by Mickey Ruskin, where the beautiful people could mix with the trash. Touring name acts like Aerosmith and Bob Marley played Max's small live music room. The New York Dolls weren't even let in at first, eventually becoming one of the few local bands permitted to play there. The Fast had no chance of being booked at Max's, but music isn't the only way to perform.

"By this point I'm about fourteen or fifteen," Paul recalls. "So I'm very, very young. My brothers are a little older. We go to Max's; Mickey Ruskin was standing at the door, and for some reason he likes us. I think it had to do with maybe I was a fourteen-year-old boy with long hair dressed in glitter and makeup, and that helped us get in and got us into the back room."

The boys became part of the scenery in Max's famous Back Room, where

Miki. Photo courtesy Paul Zone.

local freaks like the Dolls rubbed elbows with Alice and Iggy and Bowie, who was at Max's every night the week he came to town to do Carnegie Hall.

"Of course," Paul recalls, "we went to see Bowie on his first show at Carnegie Hall in New York. These were all really turning points and almost every week seemed like a new transformation in our life, a progression. It was very exciting."

By '74 things had changed a little bit, but there were still no solid places to play yet, no CBGB's, no Max's for a local group. The bands looked for alternate venues, and one opened up when the New York Dolls played a show in dresses and high heels at Club 82, a drag joint that decided to have rock shows once a week. The Fast

were in the audience, and at that show they met a number of people that would become big parts of their lives, including Debbie Harry and Chris Stein, who had just left the Stilettos and were starting Blondie. That show was a turning point, where the boys got involved with, and accepted by, a crowd in which they really felt they belonged. Soon the Fast were playing at Mothers on Twenty-third street (a gay bar transformed by Peter Crowley into a rock club) with Blondie as their opening act. At a place called Performance Studio, a rehearsal hall where the Fast would put on shows, the Ramones had their debut opening for the Fast, Milk and Cookies, and the Planets. Around this time they also met Lance Loud, most famous for coming out on national TV in PBS's *An American Family*, the documentary that heralded reality TV by showing the underside of a "typical" family. His band, the Mumps, was another group of misfits struggling in the pre-Max's/CBGB's punk scene. Debbie Harry and Lance Loud became good friends with Paul and Miki. Blondie and the Fast, it turned out, would have an extremely significant influence on each other.

When Blondie was looking for a keyboard player, Paul introduced them to Jimmy Destri, a Brooklyn kid who was the brother of a girl Paul went to school with. Though Donna Destri (who went on to sing backup with the Fast, as well as perform with Voodoo Shoes and record disco with Man Parrish in the '80s) hung out in the city, Jimmy's first trek over the Brooklyn Bridge was to be introduced to Chris and Debbie, an introduction that helped form one of the top new wave groups in the world.

In return Debbie, while hanging with Lance Loud and Miki, made a suggestion that would change the course of the Fast. She suggested Paul should be the lead singer.

Miki's vision, it seemed, worked on two levels. On the one hand, his leadership, his concepts, and his power had to stay intact. The Fast were a band that made straightforward, humorous pop tunes that celebrated absurdity and showcased Miki's talents, and that would never change. On the other hand, they also were a band that *had* to make it. Whatever decisions would make the band a success Miki would institute, as long as his vision remained intact. This led to a series of moves over the years that were both incredibly calculated and incredibly naive. Major band moves would be made to give the people what they wanted. More often than not, Miki's concept of what the people wanted had absolutely no grounding in reality. This decision, though, worked out fine.

The concept of making Paul frontman made sense. Not only did Paul, with his long curly locks and chiseled features, look like a frontman, but his public persona made him a natural resource to draw an audience. He was popular, a social butterfly who loved hanging out, being with people, making friends with stars, and going to clubs. He was hairstylist to the scenesters, an amateur photographer who occasionally published shots in magazines like *Creem*, *Punk*, and *Rock Scene*, and a general schmoozer. People were already coming to see the Fast and saying to him, "I thought that was your group." To top it off, he was still a teenager, and three years of extra youth is a lot in rock age. So in 1975 Armand took a blow to his ego and gave up lead vocal duties to become full-time keyboardist.

No records were released during the Armand lead singing era, but Paul's personal cassettes of early shows, Armand's backing vocals on vinyl, two live songs recorded for an exploitation movie, and his later solo work help facilitate a comparison between the two singers. Paul was clearly more of a frontman, his Paul Stanley looks more magnetic than Armand's dark Gary Numan–meets–Johnny Cash vibe, but it's hard to say he's a better singer. Though some called his vocals screechy, Armand clearly had a better range, his melodramatic falsetto a worthy opponent for Miki's guitar histrionics (and whether by design or pitch problems, his singing at times was gloriously adversarial toward the music). Armand could also convey emotion in his vocals in ways that Paul didn't. Peter Crowley, who booked the band at Mother's and at Max's, recalls seeing Mandy playing years later with another band. He performed a song he wrote after a boy broke his heart, and, "the whole audience would be crying. It was like listening to Billie Holiday or something." I think it's fair to say Paul couldn't have pulled that off. However, Paul's greatest vocal gift was his in-song acting. Though his range was limited, he knew how to become the characters the songs needed him to be, helping get the point across in two and a half minutes. As far as pure singing, a good analogy might be to the midlevel male vocalists in the lounge genre. While a Sinatra or a Bennett had a little extra something vocally, a Jack Jones still got the job done. And, of course, in rock 'n' roll, pure singing isn't what it's about. Paul was a genuine rock 'n' roll showman.

The next few years would be the prime of the Fast's popularity. With Miki's antics balanced with Paul's dancing, posing, and strutting, the band stood out. "I grew up with Bowie and Alice Cooper and Mark Bolan," Paul explains. "They were the three guys. So, I just thought morphing those three together would do it. Miki was the only other person on the stage that had an animated sort of thing. I can't think of another guitar player that would put together Pete Townsend and Roger Daltrey, but he did." And it worked. Of all the bands on the scene, the Fast were said to have the biggest screaming girl, teenybopper-style following.

Visually they had gone beyond glam. They developed an "Op Art" aesthetic, wearing big, bold polka-dotted suits, checkered outfits, and zebra stripes, with panels of the same fabric hanging behind them. They combined mod and glam aesthetics with '67 pop art. Other costumes also derived from the musical material. As Miki explained in 1977, "Our act is put in sections . . . racing cars, fantasy, and pure power pop." So songs like "Donna's in the Death Seat," "Moped Man," and "Motorcycle Mania" from the "racing" section got the band into Brando / "Wild One" duds (and an on-stage motorcycle!). "Fantasy" tunes like "Cops and Robbers," "Teenagers from Outer Space," "Comic Books" (inspired by Armand's huge collection of '60s and '70s D.C. comics), and "Cowboys and Indians"–inspired Western wear, sailor suits, and Armand's (inspired by the Sweet) Nazi outfits. They even had special instruments for special songs. Miki used a double-neck guitar for "Siamese Twins." In fact, Miki's array of guitars was one of the band's trademarks, as he had up to ten different-colored models at a time and would use as many as he could in each show.

Not long after Paul joined the band they went into the recording studio with a guy from Yonkers who used to come see the Fast all the time. Eighteen-year-old Bobby Orlando, who would become dance music kingpin Bobby O later in the decade, helped run SBS Recording with his father, Jerry. Jerry was impressed with the Fast and fancied himself their manager for a short stint. The vibe between the Orlandos and the Zones was good, and everyone was very pleased with the songs recorded in that session, including a new one Miki wrote especially for Paul. This tune, "Boys Will Be Boys," was a bouncy, swishy power pop confection that makes "In the Navy" seem straight as a laser beam. Orlando convinced the boys he could get label interest, but nothing developed. However, other record deals and management offers were looming.

Meanwhile, a development occurred on the scene that would change the fortunes of many outsider musicians. Mickey Ruskin got out of the Max's Kansas City business, and Tommy Dean opened the new Max's. With his visionary booker Peter Crowley, all of a sudden the strangest, wildest, most out-there local bands were suddenly being booked on prominent nights and treated with dignity. This would become the Fast's headquarters.

Tommy Dean loved the Fast and wanted to be their manager. They became the house band, playing on weekends and being put on salary. Paul (thanks to an awesome record collection) became a DJ at Max's, alternating nights with transgendered scenester Wayne/Jayne County. The Fast had definitely arrived.

Though they were still getting little critical notice, after Jayne County began playing the tape of "Boys Will Be Boys" during her DJ stints in May of 1976, the buzz was on. *Trouser Press* called it the best demo of any New York band. That song would open many doors for the Fast.

There are three levels on which "Boys Will Be Boys" works, and all symbolize aspects of the Fast that made the group so special.

First and foremost, it's a great pop song. It's an amazingly solid piece, with Miki's guitar and Armand's keys providing a deceptively simple foundation that actually demonstrates some very unusual decision making. The chorus and hooks are infectious and every aspect of great bubblegum music, including deviance wrapped in wholesomeness, can be found in this sounds-like-a-hit tune.

Also contributing to the song's artistic success is the whole "regular guy" angle. A theme throughout the Zones' careers was the juxtaposition of Brooklyn neighborhood dudes and Freaks. They'd paid homage to their Italian upbringing over the years in lyrics, costumes, and even with their publishing companies Bruno Beats ("The name Bruno had that sort of a ethnicity," offers Paul) and Pizza Publishing. This was an aspect not lost on their fans, especially the Italian American ones. Anthony Illarde, who went on to drum in Rights of the Accused and Chamber Strings, recalls going to see the Fast as a twelve-year-old when they came through Chicago. "Try as I might, I just couldn't look like these British punk guys. I can't tell you how excited I was to see these *dagos* rocking! After seeing Paul Zone wearing one, I must have worn a 45 adapter around my neck for the next six months!"

In "Boys Will Be Boys" the neighborhood dudes are the subject, as Paul rattles off a litany of things "*some* boys" do, like get married, have a baby, get a *divorce*," all with a delivery that mixes innuendo, disdain, and delight in baffling proportions. And the fey voice that's delivering these lines introduces the third aspect of the Fast formula, an aspect that is perhaps most important, but also can be a bit confusing: the gay factor.

Now to say there's any confusion about the gay angle of the Fast seems ridiculous, but when talking to Fast fans from that era, several told me that despite the content of most of their songs, the band members' sexual preferences were not things they thought about. Vector, a fan who told me he perhaps went to more Fast shows than anyone else in history, was surprised when I mentioned it. When we spoke later he opened with an apology. Of course, in retrospect, he realized what was going on, but he honestly didn't think they were gay at the time. And with good reason.

"We weren't basically gay at that point," explained Paul. "Well, yeah, we were. But at that point we weren't. We were completely living bisexual lives. It's funny, because not until very later, like in the mid-eighties, did myself or my two brothers ever even discuss the fact. To me it was an understanding. As long as I could remember, from being thirteen on, I considered myself an active bisexual. Especially going to those places. In that scene whether you had any homosexual or bisexual tendencies, it didn't matter. You acted like you did. It was just part of the lifestyle. There would be times when we would go to places, and we would see David Johansen and Arthur Kane making out. Clearly these boys aren't homosexual. But those days, who knew . . .

"I think I was probably more actively bisexual in the early '70s in New York than my brothers were. Because they would have girlfriends, and I would just be having sex with everyone . . . and I was fourteen, fifteen. It was never like something was hidden or closeted. It was something that was just never discussed. When I was like eighteen, nineteen, I started realizing that when that whole phase, that whole fad, started to go away, to me it never really stopped."

Though it seems rather unusual for all three brothers to be gay, that turned out to be the case. "Well, who knows what it is?" shrugged Paul. "It might be the gay gene, or maybe the culture; it may be the alienation of our father; it may be my mother's overprotectiveness." Whatever the reason, eventually their gay identities would be integral parts of their musical success. But in the '70s Max's era, it just made them part of the pack.

Max's Kansas City was an amazing brand name during that period. Even when the club sometimes struggled with a draw, it maintained the kind of name recognition that would be spun off into Hard Rock proportions if it had come up in the '90s. Tommy Dean decided to capitalize on this and started his own record label, Ram (later Max's Kansas City Records) to release a compilation album of Max's bands. The incredible record, *Max's Kansas City 1976*, features as the showcase track Wayne County and the Back Street Boys' theme song for the club, a name-dropping delicacy with a Lou Reed rip-off vibe. Pere Ubu, Suicide, and Cherry Vanilla all have great tracks on the album, but the Fast steal the show with "Boys Will Be Boys" and the fun "Wow Pow Bash Crash." In fact, when CBS rereleased the album in 1978 as *Max's Kansas City New York New Wave*, they released the Fast songs as a single in England. One day after the album came out the boys felt they were rock stars, and hit the road for their first West Coast swing, crossing the country to play the Whiskey in Los Angeles.

Photo courtesy Paul Zone.

Back home the Fast became the big group at Max's. Though they played rival CBGB's a couple of times, they had to play Max's because Tommy Dean was now their manager. They were selling out two shows a night on the weekend, and they even had a drink named after them on the menu ("THE FAST $2.50 — Tequila gone bananas. Drink it FAST!"). It seemed success was on the horizon!

"Every record company is coming to see us," recalls Paul, "just like they're going to see every other group. Signing other groups. Doing things with other groups. Little did we know that Tommy Dean would scare the record companies away because he would say if you want to sign the Fast you have to sign Max's record label." It seems Tommy Dean had big plans for his own label and wanted to use the Fast as a conduit for his success.

While everybody else from the scene was already making their first record, the Fast, for reasons unbeknownst to them, only had the compilation tracks. Richard Gottehrer, who did the first Blondie album, was a big Fast fan and was anxious to record the band. Tommy Dean made arrangements for the recordings, and Gottehrer offered to arrange a record deal with Private Stock, Blondie's label.

"When Private Stock came to Tommy Dean, he insisted the label had to take on Ram and other artists he brought them," laments Paul. "So there went our record deal with Private Stock. So at this point we get freaked out, and we told Tommy Dean, 'We have to have a record deal within the next few months, or else we're going to move on and do something else.' We never had contracts or anything like that with him."

Tommy Dean brought in Ritchie Cordell to produce the band. Cordell had just recorded a Tommy James record the boys loved, and this was a very exciting time for them. Cordell oversaw three weeks of rehearsals, five days a week, preparing them to do two originals and some Gary Glitter covers that seemed like they would go over as pop hits in the U.S. (a few years later Joan Jett had success with one, "Do You Wanna Touch Me").

One day the band came to rehearsal, Cordell was supposed to be there, and he wasn't.

"Ah, Ritchie won't be coming any more. It didn't work out," Paul recalls Dean saying.

That was that. The band was completely discouraged with Tommy

Photo courtesy Paul Zone.

Dean, who, like most of the scene, was a full-fledged coke addict at the time. The boys were merely pill poppers, downing Black Beauties, and Yellow Jackets, speed freaks in the tradition of the Who. They no longer had patience for Dean's coke-fueled screw-ups.

In an attempt to satiate the band Tommy Dean released the Gottehrer tracks himself as a single on Ram. The florid "It's Like Love" with Mandy's funny keyboard effects and Paul's pseudo-Brit enunciation, and the power pop manifesto "Kids Just Wanna Dance" made up the fine 45. The band even made a low (l-o-w) budget video for the "It's Like Love," with a bizarre cartoon vibe. As Miki and Paul move around in yellow galoshes and thigh-high leather boots, respectively, animated words and images flash across the screen. With Dean's poor business savvy and the Fast's luck, of course the video was never shown anywhere, and the single did nothing.

That was the "last straw." But for a band that never quits no matter what, there really is no last straw. Their punishment to Tommy for failing to make them famous was that they "left" Max's. Which means they played every other club in the city, while still playing Max's. And Paul still worked as a DJ at Max's. And Tommy was basically still their manager.

By '77 Max's was changing. The best bands were gone. Blondie was opening for Bowie; the Ramones were touring Europe; Jayne and the Heartbreakers relocated to England. Peter Crowley had a good ear, and the next generation of Max's bands were an impressive bunch, but it wasn't the same for the Fast. Though they befriended the Cramps, Lydia Lunch, and the "No Wave" bands, by this point the fact that they were still there while everyone else "graduated" was a problem. There were still highlights, like the B-52s playing their first New York show opening for the Fast, and the Damned telling them they were the only group England was waiting to see. And, in truth, Miki really believed in his greatness, saying at the time, "I want to have eight albums out (in the next five years) . . . album titles are gonna be fun!! 'Fast Fast,' 'Real Fast,' 'Faster Than a Speeding Engine,' 'Faster . . . Faster . . . Fastest' . . . I want us to be playing M2 Garden . . . I know we can do it, I feel we have all the talent of a Queen, Roxy or Cooper!" And if that wasn't enough of a show of confidence, he even continued to boast of his pet project, "The Magic Seashore," a rock opera he'd been working on since 1972. The epic is about a mermaid who loves a human, gives up her tail, then finds her new man to be a drip. But rock operas aside, the Fast was in a rut, and at this point just playing the same circuit wasn't enough.

The band continued to tour the country. "The Ramones and Blondie would play in those same towns, at the really good clubs," recalls Paul, "and we were playing at the really cheesy, horrible places. But the same crowd was there. Last week they went and saw Blondie someplace else. They would come see us 'cause we were from New York. To them we were just an up-and-coming group, that's all. We were gonna break, any day now." *(laughs)*

The frustrations the band was facing became too much for Tommy Mooney. After half a decade in the Fast he left, and drummer Peter Hoffman's brother Robert was recruited on bass. To illustrate the bizarre mechanisms going on in Miki's brain, the bass player they actually wanted was Louis Bova, a great friend and a better musician, but Miki figured the gimmick of two sets of brothers would be better for business. More significant personnel changes were on the horizon.

In 1978 Armand started rehearsing with other people. He was a songwriter and he was a singer, but in Miki's band he would never be able to fully explore those talents. Perhaps the glories of being a co-frontman prior to Paul joining compensated for the creative limitations, but as a support player he was frustrated. Miki wanted to be Pete Townshend, the captain sailing the ship and writing all the songs. Though he'd certainly admit that without Armand and Paul the band wouldn't be what it was, it was crucial to him to get songwriting credit and to be recognized as the creative force.

"We all came to the conclusion that we didn't need Armand anymore and he didn't need us anymore," remembers Paul. "We loved the idea of him starting his own band and writing his own songs; it took guts to leave a band with a good following."

He started his own band, Ozone, a poppy, strange unit that showcased his dramatic vocals. Armand took the bass player, Robert Hoffman, with him, opening up the spot in the Fast for the patient Louis Brian Bova. Hoffman's tenure was short lived and soon original Fast bassist Tommy Moony was in Armand's band. From 1978 through the early '80s they played the circuit, fully supported by Max's booker Peter Crowley, a huge fan of Armand's. They recorded for the Max's label, and later (proving no hard feelings existed) Armand would do work produced by Paul and Miki and released on the Fast's own label.

The Fast now was a four piece. It was a big time for changes, and as Paul explained, "We figure now we're really gonna be the Who!" One change was that Paul cut off his flowing locks around this time. Another change was the sound, a harder version of the old pop. "A lot of things *(we do live)* I would consider heavy metal," Miki declared at the time. A more significant development was a name change. So as not to be confused with the five piece, and to give Miki some of the glory he craved, the band changed its name to the Miki Zone Zoo.

"It showed people who was behind the Fast," Miki told *FFanzeen* magazine in 1980, "which I wanted to see happen." They released a single (produced by Miki) with their signature live pencil-solo tune, "These Boots Were Made For Walking," and a fun, wacky soundtrack to an imaginary movie, "Coney Island Chaos." The raw, playful guitar on this song is a treat.

In New York they played under the new name, but on the road they still had to be the Fast, or they couldn't get booked. So it was the Fast that took the stage for a fateful show at the legendary Rat in Boston. The band had been going to Boston for years, and had a good following. On this trip, though, the full house included Ric Ocasek, lead singer of the Cars. The Cars were one of the biggest bands around, and his presence made the boys nervous, as the band was playing their first show outside of New York in the new incarnation and were not fully confident as a quartet.

The nervous energy translated into a great performance. As they came off the stage, the crowd roared for an encore. After their return to the stage they retired to the dressing room, chests puffed out.

Miki turned around to the band and declared, "The next knock you hear on that door will be Ric Ocasek coming in and saying he wants to produce us."

There was the knock. It was Ric Ocasek. He came in and said he wanted to produce them.

"Listen, I'll give you a call next week. I'm going to be in New York; I'll call you a day or two before time and we'll set up some studio time." Ocasek told them, and left. Then he came back in, and asked, "Sunday we're doing a show up in Maine; do you want to come and open up for us?" It was Friday.

Two nights later, Halloween, they were in Portland, Maine. The Miki Zone Zoo was dead. It was the Fast who were playing the Cars' equipment, rocking out to 20,000 people, and getting a great response. The band was looking cool on-stage, out of their Op-Art stage, but still, to quote Paul, "very animated." Miki wore a bolo tie, had a pencil-thin mustache, and, like the rest of the band, sported black leather. Paul sported a handsome fringed ensemble. They opened with "Mickey's Monkey," did their new harder version of "Kids Just Wanna Dance," and basically had a blast for forty-five minutes. The Cars watched from the wings and loved them. It was a high point for the Fast, and they were certain, at this point, they were on the road to success.

They went back to New York and a week later Ocasek called them. He booked five days at Electric Ladyland, where the band recorded five fantastic tracks. The session was stocked with "tons of all different types of Hawaiian marijuana" (though Miki avoided that "hippie shit") and the Fast certainly, for that week, were living the true rock star life. Hopefully they enjoyed it while it lasted.

As the 1980s broke there were several sparks of hope for the Fast, including one Ocasek track appearing on a major label compilation, but after that didn't develop into anything, chances for real success seemed slimmer and slimmer. As New York's landscape changed in the post-Max's era, the name the Fast was almost a burden. Meanwhile, the boys needed to make money, there were few opportunities to play in the city, and there was no DJ gigs for Paul anymore. That meant staying on the road. Though far from their peak of success, the band was touring relentlessly as the Reagan years dawned. In '81, perhaps a low point of their popularity, a tour docket from January through mid-September listed over ninety dates. This wasn't a sensible itinerary, either, but rather Boulder to San Francisco to Texas. Detroit to Minneapolis to Chicago. Though they were able to make friends with a lot of celebrities and pseudocelebrities (always a favorite pastime of Paul's: in Chicago they knew punk pioneer Skafish and Cheap Trick) overall these tours, in a van or a broken-down station wagon, were rough.

Far from the major label debut they'd dreamed of, the Fast's first LP was a self-released compilation of previously recorded tracks packaged in a black-and-white sleeve. Though it was mainly released to have a product to sell at shows, rather than as something they felt would be a hit album, it was a nice package. Modeled after one of the Zone boys' favorite albums, *The Who Sell Out*, *The Fast For Sale* featured four big individual pictures of the band members, parodying the cover art of the original. Instead of Roger Daltrey in a tub of beans, Paul is in a boiling bathtub full of crabs to illustrate the Fast song "Wet & Wild." Instead of John Entwistle as a caveman hugging a blonde cutie, Louis Bova in "T-Shirt & Tight Jeans" (another Fast song title) hugs Jill Monroe, a transsexual porno model. Instead of a shirtless Keith Moon applying a giant tube of zit cream to a pimple, new drummer Joe Poliseno has oversized toy cars crashing on his neck, causing a giant stream of blood ("Cars Crash" was one of the band's signature tunes). Eschewing Pete Townshend's pose altogether, Miki appears as an amazing sexual Satan, to illustrate the tune "Sizzler." The band also adds a jingle for "Max's Kansas City" to the beginning of "Boys Will Be Boys," an homage to the Who's intersong jingles. Completing the take-off of the album was the title of the band's vanity label, Recca (saluting the boy's love of record collecting) to mimic the Who's label, Decca. This would continue to be the label name for the rest of its considerable tenure.

Miki and Paul's relationship with *The Who Sell Out* is actually worth noting. As Paul explains, "It was such a un-commercial album and never really amounted to anything in America. We would always notice that every bargain bin would have *The Who Sell Out*. So Miki and I started collecting it. We have about sixty-five copies of *The Who Sell Out*, because we would just keep buying it. We would see where we could find it the cheapest. And I would say, 'I found it for 59 cents'; he'd say, 'I found it for a dime,' and written on it was 10 cents."

The album itself received good reviews in the small press (*Illinois Entertainer* called it "Four Rick Nielsons in Sparks drag," and *East Village Eye* called it "Killer"). The biggest criticism most people had about the album was its diversity, as this pastiche of tracks from various years varied greatly. The airy "It's Like Love" contrasted quite a bit with the new heavy Ocasek-produced version of "Kids Just Wanna Dance." And "Love Me Like a Locomotive," with its would-be menacing vocal delivery and graphic lyrics ("pump my piston; make it steam") is worlds apart from the sweet double-entendres of "Boys Will Be Boys." But overall, there is a great deal of unity here, as well. The choo-choo train sound effect vocals on "Locomotive" fully relate to the humor of "Boys." And throughout all the tracks the

same solid pop craftsmanship, tasteful lack of flashy solos (great for live shows, bad for pop records, they figured), and surprisingly nongeneric decision making make everything fun to listen to. Highlights include the driving Ocasek track "Sizzler," and "Cars Crash" (also released as a single prior to the LP's release), produced by Miki and Ian North (of Milk and Cookies and Neo; he would soon join the Fast as bassist). "Cars Crash" is a truly weird, dramatic tune that combines oldies radio teen tragedy tunes, J. G. Ballard, and plenty of pure Zone-isms.

Though *Fast For Sale* featured the fun, pop sounds of the '70s Fast, the band that was on the road selling this LP in the '80s was a darker, harder beast. They were reading about goth in England, and the look of Alien Sex Fiend seemed to relate well to the dramatic animated vibe in which the Fast found its foundation. This also seemed to relate to the deviant, underground, leather scene that was happening in New York at the time, a scene the brothers were definitely a part of. The new concept of the Fast was to combine what they thought was goth with a musical interpretation of the leather underground. It was also a time to take the homosexual themes away from the

95

The Fast

playful, ambiguous "everyone's gay" concept of the Max's era, and overtly acknowledge who they were.

"At this point there was no more girlfriends," recalls Paul. "All the years before this we never would go to gay bars or have those sort of aspects of gay life. Any gay life we had was in the rock 'n' roll life. In the early '80s was when we really started to understand and develop; we became a part of the West Side leather scene. We had a following with the gay leather people that weren't into disco, the hard-core, leather scene that wasn't listening to Gloria Gaynor. They liked heavy music, dark and deviant, to go with their dark and deviant lifestyle. And in reality Miki and I did have a dark and deviant lifestyle then because of drugs."

Soon after they worked with Ocasek and morphed into their leather boy stage they became influenced as much by crystal meth, coke, and opium as by Alien Sex Fiend. On stage the period was defined by Paul in a leather straight jacket and loincloth, with everyone draped in capes and chains. Off stage it was the band's heaviest period of drug use. In their pop days they were "popping" uppers, engaged in playful, almost wholesome drug use, with Miki ordering pink caffeine pills out of comic books and sharing them with Jayne County. During the leather period the cocaine and meth abuse was becoming dangerous and ugly, as Paul would find out.

"I remember we were doing a show in Providence, Rhode Island, and just after a night of doing all of these drugs, I felt really, really bad on our drive back to New York. I arrived back at my place after driving all night. I couldn't breathe; I felt like I was having a heart attack. I went to the doctor, and the doctor examined me, took some x-rays. The x-rays showed that I had collapsed both of my lungs and was ready to have a heart attack. I had to have my sides opened up and tubes stuck into my body and was hooked up to machines to pump my lungs back up. I stayed in these machines for about two weeks. I had overdosed, obviously, and was right next to heart failure. Needless to say, that was my last encounter with drugs. I think basically why I survived throughout the '80s is because I never did drugs again."

The experience didn't change his brother's habits at all. Miki continued with his reckless leather-bound, drug-hazed lifestyle.

It was during Paul's transitional phase that a more sinister-sounding Fast returned to the studio. Recorded on eight tracks on a shoestring budget, *Leather Boys from the Asphalt Jungle* is a bizarre album, sure to disappoint many pop-minded Fast fans, and sure to confuse almost anyone who has the rare opportunity to experience the record. It's a dark concept album about negotiating the treacherous urban landscape as a leather boy, with continuous jungle references and a number of racial overtones. The lead track, "Jaguar in the Jungle" is about the Atlanta child murders, and posits some of the most confusing social-science theories imaginable. Closer to home they "Ride on the Wild Side," where one goes on safari for a Leather Lioness and wildebeests (?). On another track they pose in their "Black Leather Jacket" as rebels in the night, West Side Highway studs.

Photo courtesy Paul Zone.

They also revisit their Brooklyn youth with both "Boro Boys," exploring the dark side of the neighborhood guys, and the great "Skinny Kids and Bigger Bullies," which is almost an origin tale for outsider kids turned freaks. Perhaps their most blatant attempt at goth is "Ritual Sacrifice" which, with its shopping list of chicken gizzards, goats heads, and lizard quarters, comes off more akin to Screamin' Jay Hawkins's "Alligator Wine" than to anything Siouxsie would sing. What does have some relation to the dark side of British new wave is the spare sound, and an electronic angle is explored as Armand returns for a track to add an eerie synthesizer vibe.

This mix of leather and the boys' version of goth is mighty bizarre, and the cover art matches the musical weirdness inside. At this point the lagging popularity and the hard-core touring put strains on personnel, as drummers and bass players didn't want to leave New York. The rhythm section was rotating so quickly the Zones didn't even bother to list or picture any other band members on the sleeve. To make it seem like a real band, however, Miki and Paul each appear twice on the cover, as leather-and-chain-clad clones in robotic oversized shades. Choosing to become a duo would be Miki's most crucial decision since anointing Paul lead singer. It also was an economic reality.

But simply breaking down to a duo wasn't the only change the band needed to undergo. At this point it was becoming increasingly difficult for Paul to perform as the dark, leather character in his drug-free state. "It was a little hard for me to be the same persona that I was, hanging from the rafters and crawling on the floor and wearing leather loincloths." But even without conviction, Paul probably would have bit the bullet and stayed "leather" if more people liked the material. However, what the Fast called "goth" just wasn't going over in Nebraska.

So metal didn't work, goth didn't work, they didn't have any band members, and they couldn't conceive of giving up and getting "real" jobs. It was time for their influences to change, for the band to take a different direction. Inspiration came when they saw Depeche Mode play with a big reel-to-reel tape recorder spinning on stage.

"What we did," laughs Paul, "was we went into our friend's recording studio and recorded drums and keyboards on a tape for our songs, a full tape of a set, and Miki and I, we would grab Donna Destri or another keyboard player, to come with us and do shows. The big tape recorder on the stage, in the back, I would go over and turn it on, out we'd come, these cheap little boombox beats, with keyboards on it. We toned down the leather, wore tailored, vinyl skintight suits with penciled mustaches and hats. We'd bring another keyboard player with us, Miki would play guitar, and I would stand in the center. And soon we wouldn't even use the keyboard player; it was just Miki and me with the tape recorder. The Fast gone electric. I don't know how we got the shows, but they booked us."

"The Fast gone electric" found inspiration in another duo as well. Shortly after Soft Cell hit with "Tainted Love," the Fast recorded and released their audio document of this phase, the "Moontan" single. The record arguably has the best artwork of anything the band released, a florid Tom of Finland–esque drawing of the boys as erotic, muscle-bound mermen (perhaps a reference to Miki's rock opera). Though Paul actually had been working out at home and the YMCA ("No jokes, Village People are friends of mine") since his near-death experience, he couldn't hope to match the physique in this artwork! The A-side is a low-budget electronic tune with a sound only baby steps from *Leather Boys*, yet fully recognizable as a part of the new synth frontier. The lyrics are pretty great, boasting of (in place of a white-hot suntan) a "black-cold moontan." But the genius is the B-side. Minutes after hearing Soft Cell's electronic gay take on the girl group sound with their "Tainted Love" / "Where Did Our Love Go" medley, Miki and Paul dipped into the Supremes song bag for "Love Is Like an Itching in My Heart," crafting a masterpiece of ridiculousness. Spare, tinny beats and a synth that sounds more Pac Man than Mantronix are married with ludicrous sped-up falsettos to create a song that sounds closer to Weird Al Yankovic's "Another One Rides the Bus" than anything else. When the tune ends with shrill yelps of "I've been bitten by the love b-u-g!" it's clear this is an amazing example of the futility and brilliance of the Zones. Futility because 90 percent of the time they aren't doing anything near what they think they're doing. There's no genre this fits into. It's too thin to be a dance record, too humorous to fit into the moody English synth movement, and too cheap to be a true pop hit. But its brilliance is in its pure, joy-soaked absurdity! So what if it's an anomaly? It's an amazing anomaly.

Though they weren't exactly the hottest act in town at the time, the boys still believed in their work, and in some ways, knowing they weren't about to be signed liberated them to record and experiment and release records. Miki began performing without Paul as Bruno Beats and released material on Recca, including a Christmas EP. He also did club dates as "Miki Zone sings Gene Pitney," decked out in full tux! They released a Recca record of Armand Zone (dressing as a Phantom of the Opera–type swashbuckler). At this point they felt it was important to document their look and sound, so though they didn't expect the singles to gain them glory, as artists (and I'm sure as record collectors) they were proud to have product.

Little did they know that their next phase of recording would bring their

FAST

moontan
love is like an itching in my heart

PRINTED IN U.S.A.
RECCA
R 2002

he fast : miki zone(instr./voc.) paul zone(ld.voc.)
ecording : i.n.s MCMLXXXII
over : richard rosenfeld photo : emile greco
gent : mitchell karduna (212) 241 - 2168
ECCA RECORD : 134 CHESTER AVE. BKLYN, N.Y. 11218

Illustration courtesy Paul Zone.

record-releasing activity outside of the masturbatory realm. Bobby O, with whom they had done early Fast tracks, had become a big name producer in the dance biz, having done outstanding work with Divine that seemed particularly akin to the Zones' sense of humor and theater. Many people familiar with the late Divine as the obese transvestite lead actress/actor in John Waters' films don't know about her parallel career as a gruff-voiced disco diva. Divine's records were huge in the worldwide dance scene in the '80s, and in Chicago they were frequently played on mainstream black radio. Most connoisseurs agree Divine's work with Bobby O was her finest.

"Bobby Orlando, right," recalls Paul, "Let's call him up and tell him that we want to be a dance act now. We'll do country and western at this point, forget it. We paid too many dues and we've tried too many things. At least dance music can be pop. To us it didn't sound like disco, it sounded like pop music. So we call up Bobby Orlando."

"To me, this is when it really became fun for the first time since so long ago. We had a reason again."

They went to Bobby Orlando's studio and recorded three over-the-top electronic dance songs. "At the Gym," a riff on Village People's "YMCA"; "Unisex Haircut"; and "Male Stripper." The latter was pretty much "Numbers" by Kraftwerk with lyrics celebrating exotic dancing sung over the loop. Bobby decided not to release the tracks on his label, O Records, but he was impressed enough to introduce the Zones to Denny O'Conner, a gay record promoter and DJ in New York with a finger on the pulse of the scene. He suggested a name change, and the Fast became Man's Favorite Sport (named after a Rock Hudson movie). Denny got the Zones in touch with the owner of Media Sound, a 24-track recording studio. He in turn hired the boys as in-house producers, really a glorified house band coming up with tracks for would-be disco divas. They were paid for each demo they did, so that took care of the touring revenue they were losing. But more importantly, he gave them as much free 24-track studio time (with engineer) as they wanted. This sweet gig lasted for over a year.

Though none of the demos they did for other artists were ever released, the music they recorded for themselves was getting better and better, and they owned the masters and music. They finally felt they really had something when they recorded a dance version of Frankie Valli's "Walk Like a Man."

With that under arm, they took an opportunity that arose to go to England. Through connections they were able to perform at Heaven, the primo club for this type of music, lip-synching to their tracks. More importantly, they brought "Walk Like a Man" to English dance labels trying to swing a record deal for Man's Favorite Sport. They went from label to label, pimping the track, but left without any interest.

Frustrated, they returned to New York, and continued to work in the same vein. About three months later, Divine released "Walk Like a Man," an exact duplicate of the Zone track, down to the breaks. Using the demo the Zones had left with them, Divine's British label had copied every aspect of their recording and had a Top-40 UK hit.

Though they felt ripped off, they were also encouraged. If their record could be a success, even if it wasn't for them, it meant that finally, after years of being too early, too late, or just plain wrong, they were on the right track.

At this point Miki and Paul's personal lives outside of music had diverged greatly. Miki was still attending hard-core West Village leather gay clubs and bars, while Paul was reveling in the gay chic of the hottest clubs in town. When Keith Haring and Jean-Michel Basquiat held court at Paradise Garage, Paul Zone was there. Though he was a bit of an outcast because of abstention from the coke and speed that defined that scene, he also likely escaped the same fate of top scenesters because he had his full faculties at the peak of AIDS recklessness. His brother was far less controlled. At this point they shared few mutual friends outside of the studio. Almost none of their rock associates could relate in any way to the genre in which they were now rising stars. Though a few of their best friends from the Max's days (Blondie, Lance Loud, the Ramones) were still social with them, literally none of the fans who followed the Fast were loyal to Man's Favorite Sport.

"Some of them had come at the beginning when we started doing the electronic stuff, because we'd play at the Pyramid in New York, the Mud Club, and some of them would come and see us, but they would say like, 'Man, you know you gotta get those guitars back.' They hated it. But it was fine, we didn't care. It was over; that aspect was over."

Man's Favorite Sport's next step was to enter the studio of their friend Martin Vecsey of Material, who has worked on hits from artists as varied as Herbie Hancock, White Zombie, and Smashing Pumpkins. The track they did, "Hottest of the Hot," is a hilariously blatant lift of Donna Summer's "I Feel Love" sped up to the tempo of Hi-NRG, the wave of dance music that was the rage at the time in gay clubs. One of the most striking elements of the dance records is Paul's delivery, and "Hottest of the Hot" is a fine example. The Jack Jones / lounge vocalist analogy is now in full effect, as all rock 'n' roll inflection is removed at this point, and smooth, smarmy, resonating vocals take over. You almost expect a wink at the end of each verse.

Taking no chances with rip-off artists, they released it on Recca with "Walk Like a Man" as a B-side. Having had little luck with Man's Favorite Sport, they opted for a new moniker. The record was released as Man 2 Man.

Denny O'Conner, now acting as Man 2 Man's manager, helped promote the record and put the brothers in touch with distributors. Being a DJ himself, Denny knew every gay DJ in New York in the '80s. "It became actually a song that everybody would play, so it was fantastic," explains Paul. "It was inconceivable to us that we could go to a club and there would be a thousand shirtless guys dancing to our record. But this was real, and when we'd tell our old friends, old rock 'n' rollers, they would just look at us like, 'you're crazy. That doesn't amount to anything. You should be embarrassed about that, and you're bragging about it!'"

Soon they'd have a lot more to brag about. In early 1985 the records were moving merely by the dozens, but a long-distance call soon changed the fortunes of Man 2 Man. Peerless/Mastered, a Mexican label offered to buy the rights to the record and release it. Apparently Hi-NRG was pretty hot at the time in Mexico, and icons like Divine and Sylvester were playing to huge crowds. The Zones licensed the record, not knowing what to expect. They couldn't possibly foresee what happened next.

"Hottest of the Hot" went to number 1 in Mexico.

The next thing the boys knew they were flown below the border, put up in a hotel, all expenses paid, and were given carte blanche to live the next six months as pop stars.

"Dos Hombres" or "Man Dos Man," as they were known down Mexico way, had it both ways. Kids were outside their hotel rooms screaming for them as if they were the Backstreet Boys. At the gay clubs they had their pick of whatever they wanted. They would play to 200 people in gay clubs and then play to 5,000 at festivals with Sylvester, Jessica Williams, and Divine.

The greatest documentation of this era are tapes of the TV shows they visited. The boys were on the tube twice a week. On these shows they lip-synched to the same two songs during every appearance, not just because these were the popular songs, *but because they didn't have any other songs*! They appeared on children's shows, dance shows, and the great *Hoy Mismo*, a *Good Morning America*–type program that also appeared on Mexican stations in the US.

"We would be calling all of our friends in America and telling them to turn on channel 64 at six in the morning because we're going to be on *Hoy Mismo*!" enthuses Paul "These would be the strangest shows. It was like we went to another planet and became pop stars."

The *Hoy Mismo* appearances are out of this world. When the boys first arrive they are wearing black thrift-store clothes, mesh shirts, and big black hats, looking like Hassidic perverts. By their late appearances they're basically wearing full bullfighter outfits. Paul almost looks like a real live pop star in these clips, and a few of his moves bring to mind Madonna. In fact, on one appearance when he removes his jacket he seems to have on, garment for garment, the exact outfit Madonna wore in the "Lucky Star" video. Miki on the other hand, with a rather bushy mustache at this point, looks like Father Guido Sarducci. Seeing these two unlikely stars lip-synch lines like "Your love is like a lubricant, it soothes the soul inside" for happy middle-aged Mexican anchormen and anchorwomen is beyond surreal. Miki uses whatever they have in the studio to ape his keyboard lines, be it a Casio, a baby grand piano, or an accordion. Talk about animated!

And the interviews! Forget it! While they fake Spanish and the interviewers struggle with English, classic lines are bandied about in Brooklyn-ese including this explanation of their synthesizer skills: "We're electronic geniuses!" They pretend to understand what teenage girl callers are saying about them, and when offered Mexican bandannas by the hostess they fight over the lavender one. What's most noticeable about the clips is that even though they do the same songs over and over and over, they never seem bored. As they do the minimal choreography, jumping around and dancing a bit, they are having so much fun, and are so happy, it's palpable. Little wonder their commitment to Man 2 Man's success at that point became total.

After returning to New York, Paul and Miki ran into Man Parrish on the street. At that point Parrish had already become an underground star. He'd done production for a number of people, including brilliant work with Klaus Nomi. Parrish's solo stuff, particularly the single "Hip Hop Be Bop," was big in the UK. The Zones knew Manny through a record he did with their friend Donna Destri, and were excited to tell him about their disco success South of the Border. Eager for another Mexican hit, they arranged to get together and work on some tracks.

Man Parrish's recording empire consisted of a little 8-track recorder in his bedroom. It would prove more than sufficient. Miki and Paul brought their favorite records, told Parrish what they were interested in emulating, and they set out to construct a new version of "Male Stripper." The catchy ditty they came up with was part tabloid tell-all ("I was a male stripper in a go-go bar . . .") and part ode to beefcake ("ripples on my chest, never got a night's rest . . ."), with a humorous vocorder robo-chorus. The Hi-NRG disco groove and the oddly wholesome gayness of the song is as good an example of Man 2 Man's magic as anything they recorded. When it came time to release the next Recca 12″, "All Men Are Beasts," they decided to put "Male Stripper" on the B-side.

Between going back to Mexico to reap the glories of "All Men Are Beasts," Miki and Paul also were taking care of Recca business in New York. Soon they started getting more and more orders. "Send us a box of the 'Male Stripper' record."

To which they responded, "Well, you mean the 'All Men Are Beasts' record."

Another distributor: "We need a hundred 'Male Strippers.'"

"A hundred? Where are you sending them?"

"Well, we're sending them to this record store in England and they're snatching it up." The next week, "Send us another hundred." The next week, "Send us a thousand 'Male Strippers.'"

Of course, despite their Mexican good fortune, the boys couldn't afford to press 1,000 records on the spot. That would have cost them around $4,000, as they informed the distributor. He hung up. A short while later the phone rings. It's the distributor. "OK, I'll pay for them."

A phone call from England soon followed. Bolts, a small label, was interested in releasing "Male Stripper." They struck a deal, and then the fellow reminded our heroes of some previous business they'd done together.

"You know, you guys know me. Remember you came and you played 'Walk Like a Man' for me that time?"

"So you're the fuck that stole . . ."

So that was the fuck they signed with. And as it turned out, after getting a (perhaps too) modest advance, he turned out to be very honest with everything, and Man 2 Man was always paid well for "Male Stripper."

The song went on to be the number-1 disco record of 1986 in England. Though the dance charts represent only underground success, it did translate into thousands of dollars in English sales, in sales of the Recca version, and in foreign licensing. A monthlong summer tour of every gay club in England and Scotland earned them £10,000 a show, a fee only garnered by two other performers on the circuit, Sylvester and Divine.

Nothing could go wrong at this point, or so it seemed. During the late summer, however, Paul began to notice that Miki wasn't at his best. Nothing terrible, he was just a little sick and acting weird. Paul wrote it off as too much cocaine, and soon Miki got better and seemed fine. Anyhow, it wasn't a time for worrying. It was a time to enjoy the success the Zones had been working nearly two decades to achieve. Though they weren't popular in the US at that point, they were more than prepared to squeeze whatever juice they could out of the fruits of their foreign success. In a move poetically representative of their humorous pandering, the next Recca 12″ was "Energy is Eurobeat" b/w "Mexico." They simply made records *about* the places where they were popular . . . and it worked. Every single they released that year was a success.

The first four 12″ records were compiled into an LP in Mexico. The record has the unfortunate title *Malenergy*, a would-be rip-off of Patrick Cowley's "Menergy" that is betrayed by a silent *e*. The album is a fantastic document of the era because, unlike the 12″ records, you get photos of the boys on the sleeve. On the front cover they look like extremely typical gay models, with neat hair and mustaches, tight white "wife-beater" undershirts, trim black slacks, and accessories (suspenders, studded leather, a cravat, tattoos) that leave no doubt, but also show little originality. On the back cover, however, they're standing in front of a wall of fake reel-to-reel futuristic computers, each holding a Casio, and dressed as a bizarre variation on some kind of Greenwich Village Batman and Robin. Both wear "animated" oversized leather hats, predating the raver Dr. Seuss look by nearly a decade. Miki is wearing an all leather sleeveless ensemble . . . with super-hero cape! Paul wears snug shorts, a tartan vest, a black trench coat, white fingerless gloves, a tux shirt, and a bow tie. And the real kicker is that the front cover was the costume! The back cover was far more representative of what they would wear onstage, or even on the streets, than the *Blue Boy* front cover.

"That front cover to us was just like, OK, let's be a little bit normal here for maybe the hard-core gay people who want to see just normal disco-looking things," explains Paul. "So maybe we calmed it down for a shot, and that's what they used as the front cover. But all in all we were more or less doing the more animated thing in the early '80s."

After the release of "Energy Is Eurobeat," which did well, but was no "Male Stripper," the boys returned to New York and got together with Man Parrish to formulate their next plan of attack. Paul recalls, "We just tried to figure out what can we do that could be as blatant as possible, and as embarrassing as possible? What could we do? And, really, I don't know if all three of us said it at the same time, but we just came up with the idea to do, 'I Need a Man.' We said, this is going to be the funniest, gayest, biggest record. There's just no way that a DJ isn't going to play this record. The only people that played 'Male Stripper' were gay DJs. They'll have to play this record if we do it. And we did it, we just loved the fact that we were doing it, and laughed the whole way through the whole record."

The over-the-top Grace Jones cover song was in the can when they went back to England. They planned to release it at the beginning of the year, figuring "Male Stripper" had run out of gas. It was December 1986, and all the year-end charts were already out, but they were prepared to take the 1987 dance music world by storm. They even made plans to revive Miki's rock opera, "The Magic Seashore," as the first Disco-Opera! Unfortunately, their New Year's plans would change. When Man 2 Man went back to England, Miki wasn't doing too well.

"He just looked like shit," Paul explains, "and I was like, Miki, I think you're really sick, when we get back home, you gotta go to the doctor and you gotta face all these things."

Paul knew, but Miki was in addled denial. He was always on coke, always getting high, and to add to his drug haze, at this point he was having bouts of dementia. In England they did shows at Heaven and a few other clubs. At points during these performances, Miki backed up and sat down on the edge of the stage, barely able to move. "He was actually comatose in a way," explains a choked up Paul, "It was really, really very hard to see him like that."

On the twenty-third of December the brothers flew back to New York, Miki vomiting the entire flight. Paul carried his brother off the plane and took him directly to his parents' house, then to the doctor who immediately sent him to the hospital. There the staff didn't even need to determine if Miki had AIDS, only what was wrong with him from having AIDS. In addition to lesions on his legs and dementia, they diagnosed spinal meningitis. The only silver lining at this point was the fact that Miki didn't know any of this.

"Paul, where are we?" Miki asked his brother from his hospital bed.

"We're in the hospital." Paul responded. "You're not doing too good. But you're gonna be OK." Miki went back to sleep and never really knew the condition he was in.

"So they started treating him," Paul recalls, "pumping him up with whatever they had back then, meningitis medicine, and he started coming out of it, actually. I don't know if there was brain damage; they said it was just dementia, but he'd regressed. Friends would come see him. This was like a day after Christmas, December 26, 27. People were coming. At times the whole room would be filled with all of our friends, our family, and he'd be talking to everybody. Of course I was sleeping in the hospital with him every night. In the morning I would get up and go back home and there would be other family members or friends hanging out, then I would come back at night and spend the night with him. Every night I would be there with him. Of course he never would sleep while I was there—he would be sleeping in the daytime. I'd be sleeping on the chair, and he'd be waking me, talking to all of these people in the room who would be coming to visit him. Of course the room was empty—it's the middle of the night. There would be angels, 'Don't you see them,' he'd say. 'They're right over there.' He'd be having conversations with them. And it's going on for a week, the same thing. And then on the thirty-first, New Year's Eve morning, five o'clock in the morning, I just hear him coughing, choking. I'm telling him spit it out, whatever it is. It's five in the morning, no nurses, no doctor, he's in my arm as I'm trying to help him. And he's turning blue, choking and gagging. And here I am, not wanting to let him go, pushing the buttons, screaming for a nurse. Turning blue, he dies right there in my arms. Instantaneously. They all rush in. They usher me out of the room. They start cutting him open, his neck, I don't know what they hell they were doing. And that was it. That was it.

"About a minute after that, they all walk out of the room, and I'm standing outside of the door. They said, 'I'm sorry we couldn't save him. You can go in now.' And that's it. They all left. I go back into the room, and he's just laying there. And I'm sitting on the bed next to him, like, fuck, now what am I gonna do? Who am I gonna call? What? Why is this up to me now? What am I gonna do with all of this information? I called up my boyfriend, who I had a great relationship with throughout the '80s, and he called up Lance Loud—we were like best friends. Him and Lance come to the hospital, seven in the morning, and they're sitting on the bed with me. And the three of us are sitting in the hospital room with him laying there. They said it'll take a few hours for them to come up and put him in a bag and take him out. But we were in this hospital room for, I would say, about an hour and a half, just sitting there with him. What are we gonna do? We weren't gonna leave him there. It was just, it was so animated, it was shockingly *animated*."

Paul called his family and arrangements were made. There was a closed casket funeral, and the Ramones, Blondie, and the rest of the New York punk scene's royalty attended.

"And that was it." Paul laments. "Happy New Year."

If this were a typical rock 'n' roll story, perhaps that would be it. And even if it was, the story would still have an aura of triumph surrounding the tragedy. While the reckless, self-destructive behavior that led to Miki's death certainly determined his fate, that aspect of his life was the least original. Drugs and wild sex led to many a death in the scene, but what always set the Zones outside of the norm was their unique "animated" art, and when Miki fell, it was from a stage he mounted after a tireless journey few artists would have been able to make. His unrelenting drive for pop success led him on an adventure through decades, eras, and genres, with seemingly insurmountable obstacles at every juncture. Yet amazingly he found the success he sought, with his visions of absurdity intact, and he was able to, far too briefly, enjoy the fruits of his dreams. To repeat, if this was the end of the story, it would ultimately be a tale of Miki's triumph, not his tragedy.

But the story was far from over.

Paul went home and didn't want to have anything to do with music, or Man 2 Man, or anything. He spent the next couple of months trying to get his head together. Then in February he got a call from the label in England. They knew about Miki, and respected the space Paul needed, but what they had to tell him was important.

It seems that as the number-1 dance song of 1986, "Male Stripper" already had a tiny part of mainstream England's ear. However Miki's death, coupled with reports that the computer programmer on the record, Michael Rudetski, overdosed in Boy George's presence, was enough dirt to make tabloid happy Brits take a listen. The catchy tune did the rest.

"Paul," his label rep told him, "we just got information that next week 'Male Stripper' is going onto the pop charts at number 25. We really need you to come here."

Paul returned to the UK a week later. When he landed on Monday "Male Stripper" indeed did debut at number 25 on the British Pop chart. The next week it went to number 15. The next week it was at number 7. The next week it went to number 4 and stayed at number 4 for two weeks. Paul performed on *Top of the Pops*, and got the pop star treatment. The Zone Brothers' dreams, and Miki's legacy, had been truly realized. Who knows what it means to be number 1 in Mexico? But to be number 4 pop in England, the home of the Who . . . you have made it!

Paul went back home, then went back to England about two weeks later and lived there for about a year and a half. "I liked the idea of just carrying on Man 2 Man," Paul admitted, "because now was the real time to just go and make the money at it obviously. And I really did with that tour and the record. Having a hit record is amazing. God, you make so much money. It's just sick when you hear that people have, like, so many hits, when just having just one big hit record is so great."

Man 2 Man actually had a moderate follow-up hit in the wake of "Male Stripper." "I Need a Man," the last song Miki performed on, came out in April and went to number-25 pop, "which isn't so bad for a song called 'I Need a Man,'" quips Paul. The only other chart action was with a new version of "At the Gym," which reached number 99.

And though a number-99 record may not be too representative of chart success, as far as the artistic success of the Fast / Man 2 Man vision, that record couldn't be any more perfect an example of how Paul kept the flame lit. Perhaps Miki was the genius, as the group was ultimately his baby, and he wrote everything. But even if Paul didn't have the poetic chops of his brother, one thing is clearly demonstrated by his post-Miki work: Paul *got it!* So often when an artist makes a record that revels in glorious absurdity they can't repeat the magic because they either didn't know they were being funny (the old "so bad it's good" deal, represented by the likes of Shatner and the Shaggs) or further attempts at humor seem too calculated and charmless (most novelty record artists fit into this category).

Remarkably, the Fast and Man 2 Man avoid both these traps. They know they are creating ridiculous music, yet it's so grounded in an understanding of pop that they create records that are far from mere novelties. While Paul doesn't have his brother's chops, he totally understands the "animated" vibe, and compensates for what the records don't have with elements that have suddenly become available to him as a "successful" artist. "At the Gym" is a good-natured blatant rip off of "YMCA" (Paul is friends with Village People and "YMCA" would actually be released in the '90s as a split CD single with "Male Stripper"). The record features ridiculous lyrics ("You work a sweat up in my heart . . . At the gym, that's where the muscle begins . . .") and the modest triumph of fitting the word *Schwarzenegger* into meter, and it was actually produced by the Village People's Svengali, Jacques Morali. The cover art by Keith Haring (a clubbing pal of Paul) completes this amazing package.

Every over-the-top gay theme would be explored in Paul's new music, from show tunes in "Swingin' on a Star," to mutual man-love masochism in "Hard Hitting Love" (". . . don't pull no punches back"). The latter was written by Ian Levine, who wrote "So Many Men, So Little Time," and other Hi-NRG classics. The ultimate record from this period has to be "Do Ya

Wanna Funk." The cover of this Sylvester classic (done not as Man 2 Man, but as the Zone Bros) finally has Paul and Mandy sharing equal billing, with Mandy mimicking (as much as possible) Sylvester's falsetto.

The post-Miki Man 2 Man era (also known as Man to Man and Man Two Man, depending on the country) lasted until around 1990, with Paul releasing music and touring Europe. "I just milked it, "Paul explains, "kept on putting out singles and records and nothing ever went pop of course; they all just became dance records." He picked up a couple of hunky guys as back-up dancers for his '87 tour and did some videos with them ("I Need a Man" is another faux cartoon, with Jayne County hosting a *Shindig*-type show, and Paul in drag as a Ronnette). He actually did a number of interesting videos during this era, none of which you've seen on MTV. The "Try My Love" clip, a relatively hetero number, features Paul emoting around Brooklyn like a male Madonna, wooing a pre–*L.A. Law* / *Goodfellas* Debi Mazar, a round-the-way girl Paul knew since the early '80s.

After retiring the name Man 2 Man and releasing a few records around Europe as Paul Zone, he settled back in the states, moving out to L.A. around 1992. Though he isn't still with the boyfriend who helped him through the loss of Miki, like his pals Chris Stein and Debbie Harry from Blondie, they have maintained a close friendship postbreakup, and live a few blocks away from each other. For a social butterfly like Paul, Hollywood works out just fine, as he gets to run into old famous friends like Mazar and Rob Zombie.

Unlike many of the folks who had a bunch of hits that end up destitute on *Behind the Music*, Paul used his loot well. "Back in the '80s I bought a couple of apartments in New York when I made chunks of money. I own some property and rent it out and that's why I moved here to Los Angeles where you can live a much nicer life and it's less expensive. My apartments in New York I can rent out for a hell of a lot of money, and they basically pay my living expenses someplace else."

Though he hasn't really had to have a regular gig over the years, he has done some DJ-ing (not dance music, but rock stuff harking back to his Max's DJ days) and has built a studio in his house. Paul's been working on various projects in the studio, including collaborations with old cohorts Man Parrish and Dee Dee Ramone. Though he doesn't see what he's doing now as necessarily an extension of the earlier Zone Brothers incarnations, he has been revisiting that era quite a bit over the last few years as more and more interest has been building.

In addition to a steady stream of reissues and compilation appearances of the Man 2 Man stuff ("to this day I get royalties"), there's actually been a bit more interest in the Fast. ROIR reissued the Max's album on CD a few years ago, and a volume of "Back to Front" (one of the countless low-run vinyl compilations of rare '77–'79 punk singles) bootlegged "Kids Just Wanna Dance."

Sadly, Armand died of AIDS four years ago. He had continued to work in music, and everyone I interviewed for this article remembered his personality and his talents with great respect and fondness. Paul is the last surviving Zone brother, but their music, regardless of how obscure, lives on. When viewed as a whole, the output of the Brothers Zone makes up perhaps the most noble, absurd, body of work ever assembled by a single group. It's an understatement to say it stretches the definitions of "pop."

Photo courtesy Paul Zone.

"I could listen to anything *(we've)* done over the last twenty-five years and it just has some sort of a power pop thing. I really feel that the Fast didn't even end," muses Paul. "Even our disco days we still were not so typical, a little avant-garde here and there in a strange sort of way."

A strange, sincere, bizarre sort of way.

A very animated way.

Update

Though Paul Zone has released a few songs under different names, he has been relatively inactive as a musician since the publication of the article. However, interest in his back catalogue has been on the rise, as a Fast compilation CD was released on a Canadian power pop label, with a 220-gram vinyl version released in Spain (a version of this article was used as the liner notes), and a deluxe Man 2 Man retrospective double CD was released in the UK by Sanctuary Records in 2007. Zone has also made most of the Fast recordings available on CD Baby and iTunes. In 2009 grindhouse auteur Carter Stevens's lost 1977 sexploitation film *Punk Rock* was released on DVD, featuring two powerful live performances by the Fast, probably the best visual document of the band in its prime (and the best audio document of Armand's intense vocal contributions to the group). Paul Zone's nonmusical seventies activities have recently become his primary interest, as he has been exhibiting his photographs from that era and is currently working on a book of his intimate images of Blondie, Suicide, KISS, Alice Cooper, the New York Dolls, and their contemporaries.

Sugar Pie DeSanto

Though Chicago's touristy, pandering blues club scene has many unpleasant aspects, one nice thing is that if you're a gigging artist you don't need a big name to fill a room. People will come to see you in the name of blues. Several years back, when Sugar Pie DeSanto played Legends—the hopping blues bar owned by her former Chess-mate Buddy Guy—it was a solid bet that 95 percent of the full house didn't know Sugar Pie from Sugar Ray. But she rocked the crowd all the same, and while she didn't perform many of her classic R&B sides like "Soulful Dress" and "Go Go Power," she nevertheless put on an incredible show, demonstrating the dynamic stage moves and tough attitude that earned her the nicknames "Lady James Brown" and "Little Miss Dynamite." Though the tourists may not have known it when they walked in, they sure knew the name Sugar Pie DeSanto when they left.

Born Umpeylia Marsema Balinton around 1935 in Brooklyn to an African American mom and a Filipino dad, Sugar's family (ten children in all) relocated to San Francisco's Fillmore District, where as a teenager she began winning singing contests. Her professional career began before she hit twenty after she was discovered at a talent show at the Ellis Theater by the legendary Johnny Otis. Otis renamed her Little Miss Sugar Pie, and immediately whisked her down the coast to Los Angeles to cut her first record. Otis, the self-described "Godfather of Rhythm and Blues," had just struck gold recording Umpeylia's childhood friend Etta James declaring "Roll with Me Henry," and in Sugar Pie he had found another fair-skinned, beautiful powerhouse. Though she was young, her age wasn't the reason she had to stand on a phonebook to reach the microphone during her early sessions . . . four feet and eleven inches was as big as Sugar was ever going to grow. But over the years she would go on to prove that mighty things come in small packages.

After recording several singles with various members of the Otis posse, Sugar Pie hooked up in 1957 with guitarist/singer Pee Wee Kingsley (professionally and romantically; he became a bank robber after their partnership and marriage broke up). Working with Bob Geddins they went on to record her biggest hit, "I Want to Know" (number-4 *Billboard* R&B in 1960) for Veltone Records. The simple, solid tune (with Sugar's fine vocals and lyrics that hint at the tough attitude that would later become her signature) allowed her to tour the Chitlin' Circuit and large black entertainment palaces, and attracted the attention of James Brown. She spent the beginning of the decade touring with Brown's revue, and stole his thunder several times with her acrobatic stage act (including back flips!). Reportedly the two of them ended some shows by simultaneously jumping off pianos into splits.

Sugar Pie eventually settled in Chicago, recording and writing for Chess Records, who picked up her contract on the strength of "I Want to Know."

Artists she wrote for include Little Milton, Fontella Bass, and the Dells. Soon after arriving at Chess, DeSanto's straight razor tough style emerged. It's seldom that female artists projected rough-and-tumble take-no-shit personas in the sixties, but the few who did recorded for Chess. Koko Taylor promised she'd "love you like a woman, but I'll fight you like a man." Even when they sang ballads, Etta James and Laura Lee were hardly passive sob sisters. And Sugar Pie? Studio rats like Maurice White (later of Earth, Wind & Fire) remember her using cuss words that hadn't been invented yet. And the songs? Fierce musical threats, and bold boasts of sexual prowess. Her diminutive height wouldn't hold her back, as she shouted out "Use What You Got" ("Yes I got everything I know I need to keep my man satisfied / 'cause if you know how to use what you got it doesn't matter about your size."). Her fine threads and beauty could get her what she wanted, as expressed in "Soulful Dress" ("Don't you girls go getting jealous when I round up all your fellas / 'Cause I'll be at my best when I put on my soulful dress"). And in her classic "Slip in Mules" (a hilarious answer record to "Hi-Heel Sneakers") she explains that in addition to comfortable shoes (high heels hurt her "toes-es") she's wearing a sharp dress, "and it ain't the back that's cut too low." And if you fucked with her, watch out, as expressed in "Jump in My Chest" ("Shut up when I'm talking to you . . . If you don't believe what I say, then jump in my chest!").

Her baddest single may be the one that teamed her with old friend Etta James. The two wild girls letting loose about the raucous party on "In the Basement" parts 1 and 2 resulted in one of the best Soul/R&B cuts of its day (number-37 R&B, number-97 pop, 1967). And though she only released one LP and sporadic singles at Chess/Checker during her years based in Chicago, she toured with prominent acts, and was featured in a European touring festival of American folk blues. Ultimately, however, she never achieved the national success she deserved (some of her best Chess recordings were shelved, and not released until years later), and left Chicago for her native San Francisco. She hooked up with James Moore, a carpenter turned manager / record label honcho, and recorded the regional hit "Hello San Francisco" for his Jasman label. DeSanto became a staple on the Bay Area blues circuit starting in the seventies, and continuing until today, earning the nickname the Blues Queen. She's become a hero of the local Filipino community, and because of her protofeminist ass kicking, she's become a icon to San Francisco's lesbian music community. And though she never reached superstar status, her legacy of roughness, rawness, and power resonates in the female stars that followed her, from the toughness of Denise Lasalle to the saltiness of Millie Jackson, and subsequently Lil' Kim, Foxy Brown, and the current crop of ruff-neck divas.

I first heard about Sugar Pie when I was ten years old, and a girl I went to school with laid a mess of ancient 45s on me that her folks didn't want anymore. One of them was "I Want to Know." My musical tastes then were fairly broad-minded, but even at that age I figured she was on to something. Years later, during my college days, I saw her live at the '86 Chicago Blues Fest. Organist Bill Doggett ("Honky Tonk") was there that day, along with Jimmy McCracklin and Johnny Heartsman. I also remember that it was a sizzling 100 degrees. Heartsman was wearing a double-breasted suit and a Panama hat. Even though his head was bald as a doorknob, the man was sweating bullets. And Sugar Pie made the most of the heat by wearing amazing purple hot pants!

I was impressed, but hardly surprised. I had heard that Sugar Pie does not shy away from the spotlight. This was fresh in my mind when I entered Buddy Guy's Legends. Bypassing the rock-blues opening act, I stepped outside for some air, when from the corner of Eighteenth and Nowhere, a cab pulled up, and who walks out but Sugar herself! She was gracious enough to invite me to her dressing room, where I hung out with Sugar, her manager, and a bunch of former Chess Records studio musicians who knew her from back in the day. Rumors of Sugar's salty language were quickly verified, as she kicked back and reminisced with old friends. After a remarkable fly-on-the-wall experience watching these legends tell fantastic stories of the old days, Sugar kicked everyone out so as to change into her soulful stage dress. Soon the over-sixty siren was dancing around the stage like an R&B cheerleader. Use what you got, indeed!

I spoke with Sugar not long after, as she graciously took time out from her game (an NFL playoff) to talk a while. In the years after our conversation Sugar released strong new material on Jasman (writing most tracks herself), won awards, and saw her stock rise with English "Northern Soul" collectors. However, she has also faced some incredible challenges in the twenty-first century. In 2004 DeSanto was in an accident that physically limited her mobility (she still does splits onstage, but no more back flips). And she experienced a horrible tragedy in 2006 when an electrical malfunction caused DeSanto's apartment to catch fire while she was sleeping. Jesse Earl Davis, to whom she had been married for twenty-seven years (minus a brief divorce, followed by a remarriage), was killed trying to put out the fire after rescuing the singer. DeSanto lost her spouse, home, and all her possessions, and was living on relief and battling depression, but with the support of longtime manager Moore and her fans, DeSanto returned to the stage in 2007 as a featured act at the Berkeley Jazz Festival.

In 2008 I was delighted to see her return to the Chicago Blues Fest, bombastically kicking off the festival as the main stage's first act. Not surprisingly, Sugar Pie put on an absurdly fun set featuring glittery couture, a lot of skin during her high kicks, and some flirting with male audience members that climaxed with her climbing into the crowd in what one might call a septuagenarian stage dive. Since then she has concentrated mainly on the festival circuit, supplemented with a few awards show appearances, picking up a Pioneer Award from the Rhythm & Blues Foundation in 2008, and a Lifetime Achievement Award at the San Francisco Bay Guardian's "Goldies" ceremony in 2009.

Considering the major tragedies and triumphs DeSanto has experienced in the last decade I decided, in 2009, to pick up our conversation where it left off, and what follows is a composite of my two conversations with Little Miss Dynamite.

James Porter: *If you don't mind, I kinda want to take it back to the beginning of your career. I understand that you grew up in San Francisco and you started out singing in a church group.*
Sugar Pie DeSanto: Yeah, in and out. I never was really very churchy. I did some singing in church. Not a lot of it.

So how did you make the jump from that to doing straight secular music?
Oh, because my mother—I learned all my stuff from my mother. She always taught me music, to sing while she played. You know, it was one of them family home things. I was singin' since I was a little bitty girl. My mother was a concert pianist at the age of five.

So how did Johnny Otis come to discover you?

I used to do the talent shows here in San Francisco. They had these talent shows here every week at the Ellis Theater and I would do it maybe every two weeks, something like that, and he happened to be listening. He came through looking for talent, and that's how he picked me up.

So, what was Johnny Otis like to work for?

Oh, he was real nice to work for. He's a real easy person.

OK. Somewhere down the line, I think you made your first record with a guy named Pee Wee Kingsley. "One, Two, Let's Rock."

Yeah it was Pee-Wee and Sugar Pie. That's what we was known as.

How'd you hook up with him?

We was playing some clubs in Stockton, California, and I was playing one club and he was playing another and he came to hear me sing and I checked out his thing and that's how we started out.

And was it right after then that you got your first big record, "I Want to Know."

That came in 1959 with Bob Geddins out of Oakland. Yeah, that was Bob Geddins. But he's deceased now; he just died recently, you know, couple of months, whatever, but he recorded my first hit. That was Veltone Records.

I noticed that even early in the game you were kind of doing these tough-girl songs. Even though "I Want to Know" is not necessarily that tough, it's got that one line "Please don't start no stuff 'cause I don't want to get rough. I want to know."

(Sings) "I want to know." (laughs)

Like you're about to jump in somebody's chest. Was that pretty ballsy for the time; did you have any problems with anybody thinking that that was a heavy thing for a woman to say?

No. It went real well. As a matter of a fact, it was a smash. It was like 2,000 from gold. I did pretty good. Well, 5,000 from a gold. I traveled on that for years, from '59 all the way up there to '65, something like that. That's when I played with James Brown. I went to the Apollo in New York, and he picked me up after seeing me appear there on my own hit record. Yeah, see me and Tina *(Turner)* was on the same show at the time and she had "You just a fool, you know you in love" *("A Fool In Love")* and I had "I Want To Know," so we had star spots at the Apollo and that was in '59 and '60.

Oh man! They are too tough for me. If you ain't nothin' there, you'll know it buddy. They'll throw rotten eggs and tell you to get off. And they got a man that jumps out of the ceiling and hooks you with a cane and pulls you off, if you bad. See, 'cause most of them is talented. Most of them that's looking at you can sing themselves. Church singers, you know, so you can't fool. I got out with no problem. Never did have a problem stage-wise 'cause I always made my own way. Everything is made up by Sugar—I just got that soul.

You are probably the only female vocalist who worked with James Brown that maintained her own sound; all the others had that similar sound. Did James try to mold you?
No, I wouldn't let him. Because James usually liked to go with the women that played for him and I made that clear from jump street, I'll do your shows, but I won't be your woman, now you got that clear?

Brown wrote that you were the only women in his revue that he never slept with . . .
No, no, I never had no problem with James. Only thing that came up was that I was a little too much for him, pushing the envelope. If he jumped off the piano, I'd jump off a chair. If he'd do this, then I'd do that. I was just as strong as him. Um hum. The competition got a little too close, so I decided, let me get out of here. 'Cause I decided if I could hold a show, I could hold my own.

Who was in James Brown's revue with you?
This chick out of Philadelphia—her name was Rusty—she had a front line that opened the show, dancing girls. He had them and him, and Nat Kendrick the drummer, with the "Mashed Potato." *(Brown had recorded "Mashed Potatoes" under his drummer's name for contractual reasons.)* So it was James Brown, his band, Rusty and the dancers, Nat Kendrick, and me.

You were the only female singing?
I was the only one; I was always the only one. With Willie Dixon, Hubert Sumlin, when we did the festival, I was the only one . . .

In the mid-sixties the American Folk Blues Festival would tour England, and you were the most modern performer on that bill, did you feel misplaced being with all these older blues guys . . .
Yes! Because everyone was trying to hit, and to me they were too old. I never did like old, old men, and they were old, already wore out, And every-

body was trying to pick up Sugar and I said, no, no, *no!* I didn't want any of them, from Willie Dixon on down. When my husband passed he was 52 and I was 71. Never did like old men.

What was it like going to Europe where they could be really purists, after hearing these acoustic blues guys doing their thing, how did they take to you doing "I Want to Know?"

I didn't sing "I Want to Know," I did two numbers, "Baby What You Want Me to Do" and "Rock Me Baby." I did them more modern than that old time . . . they on stage with just the guitar, and oh lord, I couldn't believe it. I'm

not against it, but, ohhhh. . . . But I didn't do my songs; I did renditions of older songs, but not that down-home stuff. I wasn't wild; I was cool—no flips, none of that stuff. I kept it at a minimum. But I was so little and so pretty, not talking about myself, but I was *gorgeous*, and I just gave them my soul, it was that simple. At the time, I could sing. I was doing those notes; I was sharp. I just tore it up, and I'd tear it up again today. God gave me a gift, not so much vocally now, though I can still do it vocally, depending on the song, but the *actions*, my actions. I'm still just as agile as I was then.

Now we just jumped ahead a little. After James Brown you moved to Chicago to join Chess Records, as both an artist and a writer. You were on that label for what, like five years?

Seven. I did a lot of writing for other artists as well as myself. Like Fontella Bass and Little Milton. You name 'em, Billy Stewart. I did a lot of writing for Sam and Dave. I wrote for everybody because I'm a good writer.

What song did you write for Sam and Dave?

Something about "Come on . . ." It was called "Come On," or something like

that. I can't even remember, it was so long ago. I did some things for them.
I did a lot of writing for the artists. I was hot with my writing then.

Now my understanding is the Chess brothers used to call everyone who walked
through the door, motherfucker this and son of bitch that.
Well I walked through the door the same way: "Go fuck yourself; why the
hell did you call me here for; what the hell do you want?" I was a pistol. And
all the band members were scared to play with me. Man, you miss a note
and you in trouble.

I know Muddy Waters and them were supposed to have a cussed like sailors, but
I don't know if any of the other women around the scene were as bold as you.
No they weren't. I was one of the toughest women you would find, and a
big mouth, and I didn't take nothing from no one. I'm not crazy; I'm just
talented, and I'm smart, and I'm tired of you guys holding me back.

At Chess you were reunited with Etta James, and did some duets. Etta James was
like your childhood buddy, wasn't she?
That's my cousin as far as I'm concerned. She was raised with me and my
sister, who died at thirty-two; my sister was one of her group, the Peaches.
And we used to sit on my porch and sing.

You had similar-sounding voices. Were you ever rivals?
Yeah at the company *(Chess Records)*, they held back a lot of my stuff because we did sound so much alike, but I could knock her out the box. And
when they put us together like on "In the Basement," and two I wrote—
"Somewhere Down the Line" and "Do I Make Myself Clear"—if you was
listening to those, you would hear that our voices are so close.

Did you ever tour together?
No, we did a little thing here and there, but we never toured together.

So you never did "In the Basement" even though it was a hit?
No, not live.

Are you still in touch with Etta?
I haven't talked to her in a number of years. She lives down in the L.A. area
so we don't get to see each other. I was supposed to play with her in Italy,
not this year *(2009)*, but last year, and she got sick and didn't make it so
they sent Chaka Khan in her place.

It looks like your career kind of took the same path. You started out doing the raunchy R&B stuff then later on you were doing really jazzy kinds of things.

Right, 'cause see, actually my dream is to appear at Carnegie Hall one day and be able to sing everything 'cause, see a lot of people dub me as the Blues Queen, but I sing more than blues. I can sing anything. And I just want my public to know that I can do it all so someday, that's my dream. To have a show where they might see the real me, not just the dancing and everything, but that I could really sing, you know. All types of stuff; I like jazz and all that. I could perform that, but I don't get a chance too much because the blues, being dubbed the Blues Queen, you know what I mean?

You actually did do some touring on the jazz circuit for a while. You were singing with Count Basie and a few other people.

Oh yeah, I did a lot at theaters like the Royal in Baltimore, the Uptown in Philly, the Apollo in New York, the Howard in D.C., Washington. It just was a whole run of stage shows in theaters. I did a lot of that.

So how did you hook up those tours with Count Basie? Were you singing straight jazz in those gigs or were you doing . . .

No I did the blues; I did "I Want to Know." I had to have charts to all my stuff 'cause they didn't play nothing but with charts. Those were polished musicians. So, I did my own works but I had music for it. It was no problem for them to kick it off, you know, kick it down. I had a good time with him. *(laughs)*

I hope the old men were more respectful than on the blues tour.

Well they had a lot of younger guys.

So you were doing the chasing?

I never fooled around with musicians, because I always felt that that's part of my living and I didn't want to become tight with none of them. My thing was business; I sing, I do my thing, you give me my money, and I go on about my business.

So what was the Chess family like to deal with?

They were cool. They were two brothers and a son. It was Phil and Leonard Chess, and his son Marshall. They were pretty cool people. I will give them credit. Only thing I didn't like that they did, they didn't give me my propers, like uh, give me my rewards and stuff.

Right. What's happening now, my lawyer, my manager is suing MCI or MCA, whoever they are. Suing them for my royalties. We had to take them to court. They bought all the things from Chess. They had the gall to throw my shit out overseas and didn't tell me anything about it and I'm just spinnin' in London and shit. So we come to find out, so my manager's got 'em under suit . . . to get me my money.

So what about that one album that Chess put out here, not the one back in the '60s but the one in the '80s, Down in the Basement. *Did you get paid for that one?*
No I did not. Yeah, they kinda wasn't cool either 'cause what they had, they had this brother, Billy Davis, that was the producer for the company. He was black and the brother was cool and everything, but he didn't take care of the right business. I just recently got some bread from them 'cause they owed me so much over the years and hadn't gave me nothing. They just closed the mouth. So my manager got a lawyer. It's costing, but hey, it's worth it 'cause the checks are beginning to come in. Give me my proper dues, brother. I worked for all of that.

Tell me about "Slip in Mules"—was that your idea to answer Tommy Tucker's "Hi-Heel Sneakers?"
Billy Davis of the Chess Company—that was his idea. Buy some big ol' shoes. And then I helped him just think about it. That Tucker record was on Chess too, so that kind of gave the idea . . . It was a big one for me. That kept me traveling. Tommy Tucker sang, "Put on your red dress" and I told him my red dress was in the cleaners.

I'm looking at this back cover of the Down in the Basement *LP. Looks like you were wearing leather pants long before anybody even thought of it.*
That's right. I was wearing leather then, baby. They hadn't even thought of leather pants.

They must have loved it at the Apollo and the Regal when you walked on stage like that.
I tore it up—that's all there is to it. They dubbed me Lady James Brown. The shit get back. Yeah, she cool. Weighed about ninety-five pounds. And I'm now about 105. I still little. I don't want to be big, 'cause I need that for my strength for stage. I don't need to be no big woman 'cause I move a lot. I don't need to be having no heart attack. So go head home.

Sugar Pie DeSanto pushing on the left, with Jackie Ross, middle, and Fontella Bass, right. In car: the Radiants (Leonard Caston, driver's seat; Wallace Sampson, front passenger; Maurice McAlister, backseat in sunglasses; James Phelps, backseat, driver's side).

In the liner notes it says Maurice White, who . . .
He's the drummer for Chess but then he used to sing a little bit on the side, and then later on he left and went with this group, Earth, Wind & Fire. He was a bad drummer, man. What the hell he was singin' for, 'cause he drummed!

Maurice says that you'd be cuttin' up in the studio. You'd be cursin' him worse than the Chess brothers.
He's right. 'Cause I want it correct.

You want to get paid.
Not only that, I'm a perfectionist. It's just my way. If it can't be done right, then I don't want it done at all. 'Cause I'm dealing with pros, so they say, and that's what I want to deal with, pros. I don't want no side nothing.

I don't know if you remember this. I saw a picture of some guys in a car in a driveway . . . and there's you and somebody else pushing the car.
Yeah, it's the Radiants. That's Fontella Bass and Jackie Ross pushing with me. The company just did that. It was just Chess records. And they used

one of the brothers' cars. Just set it up. Billy Davis really did that. He's the big man of Chess records, big producer. He always took all care of all the business. That was Billy's idea undoubtedly.

So you eventually left Chicago, but the whole time you were with Chess you were living here . . .
Right, seven years.

After the Chess contract you went back home to San Francisco. Wasn't Chess already dead by then?
No no, he was still living when I left. Died later on after I was gone. But I stayed in Chicago seven years; I did my traveling. But I had my home base there. At that old Southern Hotel, and then I had an apartment on West Evergreen, Jackson Boulevard. I loved Chicago; it was just too cold for me.

I understand. So after the contract ran out, that's the main reason why you went back to San Francisco?
Uh-huh. Not that it ran out—I could've stayed, but I just chose to do something different back home. I was homesick by that time. Seven years was enough to be away.

You jumped around a little bit. You were on this label called Soul Clock . . .
Yeah, that was Ron Carson out of San Francisco. He cut a couple things

for me and then I was with Don Barksdale of the Boston Celtics; he played basketball. He was my manager and recorder for a while.

You had a local hit, "Hello San Francisco."

Yeah yeah, that was with my manager, Jim Moore. That's who I hooked up with when I got back. Me and him been together over thirty years. And I'm still recording for him, because I take care of myself, lay off the booze and off the weed and off all that bullshit 'cause I really want to do a thing this year and I want to be able to really hit it when I hit it. I also wrote to Oprah. I don't know if she gonna answer, but I'll find out.

SUGAR PIE DeSANTO
Checker Recording Artist   Galaxy Artist Management, Inc.
2120 S. Michigan Ave.
Chicago, Illinois

Wrote Oprah about getting you on the show?

That's right. And gave her all my background so she'd know who I am and I am legendary, you know. And who knows, she might help me. She helped a lot of people. She might give me a play. I go on her show that's all I need. That's televised and that's how you come up with gigs and stuff. Know you're alive. I know some niggers run up on me and tell me, "Oh my goodness, I know you; I thought you were dead!" I said, "Nigger, do I look dead?" You know what I'm saying honey, how can I be dead and I'm standing here talking to you? That really just blew my mind. That blew me up. I said, "You're kidding? You didn't ask me that?" They said, "Is it the Sugar?" I said, "You're damn right it's the Sugar. What you mean 'Is it the Sugar?' You lookin' at me!" "Yeah but I heard you . . ." I said, "Well if you see me, how could I be dead?" Oh man. But I came a long ways, my man. I really have.

You had a kind of homecoming in '86 when I saw you in Chicago at the Blues Fest. You were on with Jimmy McCracklin and Johnny Heartsman and all these other San Francisco blues people.

Johnny Heartsman was a modern man to music. A lot of these guys out here, he taught 'em. 'Cause the brother could play more than five instruments. Very talented man and I had known him for about forty years. We did things off and on over the years. Yeah, I sung at his (Heartsman's) funeral. I tore it up. Them people sitting up there . . . Oh Lord, when I got through they forgot about his funeral. Everybody was up there. Can you believe that, at a funeral? But, hey that's the way I bring 'em. My thing is really entertaining . . . I'm here to entertain 'til I die. Which won't be too soon . . . I go to the gym at least twice a week; I keep myself in pretty good shape. I'm not just laying here—I take my vitamins and my exercise; I do what I'm supposed to do. I'm gone be seventy-four this year. They sent me something in the mail talking about the Rascal scooter (electric wheelchair); I told them, "Are you nuts?" I just tore it up and put it in the garbage can. Un-uh, you ain't scooting me nowhere! I'll be walking or running or whatever, if it's His will. I think I'm pretty agile for seventy-three. I get around like a young chick.

Billy Lee Riley

More than a cult hero, less than an icon, Billy Lee Riley is the best former Sun artist to never have a national hit record. Passionate, sexy, funny, and rhythmic, his waxings of "Red Hot" and "Flyin' Saucers Rock 'n' Roll" encapsulate everything which is good about '50s rock 'n' roll. The frantic growl may have owed something to Little Richard, but the attack and attitude were pure Memphis-era Riley.

The movie-star-handsome Riley and his band the Little Green Men (J. M. Van Eaton, Roland Janes, Marvin Pepper, Martin Willis, and Jimmy Wilson) quickly won a reputation as the best show band in the Mid-South, but neither their wild onstage histrionics nor their musical excellence translated into hit records.

The booming success of labelmate Jerry Lee Lewis (who briefly played piano for Riley's group) resulted in Sam Phillips pulling support from Riley's record to feed the fires of Lewis's career. Subsequently, Riley and his band earned eating money backing nearly every act that recorded at Sun.

BILLY LEE RILEY   LEGENDARY SUN PERFORMER   1956 / 1960

So indispensable were their talents that Phillips reportedly said to Riley, "I can't let you have a hit record. If I did, you'd take your band and go out on the road."

Eventually, a disillusioned Riley left Sun to embark on a rather remarkable music industry odyssey that continues to this day. He has recorded for dozens of different labels, under many different names, and cut everything from pop to blues to novelty tunes to instrumentals, and tons of good ol' rock 'n' roll. After moving to California during the early '60s, he became a much sought-after session man, playing harmonica behind the likes of Sammy Davis Jr., Dean Martin, the Beach Boys, Johnny Rivers, and many others. Riley even sold tapes to Chess on which they overdubbed the *Surfin' with Bo Diddley* album.

Though a favorite on the Whiskey-a-Go-Go circuit, Riley quit music during the early '70s. He reemerged after the death of Elvis to fresh audiences craving to see what they missed the first time around, and he does not disappoint. Of all his contemporaries, Billy Lee Riley has the most gas left in his tank. Whether he is rockin' hard onstage or emoting gut-bucket blues in the studio, Riley continues to tap into what makes him and his music unique, even vital.

The following is a distillation of three lengthy phone conversations that took place while Riley was preparing and recording a new LP for an as-yet-unspecified label. I found him to be honest, articulate, and the possessor of a rather wry sense of humor. We started at the beginning.

Ken Burke: *I've read that you are of Native American ancestry. Is that true?*
Billy Lee Riley: I've got some Cherokee blood in me. Both sides of my family have some Indian in them; I don't know how much. I wouldn't even know how to measure it.

In a previous conversation, you mentioned that you picked cotton.
Yeah, I was raised on plantations, farms—just like everybody was back in them days, all the poor people. We were all sharecropping farmers. That was our way of making a living.

Were you picking cotton at a young age? Tell us something about that.
Oh yeah. I was about six years old. Cotton picking—well, we used to do it by hand. We'd grow the cotton in the fields and cotton would clump on what they called "cotton stalks" which would grow about waist high. Then it would bloom and then the blooms would turn into cotton bolls, and the bolls would open, then the cotton would come out, and we would pick it out of the bolls and put it in the sack. Then we'd weigh it and put it in the wagon.

And you got paid by the pound?
We got paid by the *hundred* pounds. Back when I first started picking, it was fifty cents a hundred, and it would take most people all day to pick a hundred pounds of cotton.

I take it you were picking cotton alongside black people?
We lived on plantations where black and white people worked together. We didn't see color. We lived together, we played together, we visited each other—all on one big farm with a bunch of integrated people.

This sounds like a corny question but I have to ask—is that where you picked up your feeling for the blues?
Yes, that's exactly where I got it. When I was very young, that was the only music that I heard. The only music you heard on radio back in those days was hillbilly and pop music—and we didn't have a radio. Sometimes we did, but mostly we didn't, so the only music I heard was from the people who were actually playing it, sitting on their front porch, and whatever . . .

When did you first start playing this music yourself?
Well, I started playing harmonica when I was six years old. My dad gave me

a harmonica, and I got my first guitar when I was ten years old, but it was
a couple of years before I learned to play it.

What kind of guitar did you get?
A Silvertone—used. Paid ten dollars for it.

How long were you on the plantations?
We left the farm in '47 when I was thirteen years old.

Were you able to attend much school?
Three years. Our schooling was very limited. We went to school only when
there was no work to be done. We had summer school and then winter
school. We worked when we were planting in the springtime and up into
the summer. Once the crops were all planted and we were waiting for har-
vest, we'd go to school for about two or three months. Then, when the cotton was ready to be harvested we'd have to come out of school and work
until all the crops were in. Then we'd go back to school.

Did this seem unusual to you?
It didn't seem unusual—it was normal for us. It was the only way we knew.
We didn't know any better. We thought everybody did that. A lot of people
went north to get those good-paying factory jobs, but a lot of us couldn't;
we were sort of tied down in the South—there was poor people, and then
there were us! *(laughs)* It's kind of funny today. But I have no regrets at all,
I'd go back there today if I could and relive the same life.

When did you go into armed services?
I went into the service when I was fifteen in 1949.

What? How did you manage that?
I lied about my age. I didn't have a birth certificate, so I told 'em I was
seventeen and got my sister to sign saying that I was seventeen. After that
I spent four years in the service.

Which branch?
The Army—and I never did like it. I went in mainly to have a place to live
and something to eat!

What happened to your folks at that time; were they still around?
They were still around, living in Arkansas. My dad, by trade, was a painter.
So, when we weren't farming, he painted houses. After we left the farms,
that's what he got into. A funny thing happened the day I went into the

service. I was visiting with my sister in Osceola, and my mother and father were living in Pocahontas. The day I was at the bus station, I had already took my examination, and I had my ticket and I was getting on the bus to go. My father was coming to Osceola from Pocahontas looking for a place to live, and as I was getting on, he was getting off the same bus. *(laughs)* And he threatened to tear up my ticket. But he couldn't do it—it was government property. He was very unhappy about me going into the Army, but there wasn't no war going on.

You were part of the peacetime militia then?
Well, I was—then in 1950, war broke out in Korea, and they gave me an extra year on my service.

Did you serve in Korea?
No, I never went over there, but they gave everyone in the service an extra year of duty, so I had to serve four years instead of three.

What was your job in the service?
I drove a truck. Delivering troops, taking troops out on the field. I had three or four vehicles assigned to me. I had a jeep to carry the officers around. I drove a two-and-a-half-ton truck and carried the kitchen out into the field whenever they were doing field stuff.

Our friend Tommie Wix (secretary of the Billy Lee Riley fan club from 1976 to 1990, and owner of the Wix rockabilly label) said you recorded your first acetates around this time.
When I was fifteen, and first went in the service. After I left basic, I was in Seattle and I did three acetates. You'd go into a little booth, and they had guitars there, and you sang whatever you wanted to sing. It went right through the microphone right onto the acetate.

What songs did you do?
I did some Hank Williams things. "My Son Calls Another Man Daddy," "I'm So Lonesome I Could Cry." I did a couple of Hank Thompson things. "Green Light" and others. I did six songs, but I can't remember what they all were now.

Where are these acetates now?
The Hard Rock Cafe has one. The Smithsonian has one, and Tommie Wix has one.

Well, that's kind of a nice deal. A major corporation, a major museum, and a major collector?

(*Laughs*) That's right. I gave that one to Tommie many years ago.

You mentioned Hank Williams and Hank Thompson. Who were some of the other people you liked back then?

Up until I got into it professionally, I didn't know too many names. We lived in a very rural area; the only time we saw shows was when tent shows would come through. They'd set up out in the country and have several different acts—sometimes they'd be country, sometimes minstrel, whatever . . .

Were minstrel shows still working in the '40s and '50s?

Out where we were, yeah. When we listened to the radio, of course I would listen to country music. So I listened to Hank Williams and the Grand Ol' Opry and all the guys before Hank Williams way back in the '30s. We only had battery radios in those days and a lot of times on a Saturday night, a lot of people would gather together in one house to listen to the Grand Ol' Opry. If the battery went dead, you had *no* radio—so people would kind of ration that battery. (*laughs*) See, we didn't have electricity.

When did you first start thinking of a career in music; was it during your time in the Army?

Well, I always dreamed of being in the business, but when I was in the Army, I was in some talent shows on base. I was in three different talent shows and I won first place each time—just me and my guitar, singing a country song. That kind of put the "bug" in me. Then when I got out of the service, the first band I formed was a hillbilly band.

What was it called?

It had two names. One was the Arkansas Valley Ranch Boys and the KBTM Ranch Boys! The reason it had two different names was because we had two different radio shows. We usually named a band after the radio show or the radio station. So KBTM wanted to call us the KBTM Ranch Boys, so that's what we used. We had three radio shows going at the same time. We would go down on Sunday and record those, and work during the week. So, we'd take a coffee break when we thought the show was about to come on, and run out and sit out in our car to listen. (*laughs*) And then, we'd get back to work. We had two that we'd tape every week, then we'd have the live gospel show with my bass player, his wife, and me. We'd get up at four o'clock every morning and go to the radio station and do a live gospel show. Then we'd go home, have breakfast, and go to work.

That surprises me. I see less gospel music in your catalogue than from other guys of your era.

I wasn't into gospel music. I think a lot of the other *(original rockers)* talking about gospel—that's just to make themselves look good. I don't think they were into gospel anymore than I was—that just makes 'em feel good to say that. We were not involved in church and all that like most people. I'm not saying I never did go, because I did, but we were not members of any particular church per se and I didn't know anybody that was.

So, how did you get to do the gospel radio show?

Well, I heard gospel; I even wrote some gospel songs. And this guy wanted to do it, and shoot—I was all for it.

So you had three jobs in radio with your band? What kind of day job did you have?

I was working in a shoe factory.

Man! Where did you get the energy?

(Laughs) I was young. We also played at nights and on weekends on stage shows at high schools and club dates, like that.

Was your sound different back then?

Back then we just sounded like any regular hillbilly band. We had a steel guitar, a bass, lead guitar, and rhythm guitar, and we weren't different from anybody else. My singing was a little different. Even though I was doing country, I still had a little bit of blues sound in me, even back then. Because I had played blues all my young days.

Did you ever take any heat for sounding black?

Nope. By the time I got into rock 'n' roll in 1957, most of that had already been accepted and all of the blues I was singing was in an area where there wasn't nuthin' but blues. So it didn't make any difference. It was a regional thing—everybody did it. So there wasn't any problem. Nobody ever said anything to me about it. I never did have any trouble over singing in my style.

That's really good to know, because I've read all these stories about how some of you guys went through hell for sounding black.

Elvis did. Elvis took a lot of flack, man. Most of these other guys wanted to sound like Elvis, so they say, "Yeah, we took it too." I think a lot of that, just like a whole lot of history from the '50s, is so distorted right now. It's hard to find the real truth. Everybody's telling stories. "Aw we took a lot of flack; they didn't want us playing black music." I never did see that happen. The only one I ever did hear of that happening to was Elvis. I didn't see anybody else having problems with it, and I doubt if they did. Elvis said he had problems with it, so to be like Elvis, everybody else claimed to have problems too.

How big of a factor was Elvis Presley's success in your pilgrimage to Memphis?
Well, he had nothing to do with me going to Memphis. I went to Memphis because my brother-in-law and I bought a restaurant. I wasn't even in music when I went to Memphis. At that time, I played music, but I wasn't trying to make any money at it. But I did play it, that's how I met Jack Clement, the guy who cut my first record. One Christmas, I was back in Jonesboro *(Arkansas)* visiting my folks and, on the way back to Memphis, I picked up these two guys flagging down a ride. It was Jack Clement and his partner! That's where I first met him was on the highway. We got to talking music and they told me they were building a studio over there, called Fernwood Studios, and they had a band that played every weekend in Arkansas. When I picked 'em up, I was only going to take them a couple of miles to where my mother lived, but we got to talking, and it got so interesting, that I drove 'em all the way to Memphis. While we were talking, they asked me if I wanted to play and sing in their band. I told 'em, "Yeah!" So I started singing on weekends in their band in Arkansas, then they invited me to cut a record. That's where I cut my first record in that little ol' garage studio. "Trouble Bound" and "Think Before You Go."

I have a compilation of your early stuff on the Charly label, and it says that you played all the instruments on those songs. Is that true?
No, I couldn't have. See, that's why I'm telling you—people are telling a bunch of lies when they tell these stories. You have to think back. In 1957, there was only mono. There wasn't even a two-track machine, and you can't overdub unless you have at least two tracks. We only had mono, and we almost didn't have that in that little studio. We had one track and about four mikes plugged into that one track. With that setup you couldn't overdub; you'd have to have at least another track, or another machine, to do that. On that first session, we had Roland Janes on guitar, me playing rhythm guitar, and another guitar player on there, two bass fiddles—upright bass

players on there, and a drummer. There ain't no way in the world I could play all that stuff. I would've had to overdub six times on one mono tape. So, 60 percent of all that stuff Charly prints, you can flush it! That stuff is written by *(Sun Records historians)* Colin Escott and Martin Hawkins. They'll call you up and ask, "What's your name?" Tell 'em "Billy Lee Riley," and they can write a whole story on that. I don't have anything to do with those guys. The last time Colin Escott called me, I told him that it was just best that he get out of town, that I didn't want anything to do with him. I didn't like the things he was writing, and I wouldn't give him anything. So we've never spoken again, and I never intend to speak to him again. And it's not only me, but several of the old guys feel the same way because he wrote a bunch of crap that just wasn't true.

I'm sorry to hear that.

You see, they messed up a lot of good history. And ever since I've been back in the business full time, I've been trying to straighten that up. The first time I went to England, they used all those same notes that you brought up to me, and I had to deny 90 percent of it. And that makes them unhappy, but I'm going to tell you the truth regardless, you know? I'm not going to let you believe something that's not true about me. I say, "You can believe what you want to believe, but I'm going to straighten my part of it up." That's what I've been doing, and so far, everything that I've told is the way it is. There's an awful lot of records out, people think it's me, and I've had to straighten all that out, saying "I don't know where that came from." I don't know how they would pick records with other people's names on it and think it was me.

As I understand it, these session notes are very difficult to verify, and in some cases, the labels never kept accurate notes. And what happens is, somebody will give the writer information wrong or secondhand information, which they repeat without checking.

Oh yeah, like them guys in Europe. You can tell one of them a story, and by the time it goes the full circle, it's been written into four or five books! *(laughs)* And, the artists tell a lot of things too, to make themselves look good. They want their life to look good too. So, it's not just the writers.

Were there any other artists on the Fernwood label, or were you the only one?

I was supposed to have been the first one out on Fernwood, but I never went on that label. I only recorded there. But when they took my master to Sam Phillips's studio to master it, Sam bought the master. So, therefore, I was never on that label. But there was a *lot* of good people on the Fernwood label; it became a pretty big label after that. Thomas Wayne had a big hit, "Tragedy." So, I wasn't on that label, but I was the first one they recorded in that studio.

Fernwood's sound, with the echo and the slapback, that was real close to Sun's, wasn't it?

It was about the same thing. We didn't have echo in there; we had to take our tape to a radio station to put echo on it. And the second song, after Sam bought the record—he didn't want "Think Before You Go"; he wanted another rocker. So I wrote "Rock with Me Baby." And, we actually went to a radio station and recorded it so we would have that echo.

Did you do two versions of "Rock with Me Baby?" Isn't there one with a sax on it?

No. That's "Dance with Me Honey." They *(Charly)* call it "Rock with Me Baby number 2." But that's a whole different song.

Tell us how you met the original members of your band The Little Green Men.

The original Little Green Men were Marvin Pepper, Roland

THE LITTLE GREEN MEN
FR. PAT O'NEAL MARTIN WILLIS
BR. JIMMY WILSON BILLY LEE RILEY
J.M. VAN EATON

Janes, J. M. Van Eaton, and Jerry Lee Lewis. I didn't even know Roland until I met him through Jack Clement when he set up my first session. And Roland knew J. M. Van Eaton. He got us all together, and we went out to where J. M.'s little band was playing. And we decided he was a good drummer, so we hired him. He had his own little band in high school and I think he started working with us right out of high school. Marvin Pepper was the bass man.

I'm not trying to start any trouble here at all, but in Jerry Lee Lewis's autobiography, he claims he didn't play on "Red Hot" or "Flying Saucers Rock 'n' Roll."

(*Laughs*) Well, I'd take what's in his book with a grain of salt. But he didn't play on "Red Hot"; he played on "Flying Saucers Rock 'n' Roll." And he knows it too, because I did a show with him on his fortieth anniversary. And one of the things — they had people who had been associated with him through the years stand behind the stage, and use a mike, and say something to get him to try and identify who you were. Well, when they handed me the mike I said, "Jerry Lee, it's been a long time since you and I have talked, but if you'll remember, you used to play in my band." And he said, "Billy Lee Riley!"

So he knew.

Yeah, he knew. Jerry Lee would probably tell you that today. That was probably written during them days when Jerry Lee gave nobody credit for anything.

So who played piano on "Red Hot" then?

Jimmy Wilson. Jimmy Wilson came to work for me right after Jerry Lee went off on his own.

To me it seems like Jerry Lee on "Red Hot."

Jimmy Wilson was a lot better than Jerry Lee Lewis, all around. He was the better piano player. He could play like Jerry Lee, then he could turn around and play all around Jerry Lee. Bach, Beethoven, and a bunch of stuff we didn't know. He was one of the greatest piano players in Memphis at that time. But he was crazy — we couldn't control him.

What do you mean when you say you "couldn't control him?"

(*Laughs*) He was just one of those kinda guys. . . . a weirdo. He knew it and everybody else knew it, but he was a good guy.

(Laughs) Well, sir, how did this weirdness manifest itself?

To give you one story, he used to live in the apartments right over Sun Records. We came back from Canada one time, and he brought a pet raccoon back with him. And, one night that raccoon was kinda restless and kept him from sleeping. So he just pinned him to the floor with a bayonet from a rifle. The next morning, he woke up and the raccoon was still alive, so he took him downstairs and beat him to death.

And he'd buy old antique relics, German guns and things from these surplus stores. They'd have barrels all fixed so you couldn't shoot 'em. Well, he'd dig out all that steel and buy bullets and shoot these guns. He shot an old wooden bridge in two one time.

What is it about piano players and guns?
(Chuckles) I don't know. He sure was crazy, but a great piano player.

So what happened to Jimmy Wilson?
I have no idea. The last time I saw him, he was in California in the '60s, and he got married to Nudie's daughter until her daddy ran him off. The last time I heard from him he was in Bakersfield, California. I heard not too long ago, that he had passed away since then. My other bass player, Pat O'Neil—who took Marvin's place, he died also. So there's two of 'em that have died. There was a big story in *Goldmine* recently about my sax player Martin Willis, several pages, and they had pictures of all of us in there. But they put the wrong caption under a picture of me and my band on stage—the caption read that it was Conway Twitty and his band. They ran a retraction.

How did your band achieve that unique chemistry you had in the studio?
The only way I can say it is we were all just in tune with each other. It was a "feel" thing, and we just all felt the same thing. We didn't go in there with anything planned; we'd just go in and start jammin'! It just so happened that all of our minds were tuned together, and it just came out that way. I don't remember none of us actually trying to get that sound. None of us were great musicians—we were playing the best we could play, and that's how it came out.

Your sound was different than everyone else's there—I've always considered you to be more of an R&B guy.
Yeah, more or less. I never considered myself a "rockabilly"; I always thought I was "rock 'n' roll."

Who called the shots in the Sun studios? From all the things I've heard, it sounds like you pretty much had your own way as far as song selections and arrangements.
Yeah, we pretty well did that. Sometimes Sam would pick a song, and if you didn't want to do it, you didn't have to. He picked "Red Hot," and I was very happy that he did. But we could do anything we wanted to; there was

no pressure there. Sam, in his own way, was producing, but it wasn't really producing per se. He was just sitting up there and having as good a time as we were. *(laughs)* And probably just as drunk as we were—or drunker. It wasn't like it is today. There wasn't that much emphasis on going in and cutting a hit. We went in to have a lot of fun just playin' music. Jammin'!

Was the growl you used on "Red Hot" and "Flying Saucers Rock 'n' Roll" inspired by Little Richard?
Well, once I started doing Little Richard's songs, I had to growl to do 'em, and I kind of liked that sound, so I just kept doing it. Of course, I don't have to do it—I can do just about any other style.

Oh yeah, absolutely!
But, on some of the loud stuff, I felt like they needed *(that growl)*. Like on "Flying Saucers Rock 'n' Roll," that was a pretty high-energy thing, so on those type of records—I did my best to scream. But there were other songs where I didn't need to do that, like on "One More Time" and "Wouldn't You Know," stuff like that.

"One More Time" is a helluva blues song.
That's one of the best songs I did at Sun.

I've read where Jerry Lee Lewis has said that he was always a country singer who did country music speeded up. Were you basically always a blues singer who just did the blues with a big beat?
I tell ya, that's about it. Most of my stuff was from blues songs; all I did was change the tempo and the arrangements on 'em. Most of the other guys who came to Sun were country singers who came there and changed. There's a fine line between our kind of rock 'n' roll and country. It's a mixture and a tempo thing. You can take any country song and make a rockabilly tune out of it. It doesn't matter what it is. I proved that when I was being interviewed by the Smithsonian. I took a song like "Tennessee Waltz" and sang it as country, then blues, then rockabilly and it worked all three ways.

Did they film you doing this? When will we be able to see this?
It's only going to be shown on exhibit—it's not going to be on the air. I've got a big exhibit with them. They just bought a bunch of stuff from me.

When is this exhibit going to open?
Well, I think it's going to open in Memphis this year or next year. It'll stay

Left to right: Riley, J. M. Van Eaton, Martin Willis, Jimmy Ray Paulman, Pat O' Neil; Brass Rail, Ontario, 1957.

there for a while, then it's going to Washington permanently. Part of that exhibit with my things is on the road right now. And sometime before I leave this ol' world, I'm supposed to be part of the ceremony for that.

Let's talk a little more about the Sun days. Was Jerry Lee Lewis OK to work with in the studio? Did he do what you told him to do?
Back in the '50s, Jerry Lee Lewis was very hard to get along with. Jerry Lee did things his way, and that was the only way that he ever did do anything was his way. Nobody told him what to do. If he was in a good mood, the sessions went real well. If he wasn't in a good mood, the sessions didn't go too well. It was strictly up to him, and we knew that, and we just did what we were supposed to do. We didn't step on his feet.

But you were the leader of your group.
I was the leader of my little group, but when we went into the studio as session men for somebody else, everybody was on their own. We didn't go in as the Little Green Men; we just went in as individuals. So, I wouldn't dare go in there and tell anybody what to do. Early on, Sam didn't even want me to hire Jerry Lee. He said, "You don't need no piano in a rock 'n' roll band."

This is before he even heard Jerry Lee Lewis. I was the first one who met Jerry Lee when he came to town, as far as musicians were concerned—and that's why he went to work for me. So when I told Sam about him he said (*perfect imitation of Sam Phillips*), "Man, you don't need no piano player." I said, "Yeah, I do and this guy's great." Sam said, "I don't care how great he is—piano players belong in jazz bands. Dixieland, country . . ." I said, "I'm going to put him to work anyway." When I told him I was going to use him on the "Flying Saucers" session he said "all right," but he didn't want to use him, and he wouldn't let him take a solo—he just played rhythm. He told him, "All I want you to do is play that pumpin' rhythm." That's where he got "pumpin' piano," that's where the name came from. Sam didn't really even know who he was at that time—and Jerry Lee's first record ("Crazy Arms") was an *accident*.

That's the one where you were in the bathroom.
Roland was in the bathroom, and I'm the only one on there other than J. M., and I got that last guitar note on there. Nobody even knew that record was being recorded at the time. Jack Clement had the machine going and we just sat there, messin' around man. I was standing there beside the piano with an upright bass and I didn't even know how to play it, and I wasn't miked; and I was thumping around trying to figure out how to fall in with Jerry Lee—and that wasn't working. By that time, Roland had come out of the john, and I laid the bass down, and he came over and picked the bass up like he was going to play it. He's sat there trying to hit a note or two, so I picked up his guitar and I was going to play along with J. M. and Jerry. But by the time I got ready to play, Jerry ended the song. I hit that one note—that one little chord, and that was about it. So, I was on that record, which was an accident. We were there for something else; we weren't there for a Jerry Lee session. Jerry Lee was just going to be part of the band.

Really? You know, the common story is that Jerry recorded that at his audition.
Jerry Lee did not have an audition with Sam Phillips. He cut "Crazy Arms," Jack Clement showed that to Sam, and Sam liked it. After that, he called a session and we went in and did a session on Jerry Lee. But nobody even knew the tape recorder was on, and after it was over Jack yelled out, "That's a hit!" And all of us were amazed, and Jerry Lee said, "You didn't record that did you?" Jack said, "Yeah." And Jerry said, "Hey man, we can do that better than that. Let's do it again!" Jack said "No man—it's good, we're

going to leave it like this." He wanted to do it again, but that's the only take there was of "Crazy Arms" that I know of—they may have come in later and done some more—but that take is the one they released.

Eventually, everything you guys recorded during the Sun days was released—and there's another version of "Crazy Arms," but it's from much later.
Jerry cut a lot of sides over there. We used to go in and stay all night over there. We'd get into a groove and cut things in one or two takes all night long—then sometimes we'd go in and get nothin.'

For your own sessions, did you work the same way as Jerry Lee? No arrangements, just jamming?
When Willi *(Martin Willis)* started playing sax for us, that's when we started putting some arrangements to things. Martin Willis was very talented—and before he came we'd just get in there and jam. But Willi was quite a perfectionist, and he liked everything to be done just right. I give him credit, because he would usually come up with our intros and solos, and knew when we should do this and do that.

Whose idea was it to just let the piano chord hang there at the end of "Flying Saucers Rock 'n' Roll?
Sam's. He kept turning the pot completely up until it faded completely out; he said he thought it sounded like a flying saucer taking off.

Was Sam Phillips's greatest contribution at Sun in the area of engineering or as a producer?
Well, I give most of my credit to Jack Clement. Jack cut most of my stuff. In fact, he cut most of everything after he got there. Jack understood everything that was going on—he's a genius when it comes down to it. He knew what he wanted before he even came into the studio. The only thing I actually remember Sam Phillips having anything to do with was "Flying Saucers Rock 'n' Roll" and "Red Hot." And, of course, the other sides of those two records, but that was the only time I remember Sam even being in the studio when I was recording. After Jack came around, Sam wasn't there much.

I'm trying to match this up. Here's a guy you picked up hitchhiking—how did he get the wherewithal to become a great studio producer?
Jack had been involved in music since he was young, but up until *(the Sun days)*, he hadn't been old enough to do it. But once he decided to start Fernwood and all that, he knew where he was going. He's gone all the way to the

top! He's produced some of the greatest acts in the world, and discovered some of the greatest acts in the world. So, Jack was just a *natural* producer.

Did he ever play bass on any of your stuff?
He never played on anything of mine, but he was a good rhythm guitar player. He plays mandolin—and he's a heckuva songwriter.

Why didn't Jack Clement write songs for you?
He wasn't really writing the type of stuff I was doing. He took credit on three of my songs, which he wasn't supposed to—but back in them days, I didn't pay too much attention to what was going on. And when they turned the writer's stuff into BMI, he had his name on there somewhere. It didn't matter to me at the time. At that time, I wasn't looking at the money part of it—we were just having fun. That was back during the days when everybody got cheated.

I think that "Red Hot" and "Flying Saucers Rock 'n' Roll" are two of the greatest records of the rock 'n' roll era.
Thank you. Some say they're classics. They've inspired a lot of artists. As a matter of fact, Bruce Springsteen said he cut his teeth on "Flying Saucers Rock 'n' Roll." He said he grew up on my stuff.

Praise indeed from the Boss.
And Bob Dylan said he considers me his hero. I opened some shows for him, and that's the way he introduced me: "My hero." That was good. Y'know, Bob is a guy that a lot of people don't understand, and I didn't until I met him. Once I met him and sat down and talked with him—he turned out to be a good guy. I've worked with him and worked with his son. I just opened the Hard Rock Cafe in Memphis with his son, Jacob.

How did that go?
Great man, Jacob's a nice guy. Real nice young guy—he told me, "I've known about you ever since I was a baby. I remember when I was just two or three years old walking around wearing Billy Lee Riley T-shirts." *(laughs)* So there's a lot of good people in this business, and there's some that ain't worth a crap. That's the business, man—and that's the way it is.

One of your outtakes at Sun seems like an early version of "Red Hot"; it's called "She's My Baby."
That's a *later* version of "Red Hot." I did that drunk one night. I was in the studio and I had been trying to cut an album, and everybody got com-

pletely off the subject, and we began drinking and having a party. So, I was pretty high that night, and couldn't think of anything to sing so I just started singing that. I didn't even know it was put on tape, and I didn't know it'd ever be released.

It says on these album notes that Carl Perkins's band members Clayton Perkins and "Fluke" Holland played on that.
No. Nobody played on *my* records except the Little Green Men. Brad Suggs was not on any of my sessions. "Smoochy" Smith was not on any of my sessions. Every session I did at Sun Records had Roland Janes—there were one or two that even he wasn't on, but there was J. M., Martin Willis, me, Jimmy Wilson—just my band.

Were you a bit of a rounder during the '50s?
I was *crazy!* Wild—I drank a lot in the '50s, and I was wild. I thought all there was to life was wine, women, and song—and I had my share of all of it! That was one of my biggest faults. I put all of that before my career and it hurt my career. Of course that's a long time ago.

But you still have a career.
Oh yeah—I'm having more fun and probably making more money now than I've ever made in the music business. And, I feel a lot better about it. I can control it. I can do it when I want to, I'm not pushed, and I do it on my own terms. That's the way I like to do it. I don't like to be put in a corner and be told that I have to do something.

Why aren't you on some modern independent label like HighTone or Rounder?
Well, I was working on a deal with HighTone, but it didn't come through.

Are there any other labels you'd consider?
There's so many labels, man. I know hundreds of 'em. When I'm ready with my next album, I'll pick out three or four. Alligator, Blind Pig would be good labels. I'm not really worried about it.

Are you happiest when you're recording?
Oh yeah. When I get into that studio, I'm in another world. I love it. When I'm performing, that's the real me.

What was the disagreement you had with Sam Phillips concerning "Red Hot" and "Flying Saucers Rock 'n' Roll"?
He didn't promote it—he sabotaged the record. He dropped my record

for "Great Balls of Fire." That's why I had my greatest disagreement with him. Of course, we still worked together after that, but it never was the same. But yeah, he had deliberately quit selling my record—right in front of me, with me standing there listening to him—he canceled my record. So when he did that, I lost respect for him. He just forgot everybody except Jerry Lee Lewis, and that doesn't make me feel bad at Jerry Lee! That had nothin' to do with how I felt about Jerry Lee. Whatever I felt about Jerry Lee would be personal. That's what caused me to leave Sun. The same thing with Johnny Cash and everybody else. At one time, they've all made the same statement.

Was this something you guys talked about while it was happening?
Heck yeah, we weren't afraid to talk about it. Everybody knew it. Sam denied it. Sam'll deny it to this day, but he knows it's true. But it backfired on him. He dropped all of us for Jerry Lee, then Jerry Lee put the bomb on him. He went over to Europe and screwed himself up and lost his popularity on Sun Records, then he fell. So, what goes around, comes around.

You and your band left Sun to go to Philadelphia at one point, right?
In 1958, I decided I wanted to go up and talk to Dick Clark. So, we got the band together and drove up there. We went unannounced, didn't even know if we were going to get in to see this guy. But we did; I went in to talk to him, and he was about ready to go on his show—and he knew who I was. He wanted to sign me up for one of his labels. And, he actually called a studio and set up time, and told the engineer to be there at three o'clock that afternoon because he had a band coming over there that he wanted to record. We got halfway over there . . . then decided to come right back home to Memphis! We were kids and we were scared. Scared to go out on that limb, see. I told the guys, "Aw man, let's go back to Sun. We'll feel better." It was strictly a fear thing as far as I was concerned.

Are you sorry that's a road you didn't take?
Oh gosh, I'm sorry that I didn't make a lot of moves that I had a chance to make back in them days. I could've been on RCA. Steve Sholes himself, when he was president of RCA in New York, set up a session in Canada for me. We went in there and sat around for an hour waiting for their engineer when I started getting that old feeling again, "Aw, we don't need RCA." So we got up and left. So I lost that.

I recorded "Rock 'n' Roll Money" in '83 and RCA was going to put it out.
I lived in Nashville then, and I flew to New York and they flipped over it
and they were going to buy it—but it wasn't finished. And, the guy who
was producing and putting the money behind it, he and I had a falling
out because of somebody he had working for him. This guy was trying to
tell me how to sing rockabilly—and he wasn't but twenty something years
old. Anyway, it just fell through, and he wouldn't finish the record, and we
lost it.

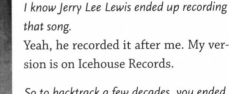

*I know Jerry Lee Lewis ended up recording
that song.*
Yeah, he recorded it after me. My version is on Icehouse Records.

*So to backtrack a few decades, you ended
up back at Sun, but things weren't the
same?*
Yeah, I went back and cut two or three
more things. I left them in '60. I think
my last record with them was late '59.

*Which one of your singles do you think
should have been your breakthrough?*
Oh, "Red Hot" should've been; it was
already headed that way. Alan Freed
told me that "Red Hot" was going to
be a Top-5 record. He told me, "This
is a hit record, man. If ever I saw a hit

record—this is it." So, Sam Phillips and Jud Phillips got to him and got with
his manager—see, he'd already booked me on a nationwide tour. That's the
reason I had closed out to come home, so I could cut an album. Sam told me
to. I shouldn't have ever told Sam I had the deal, because when I told Sam I
had a deal, he went right to work to get me off the tour and have Jerry Lee
put on the tour in my place. That's the tour that Jerry Lee and Chuck Berry
was on together and fought so much and caused a riot which made them
cancel part of the tour. So, that was another big mistake they made because
they wouldn't do right. When I got back to Memphis, that's when I found

all this stuff out. That's when me and Sam—that's when I went and tore up the studio. Did the studio in.

I've read that you poured whiskey all over the console.
(*Laughs*) I did that too. They had a big bass fiddle, I walked through that and tore a big hole in it. Poured whiskey on the piano and consoles. Tipped over the filing machines where he had all his tapes; they went all over the floor. I *wrecked* it pretty good! Then Sam came down, and took me back into his little cubby hole, and charmed me into believing that I was going to be the next Elvis Presley so I would be quiet. But he never did anything for me. And he knows it and he admits it. When we opened the Hard Rock Cafe in Memphis, he was there that night, and I walked over and spoke with him, and he told some other people—while I was standing there, he said, "Billy Lee Riley should've been one of the biggest artists I had. I wish I had done more for him. Should've done more for him—he was a great talent!" So he admitted it.

It was a little late, but that was nice for him to say.
I don't hold any regrets. What I do with people I can't get along with is I just stay away from them. I don't hold anything against Sam. If he needed me, I'd be right there. I'm sort of this way: I don't blame anybody for anything good or anything bad that's happened to me. I'm in control of my own self. Whatever happens to me is strictly up to me. I don't blame anybody, really. Sometimes I blame myself for listening to certain people that steered me wrong. Nobody makes you do anything. I didn't have to stay with Sam. I could've left Sun; I had several chances. So I can't really feel that down. It's more like I'm disappointed, because he did have something with me—he could've made some money with me. It's not like I could've made money and he couldn't. We could've all had a good thing going. He just didn't do it that way.

But "Red Hot" was a pretty good seller in the Mid-South wasn't it?
It sold good regionally. "Flying Saucers" sold more. Both of 'em were good regional sellers, and hit Top 5 and even number 1 in a lot of places in the South. That's how it worked just before a record would break onto the national charts. And if all those things would've gotten reported, and Sam would've gotten behind 'em, they probably would've hit the national charts. Then, it would've happened, because these records were what was happening at that time. "Red Hot" was—and still is—a heck of a record! I

don't care where you play it. Before I opened shows for Bob Dylan, I was a guest on one of his shows and I sang "Red Hot" and the people went crazy man. They didn't know I was supposed to be there—he called me out from the wings, and I did "Red Hot" with his band—and them people was climbing up on the chairs. So the song is a heck of a song—it always was and always will be.

Did you ever see a royalty check from Sun?
Never. Never ever got an accounting.

Just about everything you ever did at Sun has been released on Charly, Bear Family, AVI, and Collectables, and I have read that you don't get a dime from any of those companies—is that true?
We hadn't gotten anything. Just recently we started getting something, but there's an awful lot of money owed to me. There's no telling how many hundreds of thousands of dollars are owed to me that I'll never get. But, for some reason, last year they started giving us small royalty checks. But it is nothing at all compared to what they owe. They've sold millions of records on me since they started reissuing—singles, box sets, double-box sets, triple-box sets, LPs. AVI's was a heck of a selling record before somebody else picked it up. Another label here in the States had a record out with just two of my cuts on it, and I made more royalties from those two cuts than I made off any LP—so it sold a lot of records. So if that sold a lot of records, then all of my other stuff must be selling a lot. I think this new reissue of Collectables is going to bring me some royalties too.

I'm glad your stuff is back on an American label. The AVI disc was great, but I think they went out of business.
Well, they sold to MCI or somebody—then they just sat on the masters. Now this Collectables disc is almost the same album; it's got two or three different things on it, but it's basically the same album. AVI's had the best sound and I was happier with that than any reissue they've ever done on me. It was a fantastic record, man.

Do you think Sam Phillips was just spreading himself too thin—or was it just a matter of him not wanting to spend money?
Oh, he *hated* to spend money. He and Jud Phillips fought all the time because he expected Jud to go out there and perform miracles, but he wouldn't supply him with the funds. I've heard fights between the two of them many

times because he was tight on that money. He didn't really spend that much money on anybody—not even Jerry Lee Lewis, and he spent more on Jerry than he did anybody. Jerry Lee is mad at Sam Phillips too.

Jerry Lee recorded more at Sun than anybody, but it's hasn't been until recently that he has sued for back payments.
It takes a lot of money to sue. I had thought about it on a couple of occasions. I had talked to attorneys, and it takes a whole lot of money. There's also a whole lot of time involved. And it's a big deal, it don't happen overnight.

Even though you weren't paid what you were due—do you have anything positive to say about Sam Phillips?
Well, like I said, I don't hold anything against him. I'm still a friend of his. But the truth is truth. I know in his mind he believes what he says is true and that's fine, because I know what I'm saying is true. I think we've always been friends, and I hope he doesn't feel any other way about me. We've always respected each other; he just made some mistakes. I think he knows that, but he probably won't admit it.

And you don't hold anything against Jerry Lee?
No. If I had been in Jerry Lee's place and Sam had picked me to be the one to promote, I'd of been the one. Jerry Lee was in the right place at the right time with the right sound. And Sam thought he had the next Elvis Presley—and he probably would've had if he'd of handled him right, or he could've had it with me.

If he had run things differently, do you think the Sun label would've kept going longer than it did?
He didn't really have the money at the time, but if he had the money and really worked with all of his artists . . . he had the best stable of artists in the business in the '50s; he could've almost had a major label. With just what he had, he could have made that label into one of the biggest rockabilly labels in the world and really put Memphis on the map. Right now, as far as music is concerned, Memphis gets no recognition. It's like all of us, it got lost, because Memphis people don't know how to promote music.

Do they still know how to make it?
Not anymore. When we were there back in the '50s, if Sam Phillips had been as smart as Berry Gordy, he could've been as big as Berry Gordy. He

had artists who were just as good—though they were different. His stable of artists were equally as good as Berry's, and he could've gone just as far if he had acted like Berry and given everybody a fair chance. But he couldn't do it. When Elvis came by, he dropped all his blues singers. He had some of the greatest blues acts there was, and when Elvis came by—he just garbaged all the blues acts. And with Elvis, well, he could only handle one person at once. He just couldn't take on more than one act.

Tell me about the green suits that your band the Little Green Men wore.
(*Laughs*) We just decided that if we were going to be Little Green Men, we oughta wear green suits. We found a tailor down on Main Street in Memphis, picked out the material for them—they looked like they were made out of pool table cloth. After we got 'em made, we found out they weighed about a hundred pounds! They were nice looking, but they were almost like felt, and they were bright Kelly green. They looked good on stage—but the first time we were out, we got mobbed in Mississippi, and got a few buttons tore off. We used to get mobbed a lot.

What other type of promotional stunts did you do at Sun?
Well, we did a 72-hour marathon back in '58 at the Starlite club in Frazier, Tennessee. And we actually stayed on stage for 72 hours, and we had the world's record for a while, until somebody in Canada did 80 hours and knocked us down.

How did you guys manage that?
There was always somebody in the club, so we had to do it. We took our food on the stage; we had people cater food to us, making sure we had plenty of coffee. We got some TV coverage, a lot of good press in the papers. We got some publicity out of it, not as much as I though we'd get. We really didn't get the type of national coverage that I wanted—we got coverage, but not the type that helped us.

Did that bother you at the time?
It didn't mean nothin' to us; we were just crazy kids, and it was good at the time.

How did you stretch out your set?
We didn't have "sets"; we just stayed up there. We played a lot of instrumentals—long ones. (*laughs*) I'd sing until I got tired. Then, we'd just play, get something to eat, sat on the floor and played. I tell ya, when it was over

. . . we were ready to go home. The funny part about it is, when I got home and went to bed, I couldn't go to sleep!

I take it you and the Little Green Men played your fair share of package shows.
Yeah, we played a whole lot of package stuff. We played with the Sun package with all the different Sun artists. Sometime it'd be Johnny Cash and Carl Perkins, Roy Orbison, Warren Smith, Jerry Lee Lewis. We'd usually have a headliner and some of the lesser knowns. Sometimes they'd mix us up with some of the Nashville guys. We'd do shows with guys like Ferlin Husky, Hank Snow, and whoever.

Did the Nashville guys give you a lot of crap about being rock 'n' rollers?
No, they was real nice to us. They enjoyed it, and we backed a lot of them. Any band that wasn't self-contained, we backed 'em. Ferlin Husky, Brenda Lee, a bunch of folks. Ferlin was the only one on that particular show who actually thanked us. All the rest just walked off the stage, except for Ferlin, who complimented us.

I've read stuff that says the Nashville guys hated all you Memphis guys.
I don't think that's true. The fact is, they all tried to imitate us at one time. Marty Robbins did rockabilly; even Ernest Tubb did a little rockabilly. So there wasn't any jealousy; it's just that country really wasn't happening at that time. Country had been around for such a long time, then all of sudden our music started to take over, and for a while there they tried to get in on it. I think they're more jealous nowadays—of each other. They're all a bunch of jealous musicians, afraid the other one is going to make a dollar more, have a bigger stage, and be noticed more. I don't particularly care too much for Nashville people now.

What was your typical set like back then? Did you do just three or four songs?
No we did about 30–35 minutes, about eight to ten songs.

And you did your current singles and what else?
You know it's strange, but we very seldom did my singles. I did mostly other people's songs other than mine. If I thought one of my songs wasn't as strong as some others, I wouldn't do 'em. I'd do Chuck Berry and Little Richard songs, things I could really build a show with. Of course all the rest of 'em did their own stuff, but I did other people's songs—I did a variety show. I gave the fans a whole lot of stuff and we *always* stole the show! No matter who the headliner was, we got the greatest raves.

So you guys were the hot regional act?

We were hot everywhere we'd go. We went places with one thing in mind: To make everyone else look bad! We didn't care who was on stage—we knew we were gong to wipe 'em out! That was our main objective. I don't know of anyplace we ever played where we came in second.

When I spoke with J. M. Van Eaton, I mentioned that the group seemed awfully loyal to you. When you left Sun to go to Philadelphia, they followed right along. I asked if it was just a matter of loyalty and he said, "Yes, and the fact that we thought he was really going to make it. Plus, when we were splitting the money, there was a bigger piece of the pie to be had than if we just were side men." Was that your idea from the beginning, to give everyone a vested interest in your future?

Well, we were a group . . . we weren't just me. Later, when it came down to the fact that I didn't make it and wasn't going to go as far as some of the other people, they started looking for greener fields, and I did too. So we eventually broke up. Roland left before anybody. Roland left as soon as Jerry Lee offered him a job, about 1957. He worked for Jerry more than he worked with me—he just started out with me.

Were you able to replace him as a guitarist?

Yeah, with me! I did my own guitar work. When Roland played with me, I played rhythm, I had a big old Martin. When he quit, I went and bought me a new electric guitar and I've played lead ever since. I don't play much now, even though I endorse for Gibson, and I've got a house full of guitars. Now, I mostly play when I'm doing blues shows. But if I'm doing rockabilly or rock 'n' roll, something I have to bring a lot of showmanship to, a guitar just gets in my way. But I've played lead guitar on a lot of my own records and a lot of Jerry Lee records, even though Roland was there too. When I wasn't playing lead, I was playing second guitar behind Roland. I played bass on a lot of Jerry's stuff too.

Stand-up bass?

No, regular electric. I played bass on some of Charlie Rich's stuff and most of Bill Justis's album, and a lot of recordings where I didn't know who the artist was. Whenever they couldn't find a bass man, they used me. I even played banjo on a record once. Rhythm banjo—I tuned it up like a guitar and began strumming away.

How'd the record turn out?
(*Laughs*) Turned out OK. It was the first and last time I ever played a banjo, though. Just trying to get in on a session and make that ten dollars.

Was that your regular pay?
Sometimes you got two dollars an hour, sometimes ten dollars a session.

Did you get paid right after the session?
On most 'em. Everything except Sun's stuff. And we'd go in after he would release the record, turn the stuff into the union, then we'd go pick up our checks. Then we'd bring 'em back to *(Sam Phillips)* and he'd pay us two dollars an hour. He'd never pay us union scale; we turned the checks back over to him. So he kept the money; we got a little bit, but he wouldn't pay us scale.

This is the very first time I've heard something like this—it doesn't sound right.
Well . . . it happened. We'd endorse the checks back to Sam Phillips and he'd pay us two bucks an hour or ten dollars a session, whatever was going at the time.

How did he get away with this?
Because we let him. The musicians union was more lax than any other union, even though it is affiliated with the AFL-CIO. It wasn't handled like other labor unions, so they got away with murder, man. Also, none of the clubs were union, and we had to work, and the union turned their heads.

I'm going to ask you to speculate a little. If Sam Phillips had spent some time and money on you, and you had the type of success that Jerry Lee Lewis had as far as sales go, do you think you would've been able to handle it?
I think I would've been dead by now. I'm saying that because I really believe that. Y'see, in the '50s, I was young and very gullible and I drank like a fish. I wasn't an alcoholic; I was a sot. I was a drunkard.

What's the difference?
Well, an alcoholic is an alcoholic, and a sot is an idiot. That's what I was; I was just an idiot. Alcohol, I just couldn't hold it, and I got myself into a lot of trouble. But I think if I would've been successful back in the '50s, I was already drinking—maybe I would've gotten into the drug scene. And I might've drugged myself to death.

Would the music have changed any had you been more successful?
I don't think so. If I'd have been *really* successful, I mean really big national name back then—when the music changed, I'd of probably went country.

Why didn't you ever go country like so many other artists from the Sun era?
Well, I didn't want to go country, for one thing. I'm a good country singer, I'll be honest with you. I'm a good country singer and a good country writer. I'm an honest songwriter; I write good stuff that brings tears to your eyes. I'm not bragging, I'm just saying that I can do it. But I can't market it. Right now, what I've got to do in the short time I have left on this earth, is find me a road, get on it, and stay on it. Blues is the best road I can be on right now. I can sell blues. I can be accepted by blues people, because I've been considered half blues all my life. These days, I can't sell country—because country music don't want no sixty-five-year-old singer. So, that's why I didn't do it.

Did you have any trouble getting paid in the clubs?
Sometimes we got paid, and a lot of times we didn't. A lot of times we'd go out on tour and not get paid. When Bob Neal was booking us out of Memphis on the Sun package, sometimes he'd leave and not pay us. I remember going to his house at three o'clock in the morning, getting him out of bed, to make him pay us. Sometimes people would give me hot checks and run off and there was nothin' we could do about that. The union wouldn't do nothin.' That was just a different time—different era.

Does that affect how you deal with promoters and businesspeople now?
It sure does. I do it completely different now: I get paid or I don't work.

Do you get paid before you hit the stage?
In Europe I do. Over here, I don't—but I make sure that I'm going to get my money. I haven't had any problems getting money, this time around, from anybody.

What about the Home of the Blues label? What did you do for them?
That's a label that's been around Memphis for a long time, man. They have a Home of the Blues Record shop and they also cut blues records. It was owned by a Jewish lady, and I went to her and told her I wanted to cut a record—and I cut "Flip, Flop, & Fly" and "Teenage Letter" for her.

When was that?
That was probably about 1959. That was right after Sun.

Then you moved on to run your own label?

Yes, Roland and I started our own label, Rita Records. We put out two or three mediocre things. Then we put out "Mountain of Love" by Harold Dorman, which was a hit.

I actually have a copy of your "Too Much Woman for Me" on Rita, which is a pretty good hook song.

Jack Clement wrote that one. We didn't put a whole lot of time into it. At that time, I was more interested in producing than I was being an artist. But, it wasn't a bad song, it was more R&B.

What was your goal with that label? Were you just looking for the freedom to do what you wanted?

Yeah. We went into the business; we didn't have any money. We raised $5,000 and started that label and then lost it all. See, we had a lot of good chances to go with some other labels, and my job was to sell the records. That's what I wanted to do—I was also out voted on that, because I could've sold *(the label)* to Capitol. Capitol wanted it; Columbia wanted it; there were some big majors who wanted *("Mountain of Love")*. And then, NRC in Atlanta wanted it, and they were friends with Bill Justis and Jud Phillips. So, they talked Roland Janes and the other guy into letting it go there, because they needed a hit so bad. But the one thing *(my partners)* didn't know was that *(NRC)* was in the red. And when we gave 'em that record, and the money started coming in, the stockholders grabbed their money and left. I became friends with one of the stockholders over there later, and he told me the whole story about it. So I went down there to see what was going on between the lines, and I saw that they were going to take our money and declare bankruptcy. So I came back to Memphis and I told Roland and our other partner about it, and they didn't believe me, so I said well, "I'll tell you how sure I am; I sell you my part for a thousand dollars." So I made more than anybody off of *(that label)*. They filed bankruptcy not too long after that and cleaned 'em out. But "Mountain Of Love" was a smash hit— a classic, man. Before Harold Dorman died—the last time I talked to him was about twelve years ago—he said that record had sold over seven million copies.

Why don't sales figures like that get reported?

Because of the reporting people. The RIAA is the one who reports true sales, but there are a whole bunch of people in competition with them who don't tell the truth about that. That's how a lot of that stuff gets up there. They say before his record even comes out, "This guy's record sold a million—gone platinum." If you check into that, you'll find that record hadn't sold 50,000.

Did you have any connection to Rita's sister label, Nita?
I *owned* Nita Records by myself. I also owned Mojo.

Were those around the same era?
Nita was right after Rita, and Mojo came right after Nita.

During what period of time did you record as Lightning Leon?
That was on Rita in like '61.

When you were recording under other names like Skip Wiley, Darren Lee, and Lightning Leon, were you recording in a different persona or were you just being Billy Riley and putting a different name on the label?
What was happening . . . anytime I would do a speculation, I'd put another name on it. I had one name and style established as Billy Riley, and I just didn't want to do some of these off-the-wall things to interfere with what I already had going. And should one of those records had hit—I probably would've changed the label to read Darren Lee a.k.a. Billy Riley. But since that didn't happen, I just left it like it was. Those were spec records.

How well did those records do?
Not very good. *(laughs)*

So where'd you come up with the name "Lightning Leon?"
That's an old friend of mine, who I used to know when I was doing the blues as a kid. He was an old friend who played guitar and harmonica.

At what point in your career did you start including your middle name in your billing?
That was at the Whiskey-a-Go-Go in 1964.

Did you do that because you thought it would look better on the marquee?
I didn't do it. The guy that owned the nightclub, Elmer Valentine—when he found out I had a middle name—he said "I want to use that because I'm trying to get the old Southern sound in here. And a middle name makes you sound more Southern. So I want to use Billy Lee instead of just Billy." I said, "That's fine. Don't make no difference to me."

I read somewhere that you did commercial jingles.

I did that right after I left Sun. Just before I went to California, as a matter of fact, it was the last part of '61 and the first part of '62. I wrote, recorded, produced, and played on jingles at Pepper Sound studios, for three or four months.

Was that a decent living?

Oh, I made good money. If I had stayed there I'd have made real good money, because I was getting paid for everything I wrote, produced, played on. My jingles—I had one in particular that was real good.

What products did you pitch?

Anything they wanted to sell. *(laughs)* The one that did so well was up in North Carolina for some barbecue place, and it was really a *hot* jingle. *(laughs)* They liked it so well, that they hired me on the spot.

Do you ever think about going back and listening to those old jingles?

I wish I could hear 'em. I did a lot of spots for 7–11. See, I had a lot of voices, and so I did a whole segment of 7–11 Slurpee commercials in all different voices: Jerry Lee, Little Richard, Fats Domino, and everybody who had a distinctive voice. They went over so good that I did several segments of them. Later, in '68, when I moved back to Memphis from California, one of the guys who used to work for Pepper was doing commercials in Dallas. And he found out I was in Memphis, and they flew me to Dallas and I did a whole new segment of 7–11 Slurpee ads.

How did you feel about this stuff at the time?

It was fun, man, it was fun! *(laughs)* I got a chance to do everything. I produced, promoted, wrote, arranged—I can't write a note of music, but I'd sit down with a writer and arrange a whole string section, horn sections, and I'd tell the writer exactly what I wanted to do. I've done it all.

When did you decide it was time to leave Memphis?

Well, my father died in '61, and in '62 I just wasn't getting anywhere. The band was broke up and everybody was doing everything else, and I was dating this girl who was a close friend of Stella Stevens. Stella wanted her to come out there, and she kinda talked me into going out *(to Los Angeles)*. She went out ahead of me, and I packed up the car and drove out there in '62. I just went to see what I could do out there.

Was it easy for you to make a living out there?

It was hard at first. The good thing about it, Charlie Underwood *(writer of "Ubangi Stomp")* was already out there. I only had about seven or eight hundred dollars when I got there; that was my last money I picked up at the studio. So I stayed at his house for a while, and he got me in on some ten-dollar sessions and stuff like that to help me along. Then Herb Alpert came along and "Lonely Bull," and I got to play lead guitar on that.

You were the lead guitarist on "Lonely Bull" by Herb Alpert?

Yep—and I only got fifteen dollars. After that, I started doing session work. I did a lot of sessions out there.

What do you remember about working the Sammy Davis Jr. session?

I remember it as one of the greatest thrills of my life! Sammy's producer, Bumps Blackwell, used to use me quite a bit for harmonica and guitar stuff. He kinda liked me. Back in those days, for a single session, you did three songs. You did the A-side, the B-side, and then a song you called the throwaway. Just to get that extra song, and maybe later they'd put it on an album. But it was just a term we used: "throwaway song." So Bumps said, "Sammy's doing three songs, he wants to use a harmonica on the third song." So, I came into the Capitol studios, and he had a full orchestra in there, strings, brass—big band. He was doing his thing, and I was just sitting in the corner real quiet with about ten harmonicas in a little brown bag, just sitting there waiting. So finally, they got ready for me—and nobody even spoke to me except Bumps Blackwell, because they were all busy. So, when Sammy got ready for the third song, he came out and said, "Where's my harmonica man to do the last song?" I said, "Over here." He said, "Well OK, c'mon over here. You can just blow in my mike, we don't even have to set up a new mike for you. We just have a few interludes. I'll just back off and you can blow into my mike." I said, "OK." So, I stood beside him while he was singing "But Not for Me." When it came time for me to do something, I turned loose and played some good ol' funky harmonica. And *(Sammy)* just stepped back and he said, "Hold everything. I want the band to stop; everybody stop right now." He said, "I'm going to change this up! Me and my harmonica man are going to do this song." He was crazy about it, man. So he changed that whole arrangement to where he gave me the lead on harmonica—and it turned out to be the A-side of his record. Then, he got on the phone at about two o'clock in the morning and woke Bobby Darin up—because Bobby Darin had put it out before, and he played it to him over the phone. "See here Bobby, if you'd done this record this way, you'd of had a hit record!" And he did have a big record on it—all because of me. He just treated me so nice—he was the nicest guy I ever met. He was so thrilled to have that harmonica on there.

Was that on Capitol or Reprise?
Reprise. I played for Dean Martin on that label. Most of the time you didn't see the artist; that was rare. Sometimes the artists were there, and sometimes you'd do the tracks and they'd come in later.

What about Dean Martin—did you get to see him?
I didn't see him in the studio. I did his tracks and he came in later. I met him and did a show with him.

On one of your album covers, it says you once opened for Dean.
Yeah, we did a thing at the Moulin Rouge, a big benefit show for Pierre Salinger. He was having a big two or three hundred dollar a plate dinner. And, I was one of the acts on that show with Dean Martin, Janet Leigh, Natalie Wood, Eddie Fisher, and a whole bunch of 'em.

What hit records did you play on by Dean?
"Little Ol' Wine Drinker Me" and "Houston." Both of those. Dean was a nice guy, he was a sot—but a nice guy. I've always liked him, but meeting Sammy Davis Jr. and Audie Murphy was two of the highlights of my life in Hollywood. There was so many phonies out there that I wasn't too impressed with Hollywood.

Tell us about meeting Audie Murphy. (Murphy won the Congressional Medal Of Honor during World War II and went on to be a star in cowboy pictures during the '50s and '60s.)
Well, he was a songwriter, and he came in on a session that we were doing one night. And when I was a kid—he was my hero; I saw his movies all the time. The day he walked into that session, that was the only time that I was completely overwhelmed. I couldn't wait to get over there and shake his hand. I told him, "Man, you've been my hero for YEARS, ever since I can remember." It was a thrill.

What kind of songwriter was he?
He wrote country songs. I can't remember any of the titles, but I'm pretty sure he wrote some hits. He was a good songwriter.

"Help Me Rhonda."

The album version or the single?
The single. You have to listen real close to hear me—they got me pulled down in the mix—but I played on it.

Did you get a chance to meet Brian Wilson or any of the band?
No, because they weren't even there when I did that track. That's just how it was back then.

Who else did you work with?
I worked with the Righteous Brothers on their stuff—I forget what I did exactly, but it was some work for some soundtracks for them.

What about Pearl Bailey?
I did *shows* with Pearl Bailey. I didn't actually record with her. She was one of the greatest people I had ever met. I went out and did my show before her, and she stood there in the wings and listened to my whole show, which she didn't usually do. And when she came out, she hugged me as tight as she could and said, "I want you to know that you have more soul than anybody I ever met!" She said, "You are wonderful!" I thought it was real nice—she paid me a real big compliment. That was around '65.

What did you do on Ricky Nelson's recordings?
I played harmonica—there was so many things I did for him I can't remember. That was around '65.

The story that we've all been told is, once the Beatles and the British Invasion acts came to America, all you guys from Memphis were thrown out of work. Was that true?
Not necessarily. They changed things—made it hard for everybody. It was harder to find a job, but I was playing things they weren't playing—the Whiskey-a-Go-Go type stuff. I was working.

Tell us a little about the Whiskey-a-Go-Go days.
That was a great job. Johnny Rivers started playing there first. The idea was brought over from France; somebody had been over there and had seen it. And it had trios playing and there was a small dance floor. You could get a lot of people in there, but it was kinda tight. Very intimate. Rivers started out playing there and Trini Lopez was playing at PJs—both were doing the

same thing, but the Whiskey was *happening*. So, I knew the bass player in Johnny Rivers's band, and Rivers was fixing to go on the road and open some more clubs. The band didn't want to go with him. Well Joe Osborne went with him, but the drummer wasn't going. So Joe said, "Why don't you go down there and audition for Elmer Valentine. I think you can get that job as soon as Johnny leaves. We'll go down there and audition with you." So I said, "Fine, man." So I auditioned and got the job, and I had to hire a bass man, but the drummer stayed there, and he was pretty much educated on what to do there, so he taught me the ropes. So I started playing there, and heck—the guy really liked me, so I started following Johnny. Johnny would open a club in Atlanta and I'd go in after him, same with New York, San Francisco, New Orleans, everywhere there was a Whiskey-a-Go-Go. He'd open the club, leave, and I'd go in after him. I stayed in that circuit for about a year and a half.

Was that a good money circuit for you?
It was the best money circuit, at the time, that I had ever had.

How much recording did you do under your name at that time? The only thing I've been able to find is a little four-song EP of you live at the Whiskey, and this style just fits you like a glove.
There was a whole album out on GNP called "In Action." That's what Go-Go was, just three-piece stuff, and you could just about sing anything to it. I did a lot of country songs; I did Beatles stuff, Rolling Stones, Chuck Berry. During that time, doing that kind of music, you could do all kinds of stuff—just about anything would fit. I did folk; I did everything, man. And it was an *easy* job. You sat up on a stool and everybody sat up there and played. You were on thirty minutes then you were off thirty minutes.

Did you play much harmonica onstage?
I had my special harmonica rack to fit on the vocal mike, and when I got ready to play a harmonica solo—I'd just blow it. And on that Go-Go stuff, I did lead guitar on everything. All the stuff I did with Mercury and other labels too.

Who came up with the idea for you to do the harmonica LPs, which featured instrumental versions of contemporary hits?
Billy Strange and another guy. Mercury wanted them to do harmonica versions of the Beatles' songs and just a regular album. So, I was the only harmonica player around at the time. That's the reason I got all the work. This

guy called me for a session for two albums—and that's a lot of money. Before we were finished they came up and said, "We haven't got a name to put on this LP. Would you mind if we put your name on it?" I said, "Naw." They said, "Well, we'll put your name on here as the artist and get you a contract with Mercury." I said, "That's good. It'll give me a chance to do something with Mercury." That's how that happened—it was an accident. I went down there to be a session musician, and I came out of there as an artist. After that, Nick Venet recorded a live thing on me at the Whiskey-a-Go-Go.

Didn't you do an earlier harmonica LP for Crown?
Yeah—that was produced by Gary Paxton, the leader of the Argyles, who did "Alley Oop." That was a terrible album. We did things like that just to make a living, man. He needed a harmonica player, and I went down there and didn't even know what they were playing, and the stuff that ended up on the album wasn't even my kind of stuff. I just faked my way through it and they released it. That was another thing they just put my name on because they didn't have a name to go on it.

There was some pretty tricky melodies on these harmonica LPs. Do you read music?
Nope. I'd listen to it right there in the studio and then I'd play it. That was kinda hard to do, because I didn't know that many of the Beatles' songs at the time. I learned my parts in like two or three minutes. Sometimes I'd have to use three or four harmonicas on one song, because I couldn't reach all the notes otherwise. If you'll notice, on the back of one of those album covers, I'm holding three harmonicas—and that's the way I would have to hold those harmonicas when I played on the session. I had to jump from one to another; I'd play a little bit then I'd have to modulate into another key. When they took that picture—that was during a cut. *(laughs)* I had to play a lot of times like that. Their songs were pretty complicated if you're not playing chromatic—and I'm usually not a chromatic player. I played a chromatic harmonica on one of Johnny Rivers's songs.

Which one was that?
I played on "Mountain of Love," which was a big hit for him. I played on a whole album with him, but I don't remember the titles.

What was Johnny Rivers like? Did you guys get along?
We hated each other! He was very jealous of me when I went to the Whiskey-a-Go-Go. Before I went to the Whiskey-a-Go-Go, Joe Osborn in-

vited me down, said, "Why don't you come down some night and play har-monica with us onstage." I said, "Man, Johnny don't want me up there foolin' around." He said, "Aw, don't worry about it. I'll get you up there." So, I took my harmonica down there one night, and he got Johnny to call me up. And I got up there and the crowd just went wild, and that made Johnny mad. Made him jealous. So he wouldn't let me play with him no more. Then when I started playing there, he got real upset. He came down there one time when I was playing—he had closed out of one club and got back early, and came back before I closed out. So, he came out there on a Saturday night, and it was raining real hard. We had the club packed—completely full, and 300 people were standing outside in the rain, waiting to get in. And Johnny had to stand outside for a little while and that made him mad. So he came in and was raising Cain, and Elmer Valentine was saying "Hey man, don't he sound good?" Johnny said, "Well, I could sound good too if you'd give me some good mikes, like you gave him!" Elmer told me, "He was really mad because you had a house full—you had more people than he'd ever had in there." In Atlanta, I still hold the record for attendance at the Whiskey-a-Go-Go; I had more people in there than anybody.

Didn't Rivers get turned down by Sun Records?
Yeah he couldn't make it there. He was just jealous, not just of me; he was just jealous of anybody he thought had a chance to do something.

He had a string of hit records at that time—what did he have to worry about?
Yeah, he had a bunch of hits, but I guess he was afraid that I was going to get some of the gravy. There's a lot of people like that, people who are con-sumed with professional jealousy. That's how it is in Nashville—they're eat up with it.

I'm looking at this photo of you during the '60s, and you were one handsome cat. How come you didn't end up in the movies?
Well, I've had chances. I lost one chance—I could've been in *How the West Was Won*, but I turned it over to somebody else to get it for me and they goofed up. Believe it or not, man—I wasn't real outgoing like I am now. If I'd have been then, like I am now, I would have been in the movies. Tues-day Weld was one of the stars out there that had the hots for me, and she wanted to date me, and I didn't care nothin' about dating her.

Most guys would've jumped at the chance.
I dunno, she was just not my type. She used to come out to the Whiskey.

A lot of the stars used to come there to see me. Steve McQueen was there a lot; he was a part-owner. It was a hangout really, for a lot of actors and actresses. I got to be good friends with George Hamilton, and Clint Eastwood was a good buddy of mine at one time.

What was the most unusual session you played on during that time?
That had to be the one I did with Dick Contino. I played on an album with Dick Contino; he played accordion. He was an Italian dude. I played lead guitar or what they called "first chair." *(laughs)* I played first chair and lead guitar with people like Barney Kessel. I'd play lead and Barney played rhythm.

Was that a jazz session? Pop?
No, they were trying to do a rock 'n' roll thing; that's why they called me in. I also played a lot of sessions with James Burton and Glen Campbell.

What was Glen Campbell like before he made it?
He was a halfway nice guy, but he wanted you to know, in so many ways, that he was completely better than you. I was never a big fan of his, though I worked with him a lot. Leon Russell was a nice guy. He was a piano player in the group when I was doing all that session stuff. I was working most of the time with Glen Campbell, James Burton, Hal Blaine, Leon Russell, and people like that.

Would you take session work like that today?
Absolutely, if they paid me right. I'll work with anybody. I just want to get paid for my work.

How did you come to record for Gene Norman at GNP?
He knew me, he knew about me at Sun, and he knew what was going on over at the Whiskey. And when I came back into town, and the Whiskey had gone longhair and they weren't doing my type of music anymore, I started working other clubs. Well, he came down one night and asked if I was interested in recording. He rented the studio and just set it up like a nightclub, put tables in there. He served drinks to the 25 to 30 people he had in there for an audience, and we sat up there just like we did on stage and like a live album. That was the *In Action* album, and the other one—the harmonica album, we just did that in the studio.

What was Gene Norman like to work with?
Great, man. He was just fantastic. He treated me great—and he wanted

that album to strictly be me. He didn't want nobody shining in here but me. He told me "You just do it your way. I ain't gonna tell you nothin.'"

Did you have any trouble going from an environment at Sun and some of your own labels, where you called all the shots, to a more strictly controlled situation in California?

I had no problem with that whatsoever. You see, I also did some producing out there for Capitol; I produced a "monster" album for them. You know when they had "Monster Mash" out? Well, they had me produce a whole album with a monster theme; it's called *Monsters Holiday* or something like that. I got paid *good* for that.

Who was on that album? Who sang on it?

I hired all the old guys, James Burton and all them guys. It was an instrumental LP. It was filled with all ghoulish songs *(laughs)*—all crazy stuff.

Tell us something about your time in Atlanta. I have an LP that you recorded in 1966 which was basically the Whiskey-a-Go-Go sound.

Yeah, that sound stayed in style for a long time. After I got back to L.A., and the Whiskey-a-Go-Gos had changed, I was called to do a job in Atlanta at a place called the Pussycat Lounge. While I did my stint there, the Brave-Falcon approached me, and they wanted me to come out there and play. So, I agreed to do that, and when the guy at the other club found out I was going to work for the Brave-Falcon, they had my car set on fire! I had a Cadillac and someone came to my door one morning and asked, "Do you own that brown Cadillac? It's on fire." I had to have all of the interior redone and everything. They didn't burn the whole thing up, mostly the seats.

Tell us more about the Atlanta era.

Well, when I wound up in Atlanta, I stayed there for quite a while, and I produced that record you have, and then I produced some more things. There was a movie I sang in, *Speed Lovers*. It was a racing movie with Fred Lorenzen. Ninety percent of it was stock footage. I sung the title song and sang two songs in the movie. So, the guy that backed the movie, I got him to back me and that's when I produced that album at the Brave-Falcon, on Mojo Records.

Did you produce some other things there?

I also produced "Midnight Hour," which was a good seller for me.

Yes. "Midnight Hour" sold a lot of records and I was trying to get a major label on it, and I almost had it—I should've took the first offer I got. Capitol wanted it and I could've got $20,000 up front. Then Atlantic wanted it and I hung on to it and hung on to it, and I hung on to it too long, because there were seven cover versions of it that come out. One of 'em was on Herb Alpert and Jerry Moss's A&M, and it was the only one that was really hurtin' me. The rest of 'em wasn't doing anything. Jerry Moss was putting out so much advertisement that it was hurting me—but they weren't selling any records, and I was. I done sold 150—200,000 records. I looked at the *Billboard* one morning, and *Billboard* had their version at number 58. So I called Jerry Moss and I told him the situation, "You guys got all this money and all this stuff. And we were one-time friends, and I even recorded for you for fifteen bucks," and I reminded him of "Lonely Bull" and all that. Then I said, "I've got this record out, and I don't have all kinds of money, but I've got a hit record going. Why don't y'all just pull yours; yours is the only one that's bothering me. Just pull it and let me have this one— y'all go cut something else on your group." He said, "Naw, we ain't gonna do it, man. We're gonna go on with this." I said, "Well, I'll tell you what— I'll spend every dime I've got, matching you to keep you from selling." So, when I saw that in *Billboard* that morning, first thing I did was call the pressing plant. A guy named Jack and me were good friends, and I asked him, "Are you pressing this thing on Herb Alpert's label?" He said, "Yeah!" I asked, "How many have you pressed? He's number 58 in *Billboard*." He said, "I haven't pressed nothin' but a thousand records. I've only pressed samples." I asked, "Well then, how'd he get in *Billboard*?" He said, "Politics. Bought his way in." So, I got on the phone and called *Billboard*—and here I am, I'd been buying full-page ads in *Billboard* and *Cashbox* every week, $1,200 a smack. *(laughs)* I was running out of money and some of my distributors were paying me, and some of them weren't. Regionally, I was in the Top 5 almost everywhere—number 1 in some cities, and I was ready to hit the national charts and I couldn't get in there because of Herb! So, I called *Billboard* and I talked to the head man and I asked him, "How come Herb's record is number 58 and mine's not even in there? I've talked to the man that's pressing—the same company presses my record. I'm selling records and he's not." He said, "Well, you know how it is." I said, "Yeah, I know how it is. He's *paying* for it! Look, I'm buying ads in your magazine every week—how come you can't put me in there? I can *prove* that I've sold records." And he said, "He's selling records!" I said, "Man—he's not selling records. I'll tell you what I'm going to do. Next week, I'm buying a full page in Cashbox and I'm going to tell 'em exactly what you're doing, because I've already checked and I know that Herb Alpert hasn't pressed but a thousand records." He said, "You can't do that." I said, "I'll show you what I can do. I'll put it in there and I'll expose the fact that somebody's paying you to put that record in there." He said, "Wait a minute! I'll tell you what I'm going to do. I'll put you in here next week at 58 and I'll raise him up." I said, "No, that ain't going to work! If you put me in there, I want to be the only one in there, because I'm the only one actually selling records. You either take them out or you keep everybody out." So, the next week, Herb Alpert's record wasn't in there—but neither was mine. But I did beat him down, I got Herb's record out of there.

What happened to the record after that?
Well, then all the radio stations got so confused by so many covers that they just quit playing them all. So, I lost my record man, because of Herb Alpert.

Tell us a little bit about the Mojo label. I've seen a listing in some jazz catalogues for a Mojo label—do you still own that label?
I still own my Mojo label, but *(the jazz label)* is another Mojo. I never did have the name copyrighted. That other one's probably not copyrighted either. If I wanted to release something on mine, I could.

So that's a dormant label now?
Yeah.

Do you own all the masters?
Nope, I sold all the masters. I sold everything. I was going to get out of this business at one time; that's the reason I sold everything.

Tell me about recordings at some of these other labels. What about Hip?
That's Stax. After I left Atlanta, I came back and leased a record to Atlantic. And I started working for Stax as an artist. The first thing I recorded was "Who's Making Love to Your Old Lady" country style. Of course I had the Stax band plus John Huey on steel. I did that and they didn't know what to do with it. But then, Steve Cropper came up to me and said, "I've got a song I want you to do for Stax." And he produced "Family Portrait." So, I

just started working there, producing, writing, and recorded three or four things over there.

I've got one here on Hip called "Show Me Your Soul."
That was from that *Southern Soul* album. When I played it Stax liked that. The people singing behind that is Isaac Hayes and David Porter. So they pulled that and made a single out of that—they never did put no other side on that. That song was the only side.

Let's talk about those recordings you did during the late '6os in Florida, according to the notes on the Charly LP I have, you played all the instruments on those. Is that true?
When you read that on any of them, don't believe it.

You've never played all the instruments on a record?
I've done one thing where I did all the instruments; it was released but it's very rare, and nobody has one of them. The name I used on it was Sandy & the Sandstormers. It was on ERA Records and was called "Flutterbug and the Sandstorm." I was Sandy & the Sandstormers and the instruments I played on it were bass, guitar, I think harmonica, and a cardboard box! *(laughs)*

How did it sound?
Sounded good—the guy bought it.

What would you have done if you'd had a big hit with that record?
I would've changed my name and cashed them checks! *(laughs)*

For the record, how many instruments do you play and what are they?
I play guitar, harmonica, and bass. I play a little bit of piano, but not enough to claim that I'm actually a piano player.

To me, your Florida recordings are the perfect example of Billy Lee Riley music.
It's a whole lot of different stuff, everything from country to R&B.

Yes. It seemed like your sound grew up so you were able to compete with groups like Creedence Clearwater Revival.
We did a lot of that type stuff, "Working on a River," which I'm thinking about redoing for my new album.

Another one I like from that era is "Pilot Town."
That was written especially for me—God, that was a hard song to sing.

What we were purposely trying to do, and what I told Shelby Singleton I wanted to try, was touch every base on those sessions. I had about four other artists that I recorded and we did Creedence style, R&B, teenybopper bubblegum stuff, and everything else. I did a whole lot of stuff down there. Gosh, I walked into Shelby's office with about fifteen different masters at one time. And he released some of them, but he waited until later to put the rest on some reissues. I don't know what he did with the stuff on the other guys, but I never did see any of it on the market. But I produced all that stuff, I produced for Shelby Singleton for a whole year. And that's when I produced "Tallahassee," "Old Home Place," and I can't remember what else . . .

You did "Kay," which is one of my all-time favorite performances by you, and a funky disc in its own right.
Well "Kay" is what got me in—when I cut "Kay," Sam Phillips told me to take it over to Shelby. That's what I did and Shelby bought "Kay" and then gave me a year's contract to produce for him.

Whenever I hear your version of "Kay," it just sticks in my head for days.
It was a good shot. I did all the arranging and I had part of the Memphis Symphony, the Memphis Horns—I had the cream of the crop on that one. You know that was first a country song.

Was that by John Wesley Ryles?
Yes. He did his with Nashville; I did mine with Memphis. I did it Stax style.

After recording for so many labels and being so successful in clubs, what made you decide to quit?
I got to where I couldn't relate to it. My ex-wife and I divorced and I had two small children, two years old and five years old.

What year did you quit music?
Seventy-three was when I really quit. My last actual record was in '71 on the Entrance label.

"I've Got a Thing about You Baby?"
That's right—it was a Chips Moman record. Entrance was a subsidiary of Columbia, and that record was fixin' to happen big. Then Chips and Columbia had a falling out, so they sabotaged my record. *(Elvis Presley hit the charts with a version of this song which doesn't deviate much from Riley's version.)* That's my luck. Anyway, I had these two children, so I knew I had to

get out of the business and settle down, so I came back to Arkansas and went to work as a house painter. I used to do it with my dad, and it was the easiest thing to get a job at. So, I came back and settled down, went to court and got my children, and raised them. After they got bigger, I got back into the music business part-time. Nineteen ninety-one is when I got back into it full-time.

While you were still working part-time as a musician, you did a recording on the Southern Rooster label, which got a good write-up in Rolling Stone. Whose label was that?
That belongs to Sam Phillips. We did "Blue Monday" and "Good Ol' Rock 'n' Roll."

There's some real nice funky guitar work on that — whose playing that?
Me — I'm playing guitar on that.

That record got national attention; how well did it do?
I don't know; I never did get paid for it.

Did you record other stuff at that session?
We put some other things down, but they didn't get released.

Here's a story I'd like you clear up for me. In Nick Tosches's book Country: The Biggest Music in America, *the author covers Jerry Lee Lewis's "Southern Roots" session and mentions you. It says "Billy Lee Riley, the man who cut 'Flying Saucers*

Photo courtesy Ken Burke.

Rock 'n' Roll' for Sun in 1957, materialized, looking like 5,000 concentrated volts. He spread his hands before him as if holding a birthday cake. 'Man, I got me a pill this big, and when I take a bite the damn thing grows right back.'" Did that happen?
(Laughing heartily) No! That's the first time I heard that. (laughing) I didn't even know what pills were back in those days.

Were you oblivious to all the things that artists like Johnny Cash and Jerry Lee Lewis were into with the amphetamines?
I knew that Johnny Cash was doing something — I didn't know *what* he was doing. I knew that Charlie Rich and Bill Justis was popping pills. But I

didn't know about anything but drinking—I just drank a lot and I didn't know anything about pills. I was scared of 'em—I've always been scared of 'em. I'm scared to take pills from doctors when I have to. I never have been a pill man.

I can't tell you how comforted I am to hear that. Y'know, Billy, when you read all these stories, it hurts sometimes to learn one's heroes have these problems.

Well, it hurts me to know that people get all these chances to do things. They go out and become famous and make all this money, and then they blow it on stuff that goes up their nose. And I wouldn't have snorted cocaine if you had paid me a million dollars. Or take a pill off the street— no way. I did try marijuana and it made me so sick I couldn't stand it. A guy gave me some, and I tried it—had some in a little jar that he had given me. And I flushed that stuff down and when I told him about that he almost cried. I said, "Man—I don't want that crap! That'll just make you sick."

The first time I ever saw you in person was in 1979, at a benefit for Don Ezell at the Western Steakhouse in Memphis. You weren't even scheduled to perform, but you got up and set that joint on its ear.

I didn't know I was going to do anything; I wasn't even in the business then.

I remember you being so friendly. You were sitting there next to Tommie and Howard Wix talking to everybody, and I noticed that Charlie Feathers was off by himself.

Yeah, off in a booth alone. Y'see, Charlie was going to sing, but after I got up there Charlie wouldn't do it. He left after that. Charlie was that kinda guy. I've known Charlie since the '50s. I never did a show with him, but the only thing that Charlie ever did for me—or anybody else, was downsize us. *(laughs)* He was good at that—always putting everybody down. But nobody paid any attention to him; we understood him. He seemed to have an inferiority complex. He had to tear other people down to make himself look bigger—which he didn't need to do, because we all liked his stuff. He was good, he had some great stuff out there. We did the Memphis in May *(festival)*; he went on before I did. When I went on, we just tore the place up. I'll just be honest with you. It was outside; there were thousands of people there. I had three encores and they were screaming for another one when I left. And Charlie Feathers was sitting down there beside a friend of mine who heard him talking to somebody else. So here I was singing, everybody's going out of their minds, and Ol' Charlie's sittin' there saying "Riley just ain't got it no more." *(big laugh)* So what Charlie said never really did bother me. I liked Charlie; I understood him. A lot of people didn't.

When you were recording for Southern Rooster and came out with a new album on Mojo in 1979, did you find that people were more interested in you since the death of Elvis Presley?
No, the reason I even did that *(the Mojo LP* Vintage*)*—they asked me to do Memphis In May in 1979. And I didn't really want to do it; I'd been off the stage for so long, and I didn't know if I really wanted to get back into it. Jerry and Knox Phillips talked me into doing that, and we got a band, and I went up there and did it, and was very successful. And, just before that happened, I had an offer to go overseas, and I turned 'em down. I was really scared to go to Europe. But then, when I did Memphis In May, and everybody liked it so well, I turned my head toward Europe, and I told 'em I was ready to come over. I went over there for the first time on a monthlong tour; that was in the spring. Then in the fall I went

Riley, 1979. Photo courtesy Ken Burke.

back over for another month. *(Performing)* sort've got back in my blood and I started doing quite a bit of it. I was still working a job, but I was also playing every chance I got.

Were you surprised at the interest in your old material? Had you forgotten about your Sun sides by that time?
Yeah, I had forgotten all about it. What surprised me mostly was the interest in Europe. Man, them people over there—even today, they just love it! Ever since twenty years ago, since I first started going over there, they treated me like royalty! Like I was Elvis Presley. They made you feel like you was somebody—so it was great over there.

A long, long time ago, Tommie told me that you got stiffed by some European promoter.
Yeah—the guy still owes me about $7,500. And I never saw him again. *(laughs)* He gave me half my money and told me I'd get the half later. That's what caused me to change my rules. I get paid before I ever go on stage. Most of the time, I get my money as soon as I get there and see the pro-

moter. So, I haven't been and I'm not gonna be cheated out of anything else over there.

Tell us about the 706 Reunion album you recorded with J. M. Van Eaton.

That was in '91. After I moved back to Arkansas in '90. So one day J. M. called me and we got to talking and said, "Man, why don't we go in the studio and cut something just for our own pleasure? Just because we hadn't worked together in thirty years? Just some of the stuff we used to do in the '50s, and if we get a chance to sell it we will, if we don't, we won't." So we did. We split the money and went in and recorded 706 *Reunion*. We got some good response to that—but the one thing that's holding it back from actually selling, is there's no original material on there.

That's on the Sun-Up label. Who owns that?

That's mine. There is a guy interested in *(the* 706 Reunion LP*)*—we'll never get what we need for it, but eventually when somebody gives us the right price for it, we'll rerelease it.

For someone who wasn't that interested in the music business at the time, you were in pretty good voice.

Well, once I get to playing I always change. My whole attitude changes. Once I got into the studio, it felt so good that I just really got into it.

Tell us about your album on HighTone, Blue Collar Blues. *How did this come about, and was your deal with HighTone just a one-shot deal?*

Yeah, it was a one-record deal, with an option. It wasn't an intentional deal. This is how I figured it out, and I think this is the way it really happened. I couldn't swear to this, but everything points this way. The guy who produced that, I met him when I was doing the session with Sammy Davis Jr. in '64. And he's been a big fan of mine ever since. One of the owners, Bruce Bromberg. What happened—when J. M. and I cut 706 *Reunion* back in '91, I sent HighTone a copy of it, and he loved it. He said, "Man, you guys have still got it." So I said, "We ought to get together and maybe cut an album." He said, "Maybe we will." I must of dealt with him, down almost begging him, "Let's get together and cut an album. I want to cut a blues album." So, he kept putting me off. He had 900 reasons why he couldn't do it. But in the meantime, somebody had produced an album on Sonny Burgess, and High-Tone had bought it. Well, *(Bromberg)* kindly felt bad about that. So, this is my theory: when I called him and said, "I was talking to Sonny Burgess and he's got an album out with you. What happened man; I thought we were going to cut one?" Well, he gave me all kinds of reasons, then he called me a few days later and said, "Well, we've decided we're going to cut an album." So, I think he just kinda felt bad. Had Sonny not cut his album, they probably wouldn't have cut one on me. It was a situation like, here he is, one of my biggest fans, so how am I going to feel that he released a record on Sonny Burgess and not one on me. So, he decided to do it, and he spent a lot of money on it, and it's not a bad album, it's just not me.

I'm surprised to hear that because I think it's one of your best.
I didn't have anything to do with it—that was his idea—it's not really my true voice on a lot of that stuff, because he wouldn't let me sing the way I wanted to sing. So, it came out, they didn't promote it, and it didn't happen. There were two or three songs on there that did well, but it just wasn't happening. *(HighTone)* is mainly a compilation/catalogue company, anyway. They cut these things, put you an album out, then they put it on the shelf. Then every so often, they'll take a couple songs out of it, and put it with a bunch of other things and they'll sell five, ten thousand. It's not enough to pay fifteen guys royalties off of, so they keep it all, and they'll say, "Well, we don't pay any royalties under X amount of money." See, if you put all those together, they've made a bunch of money, because they don't pay none of the artists. I mean, that's the way all of 'em are; it's not just them. That's the way all compilation companies are; it's all in marketing. That's the way it works.

Tell us about the album on Icehouse Rockin' Fifties. *J. M. Van Eaton thinks it's one of your best* LPs *ever. Certainly it's one of your rockingest.*
Well, that could've been better. That was made up of stuff I had in the can. Some of it we did at Sun studios. Some were other things we had in the can, and others were only demos I had done in Atlanta. I just put all that stuff together, made me an album, and I took it over and let Johnny Phillips listen to it. I said, "Do you like it?" He said, "Yeah." "You want to buy it?" He said, "Yeah." I said, "OK, give me some money." He wrote me a check, released the album, and that's all there was to it.

I notice that you remade T. Graham Brown's "Rock It Billy, Rock It," which you first did on the Blue Collar Blues *album.*
Yeah, that's a bad version, though, because I did that in Little Rock with a band that really wasn't up to par. A guy had a studio in his house and I was way in the back bedroom singing, and he was back in another room with

his equipment. It's just stuff I had, and I didn't know if I could sell it or not. There's things on there that normally I wouldn't release. Like "Born to Be a Rockin' Man"; that's terrible. *(laughs)* I was kinda hoping that before someone got to that song, they'd be tired of listening and shut it off. I'm not happy with a lot of things on that, but I knew the record wasn't going to do anything. I knew that Phillips wasn't going to push it.

I've heard you say that you can't sell a rockabilly album. What did you mean by that?

Oh, I can sell a rockabilly album to fans on the Internet and at shows, but I can't sell one to a label. They won't give me anything for it. They'll take it, but they won't give me anything. They'll say, "Yeah, we'll give you a thousand bucks front money." I'm not giving anything up for a thousand dollars front money. I'd rather take it out and burn it. Because I get paid pretty good for stuff I sell. I've already *paid* all my dues. Right now, I'm not bitter or nothing, I just feel like—those guys have got a lot of money, and they're going to *make* a lot of money off that record. If they don't sell but 5,000 of 'em, they're going to make some money. So, I want some of it or I don't want them to have my record. I wish I were in a financial position where I could say, "Man, I'd love to just record albums and not worry about making money, just so the *fans* could have albums!" If I had the money, I'd just cut 'em and give all my fans a new record every six months. But I don't have that money. So when these people want to put out something to make money off of, I want my part of it first. Because I'm the one that went in the studio and paid the money to do it.

You've often mentioned that Hot Damn *is your favorite album. Tell us how that came about.*

Well, I'd been wanting to cut a blues album for many years. A real, honest blues album—something that didn't have to be perfect, but was just honest. Nobody would do it. In '94, I started thinking about that record. So, I started cuttin' that record in the middle of '94. I went to a lot of studios. At first I was going to do a pure acoustic thing—just me and my guitar. I went up into a Missouri studio and I worked all night—and I'm not happy with it. So, I went to another studio in Memphis. Beale Street studios. Big, big hi-tech studio. Well, that didn't work. Then I thought, "Maybe I'll just do it with me and the drummer. Maybe that'll work." This is over a period of time. The drummer didn't understand what I was doing. Now, J. M. *(Van Eaton)* and I could have done it, but I just didn't think about it. I went to two or three other studios; I even went to Sun. Still determined to do an acoustic session. But it still didn't work—I just couldn't get into it. I told James Lott, "It's not working, let's forget about it." He said, "Look, let's just book some time, and I'll get a band together that can play what you want. We'll have a session and if you don't like it; don't worry about it." So he got these guys together and it *worked*! And I was thrilled to death, man. But then we couldn't get studio time. We'd get a night here and a night there, and it took me forever to cut that album. *(laughs)* It took me forever, it seemed like. When this was finished I said, "This is the best thing I've ever done." So, I was going to release that record on my own label. That was my whole intention. (Hot Damn) was strictly a project for my own enjoyment. But when I got down with it I said, "Man! This is good enough to *sell*!" So I sent copies to four or five companies. The first one to call me was *(Capricorn)* and he said, "Man, I want to talk to you about this album. I want it." A year later, it came out. By the time it came out, they had some other stuff going that was really hot and they about forgot about me. But they never really put a real promotion budget on it—they probably spent $5,000 on the record total, which is not anything near what you have to spend to promote a record.

So were you able to promote it effectively?
Everywhere I promoted, it was effective. That's why if they'd have put some money into it, it would've sold. We'd have won the Grammy on it. It was up for a Grammy, but I couldn't get them to help me promote it to the people who vote. I needed a whole lot of ads. You need to run ads for about two months before voting time. I needed to make sure that every blues magazine and every blues person in the world knew about that record. Well, I got a lot of votes, but I didn't get enough. If I'd of had the money to promote it, I'd be staring at a little Grammy here. There's a man in New York at the Grammy association, the big man, I talked to him. He's the one that nominated me. So, (Hot Damn) had something. That just thrilled me to death and I thought, "Well, I know I'm going to win." But everybody else was buying ads and buying ads, man. And I didn't have any competition. The same bunch wins every year, it's either John Lee Hooker or Buddy Guy. It's the same three people that win, and the only reason they win is because there's no competition. Then I came out and I had something completely different from all of 'em, and it started a new blues revolution in a lot of areas. That's why I could've *(won the Grammy)*, but I didn't get no help. And they

could've got me a hit record, but they had two more new wave albums that was happening—rockin' stuff, and they were selling thousands and thousands of records. But *they* didn't even get nominated. So, Capricorn was selling so many records and making so many dollars on these other albums that, man, I just got lost. To tell you how lost I got, they had people working in promotion who didn't even know who I was! I called promotion one time to talk to my people and I said, "My name is Billy Lee Riley." and they asked, "Who are you with?" I said, "Well, I *thought* I was with Capricorn." And a lot more people have told me that they have called Capricorn about me, and they didn't even know who I was. How are you supposed to feel about people like that? But I worked hard on that record, and it was just all in vain. They never followed up nothin.' I was on the cover of this one blues magazine and they wrote a great story on me. They sent a copy to Capricorn and they never even responded.

Usually when that happens, the record company coughs up a little ad dough.
They wanted an ad, but they wouldn't give him one after they got in touch with *(the label)*. They gave me a cover story and Capricorn wouldn't even buy an ad. Then I got into a state of mind where I was going to quit. I got this close to a *record* and I couldn't get it to happen. I thought, "Apparently, it's not supposed to happen, so maybe I should just give it up."

I don't think you should quit.
Well, apparently I didn't, because I'm back in the studio. *(laughs)* One of these days, though, I'm going to have to stop. I tell you another thing that I would like to have more of—I would like for my fans to actually buy my records more. When I advertise in magazines, I don't get much response from fans that I know get these magazines, and I don't understand that. I do sell quite a few records through those, but not what I would expect to. I'd like to have more fans who are really fans—because I treat my fans right. I treat 'em like they want to be treated.

Tell us about your latest recording project. Where are you recording it?
At Sun, with the same guys we used on *Hot Damn*.

What kind of music are you doing and how much have you gotten done?
Blues, it's an all-blues album, but I'm recutting some of my stuff from the '50s too. I've about eighteen or twenty songs to choose from for the album. We've got seven or eight of 'em all finished except for mixing. We're going back in next week to try and get all the overdubbing done. I'm hoping

to have this thing finished before I leave for overseas. I'm gonna make me another blues album, and I'm also gonna cut me a couple of rockabilly albums. I'm going to rerecord my '50s stuff, and put about sixteen or seventeen songs on a disc, and do a new rockabilly album.

Do you think you'll have copies ready to sell by the time you go on tour?
I'm not going to start anything on it until I come back from Europe.

Any nibbles from other labels?
I haven't talked to anybody yet. I might keep it for myself, maybe put it on my own label, and sell it mail order or maybe even on the Internet. High-Tone had shown interest. I tried to make a deal with them before I cut the session, and they wouldn't do it. So I'm going to count them out—just because I want to. Because they showed interest then they backed down on me. So I'll go some other way.

Do you understand the industry as it is today? If you had the funds could you compete in today's industry?
I don't like *nothin'* about the way the mainstream record business is run today. Because it's not a record business; it's just a marketing thing. Half of the artists don't have the talent, and music people don't run the industry anymore.

When did you first notice that happening?
I guess it got really strong in the '70s. It's all like Wall Street. And the artists—they're not having fun; they're not doing music; they're making business deals. It takes all the joy out of it. They're too worried about the dollar. Of course you got to make the money, but first you have to create an enjoyable environment. There's none of that in the new music. There is in *my* type of music. That's still there. But in pop music and all this big stuff, everybody's fighting, trying to get them awards, and there's so much professional jealousy that it's nothin' but a big race to see who can do better and get more than the other one. They hate each other. The greatest evidence of that was the trouble and strife between Billy Ray Cyrus and Travis Tritt. That's just a small example, but they're all that way. They're all just fightin' each other tooth and nail.

I, for one, liked "Achey Breaky Heart," despite what Travis Tritt said about it.
I did too, and I was for Cyrus because he was the underdog. Everybody *in* the business thought he was a phony, but he was the only one in the busi-

ness that wasn't a phony. He was a doing a legitimate thing, man—and everybody else was sitting up there putting him down.

So there's no place for individuals in country music?
No, man.

Are you allowed to be your own man on the blues circuit?
You can do anything you want to do. You're free to do what you want to and nobody bothers you. And that's the good thing about it—that's the way music used to be. That's the way it should be. But that's why a lot of people aren't getting any breaks, because music's not that way anymore. You've got to conform to the way they're doing it or else you're not going to get anything done. I don't see it that way. I don't care about selling no ten million records anyhow. I'm not trying to make a hundred million dollars a year—don't want it. I really mean it, man. Nobody in the world needs a hundred million dollars. I don't care who you are. Because the government is going to get most of it, your payroll's going to get bigger, and you'll wind up with not much more than when you were making less. That money just causes problems. All I want is enough money to do what I want to do, and be comfortable. And, it don't take much for me to be comfortable.

You run your own publishing for your own labels, right?
I've got two publishing companies. I've got my stuff and I publish other people's material. I've got Lightning Leon publishing with BMI, and the one for my ASCAP writers—Daddy Keys. But I don't use that one as much because I don't like ASCAP.

What's the difference?
Well, you can join BMI and you don't have to pay nothin' and they treat you a lot better. ASCAP, you got to pay to be a member, and they're just not as nice people. I don't like 'em. I'm going to get rid of my ASCAP stuff.

Billy, do you have a booking agent?
No.

Do you have a manager?
No.

So you manage and book yourself?
I do it all. I use a lot of different booking agencies—I go through a bunch of people when I'm working. I mean, I've got a lot of people that I work

with—but I wouldn't sign with any booking agency that was a major booking agency.

You mean you wouldn't sign with someone like William Morris?
Well, I would, but they wouldn't sign me.

Because you're a blues artist?
No, it's because I don't have anything that they care about. They're not interested in somebody like me; they want these younger people.

Does having all this experience in the business help you?
It helps me as far as I'm concerned, but a lot of people in that end of the business don't like me, because I know the business too well. They like to deal with people who are green, so they can rook you into a lot of things. They can't do that with me; therefore they only deal with me when they have to. *(laughs)* They don't deal with me if they don't have to. It's just like in Europe, man. I'm the only person that's working in my circuit that demands to be treated like a human being. When I go over there, when they book me as a rockabilly star, then they got to *treat* me like a rockabilly star. I'm not a star and don't claim to be, but that's what they're booking me as, so I'm not going to go over there and stay in some dirty hotel and be treated like a piece of crap. When I go over there, I stay in the finer hotels, and I'm driven around in finer transportation. And I won't be treated like a flunky—and they don't like that, because that costs money and they'd rather keep the money than give it to the artist. I've got a certain price I charge for shows in Europe and I don't come down. When they call me and I give 'em my price, and they try to get me cheaper, I say, "I'm not interested. Call me back when you get some money." I'm not flexible on my price with anybody. What I charge is what I charge. Everybody knows that. So, if somebody calls me about a job, they know what they're going to have to pay. And that's just because I have my own ideas about things, and I'm not going to keep paying the dues that I've paid for the last thirty, forty years.

Are there any current acts that you like?
No.

When you're not writing, where do you get your songs? Do you have an extensive record collection?
No, I have a real good memory. I can remember back to when I was almost three or four years old. I remember old songs and I have some blues things,

not a real big collection, but people send me things. I've got old records and some of these reissue things. A lot of these record companies, when they reissue these things, I'll call 'em and they'll send me samples. AVI, when they came out with that new record on me a few years ago, I called 'em and told 'em send me something. They did and they also brought up that they had the old Excello catalogue. I said, "Man, I love the Excello artists. Send me a box full of 'em." They sent me a bunch of everything they had, which includes Slim Harpo, Lightning Slim, a whole bunch of people. All I got was songs I already knew, songs I've been hearing since the early '50s.

So, that type of blues is what you listen to for pleasure?
If I listen to anything for my own pleasure, it's either got to be blues or original southern rockabilly. I don't like no Chicago, New York, Philadelphia, whatever rockabilly. I don't listen to a lot of music, but I will listen to blues. There's a radio station in Memphis that has a couple of blues shows, and I try to catch those. At home, I may get into a mood where I just want to sit back and put my Excello stuff on, and I really get engrossed in it. Or, if I'm trying to get ready for a session, I'll take all that stuff out. And no matter what session I do, I'm going to do some blues. I may put four or five of my own things on there, but basically, I'm going to build my album out of old blues—because that's the *good* blues. That's better than anything that could be written today. I write a lot of stuff in that frame, but believe me man, you don't have writers today like Slim Harpo, Muddy Waters, Little Walter, and all that.

How do you write? Do you work off of a title, walk around with a guitar in your hand, and jam until something comes?
It just comes to me. An idea, something just comes to me. They just come out of nowhere. I may be driving down the road and something will come to me and I'll just start jotting it down—just enough to remember when I get home and put it all together. To write a song, I'll usually put it together the first time, and then I'll just lay it out. Then I'll wait a day or two, then I'll pull it out and start again.

Do you have a home recording system so you can lay down demos?
No. I just write it down on paper, and I sing it through and put a tune to it, and it goes in my brain and stays there.

Do you use the Nashville numbers system on the lyric sheets?
No, I write the lyric sheet and that's it. I don't do any number systems until

I get ready to go into the studio. Then, I'll take my songs, go into my office, and I'll take my guitar and sing it while I make a chart. The way I do it, I don't put just the numbers down; I put the bars and the beats, four beats to a measure. That way, when the guys are playing they won't have to ask how many bars, it's all right there. It's real simple. This is the way we did it out in California; that's where I learned to do it and I stuck with it.

So, when you're in a session, are you what is known as the session leader?
No, nobody's the leader. We just go in there and say, "Look, this is the song we're going to do, and here's everybody's sheet." Then I'll sing it through one time, and then everybody will start fallin' in and I'll say, "OK— let's go do it one time." Then I'll sing it again and we'll go through that whole thing where we work up the intro part we want on it, which is usually very simple, then we just put the track down. For this latest project, we put down twenty tracks in two nights.

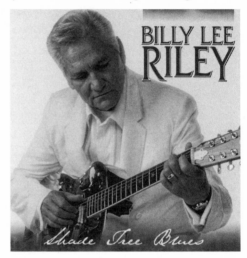

Man, that's a lot of work.
It's not a lot of work when you know what you're doing. Second thing is— the total hours was about eight. In eight hours we put down twenty basic tracks. So, the next night we'll start doing some instrumental overdubbing. The third night, I'll go in and sing all the songs and put some harmonica on it. Usually, I'll sing one and then put the harmonica on it, but this time, while we had the song pulled up and we were overdubbing, all we had to do is change channels. Usually, I'll sing all the way through four times and play all the way through four times. I'm also playing some lead guitar on a few tracks, though mostly I like James Lott's playing so much that he's doing most of it. But last night I told him, "Just for the heck of it, I want to play lead guitar on a few tracks because I want to play my new guitars."

What kind of guitar are you picking these days?
Well, I endorse for Gibson. I've got three. I've got an all steel, solid steel Dobro, and man it's got such a beautiful sound. It's got sandblast designs

all over it, Hawaiian scenes. Gibson gave that to me, and they gave me a Gibson 335, and an Epiphone 335, so I want all of those guitars on this session. So, I'm going to play at least one solo with each guitar. I've played all three guitars on the rhythm tracks, but I want to play lead on at least three songs. Y'know, Gibson wants me playing these guitars, not just holding them. *(laughs)*

How are you on the Dobro—any good?

Well, I just play it like any other guitar. Fingerpicking style, not slide. I can't play slide, but my guitar player is a real good slide man. But this Dobro has such a fantastic raw blues sound and it's got the old *gut* sound, man. James Lott liked it so well he said, "I gotta have me one of these." *(laughs)* We cut a couple of acoustic things last night, with just me and the Dobro, that I might put on the album.

Do you endorse any harmonicas?

No, Hohner wanted me to endorse, but they didn't want to give me nothin'. They didn't want to give me no free harmonicas or anything and they wanted me sign a release to use my likeness, pictures, and everything for T-shirts for them to sell, but they wouldn't give me any money for it. They wouldn't even give me free harmonicas—I had to pay almost full price for harmonicas. So I told 'em to forget it.

What brand of harmonica do you like to play?

Right now, I'm mostly playing Hohner Special 20. That's a good harp—it don't last long, but it's a good harp. I also got one, and it's been a real good harp and I might start playing it, Lee Oskar—it's the first one I ever bought because they're so expensive.

How many harps do you have?

Oh, of the ones I play, about fifteen. They're all in different keys. I sell the wore-out ones to collectors and museum people. I just save all that stuff; eventually somebody'll buy it. See, I've got a bunch of stuff that I've been selling to Hard Rock Cafe. I've sold two sets—I've got an exhibit at the Memphis Hard Rock Cafe and another at the New Orleans cafe—and they're supposed to buy something to put in the new one in Orlando. But I've still got the old clothes and the white-and-black shoes. Old guitars, I've got one guitar that was made in 1929 by the Slingerland Drum Company, and it's old and very rare. It's a small guitar. I sold a big bunch of stuff not too long ago to the Smithsonian Institute, which is going to have a big exhibit. They already got one in a traveling show right now, but they're enlarging it—they bought a jacket and trousers, shoes, a whole harmonica case—the one that I made back in '59—and an old Harmony guitar that I had. They paid a bunch of money for that stuff. That stuff's worth a bunch of money.

That surprises me because I was under the impression that museums never paid for anything.
They paid for my stuff, because I won't give it to 'em. I sold a bunch of stuff to a museum in Memphis. They were the first ones I sold things too. I could've gotten more, but I wasn't really familiar with how much they'd pay for this stuff. I found that, if they want it, money's no object.

On stuff like the acetates, have you made safety copies so you can still have the music?
Well, the one that went to the Smithsonian, they're going to do that for me. They want something they can play and also have something they can display, and when they make a copy for themselves, they'll make me one. They always make me copies of everything that they buy, pictures and films. I sold 'em an 8 mm film, the only one in existence, of me in the '50s. There's no sound, but it's me and the band in clubs around '58. Well, they wanted a twenty-second piece of it to put in a promo, and they paid me $2,500 for that. And, I still have the film and it's for sale, but it'll cost a bunch of money to get that. Somebody'll buy it one of these days and I'll make about ten grand out of it.

It's sort of like cashing in on your investments, isn't it?
I didn't know this before, but this stuff is worth a lot of money to people. Collectors are like very special people and they love this stuff, and I'm glad that I found out about this, because I probably would've thrown it all away, and nobody would've had it to enjoy. This way, a lot of people are going to enjoy it, and I'll get paid for it.

Do you merchandise yourself much?
You have to have some merchandise when you travel on the road. I make more money selling records on the road, when I've got 'em, than I do from the shows. For this festival I played up in Philadelphia, I only had about sixty CDs, and I sold them faster than I could get 'em out of the box. Now, if

I'd have had this new album that just came out on Collectables—it's brand new, but it's the old Sun stuff reissued. As a matter of fact, I just ordered a hundred of them to take with me overseas—I could've sold maybe two or three hundred of them things at twenty dollars a shot. But I didn't have 'em, people would ask me "Hey, you got any of the old records?" But I didn't have enough. I also sell a lot of pictures, overseas especially. Old pictures from the '50s.

So you're very much a do-it-yourself type guy no matter what?
If you don't do it yourself, it don't get done. I'm the one that was on the phone all the time promoting that record, and staying in touch with every-body. And that thrilled all them DJs, because the DJs that work them sta-tions never get no calls. Nobody calls 'em, because they're not Top 40.

These are the Americana stations?
Yes. So when you call that DJ, they love it. Then, when you call 'em back a second time, they feel *good*, and they'll play your record.

Tell us something about your book. I've seen chapters of it on the Delta Blues website.
That's on, I don't know how many places on the Internet, right now. Tidbits from the book. What I'm doing now is, I'm sort of restructuring and con-densing it a bit, and I'm putting it on software.

Are you working with anybody on your book?
Not yet, but I've got a bunch of people who want to work this up when I get to that point. There's one movie company that's shown interest already.

Your life would make a helluva movie.
Well, no one's ever heard my life yet. What I'm doing really, on this first book, is I'm actually going to end it just when I'm leaving Memphis for California with my car loaded down so you can't even see out of it. Cali-fornia will be the start of the next book. It's good because my book is not just starting with music. My book's going to have a bunch of other stuff in it. It's going to have *me*. Where I lived, how I lived, how I got into it, why I love the blues, where I was first introduced to blues, how I heard it the first time, and I'm going to put it all in there. I think it's more interesting if you know how the person was raised. Then, as I get on into the music part of it, then it will just all fit together well. I'm not just going to start out with *(mocking voice)*: "Well, I started recording in 1957 in Sun and I cut this

record . . ." That ain't my idea of a story. I haven't seen a book that's been written on any of those artists yet that I'd give three cents for, because they're just not complete. They're all just alike: "I bought my first guitar when I was ten, sold a bunch of eggs, and got it . . ." *(laughs)* Everybody's got the same old lines. And it's all a line—a big lie—everybody didn't get a guitar the same way. So, I'm trying to write it like it is, all the good times, my bad times. I don't want to look like an angel, because I wasn't. When I was a kid growing up, I was a good kid, and I had a hard time growing up. I think people need to know that. I think they need to know that a man can come out of one situation into another.

Recording-wise, do you have a lot of unreleased stuff in the can?
I have a whole box full of tapes in the closet and I have no idea what's on them. The reason I don't know is that I can't find a tape player to play 'em. They're either two-track, four-track, eight-track, or mono and it's hard to find anything to play those things on.

But one of these days, do you think you might lease some of these tapes out?
Possibly, I might release 'em myself. I've got enough stuff that I could put several things together. I might do it one of these days. Who knows?

Is it better to tour today than when you first started?
Oh yeah. You get more money today and you get treated better. Most of the time back in those days, we were doing schoolhouse things, drive-in the-aters with the music going out through the car speakers, and a lot of places that weren't exactly set up for music. We'd play big auditoriums with one twelve-inch speaker in a little bitty amp with a little ol' crystal mike, and maybe a setup of small speakers—but that's all we had. Everybody heard us. Everybody was happy. You didn't have to be as loud as you do today. Loud as people play music today it don't even sound like music. It's more like noise, and I can't stand that. You can't play my kind of blues loud, if you do you've lost it. You've got to settle back and play it real low.

How do you play the festivals if you don't play loud?
I have to play loud and it don't always sound good. Number 1: They don't always have good soundmen. If you have good soundmen, you could play low. You could turn your instruments down to where you can get a good sound. The mike and all that can go out to the audience loud and still sound good—but it's so loud on the stage, because everyone's turned it

wide open, every guitar is as loud as it'll go, and it just blows your head off. That's the reason I like to play smaller places, clubs that hold three or four hundred people.

As a fan, I've always preferred clubs to arenas.

You get good sound equipment and you can set back and you can play real low and everybody hears it, and they can talk. See, I like to play music where people can talk over my music and hear each other. If it's an eating place you can enjoy eating without the music knocking your plate off onto the floor. You can play up-tempo stuff, and you still don't have to get too loud.

We never did in the '50s; we never did get that loud. We didn't have to, man. Back in them days if you started playing loud, they'd tell you in a minute to turn it down. "You're too loud!" That's the way it should be today.

I'll give you the last word. What would you like to say to your fans?

Well, the first thing I'd like to say is thanks! Without them—and this is coming from me. If it wasn't for them, there wouldn't be no me. I definitely am one person who honestly appreciates my fans. Because anywhere I play, if I have an autograph session, I'm the last one to leave. But I want to thank the fans and I want to tell 'em:

Riley, 2000. Photo courtesy Ken Burke.

Watch out for anything that might be coming out on me and BUY it and HELP me OUT! *(laughs)* Keep me alive so I can keep going.

Update

Billy Lee Riley succumbed to colon cancer on August 2, 2009. To the end he was wary of interviews, hoping to save his best stories for his own book (which likely will never be published, though excerpts are previewed at deltaboogie.com) but he said he was pleased with this piece, and his long-time friend and fan club secretary Tommie Wix told him it was the best interview he had ever done (Wix passed away in 2006). The interview also got him a few bookings, appeared on some rockabilly websites, and is to my knowledge the only *Roctober* article that has been translated into Polish. Riley had released several albums in the decade since this interview, including the outstanding *Shade Tree Blues* (the blues album he discussed here) and 2008's *Still Got My Mojo*, a studio album backed by a young band from Holland. Ken Burke had a falling out with Riley, over politics and web etiquette of all things (Riley refused to stop bombarding Burke with Fox News–inspired Obama conspiracy e-mails during the 2006–8 election cycle), but after his death Burke contributed a stellar piece to *Roctober* summarizing Riley's career. The writer concluded that Riley himself ultimately sabotaged most of his shots at bigger success, as time after time, "his talent earned him opportunities that his temperament extinguished." Burke continued, "Riley was as famous as he deserved to be . . . *[he is]* the king of the *[rockabilly]* B-list. Elvis Presley, Jerry Lee Lewis, Carl Perkins & Charlie Rich, the guys he started with, were all better because—in addition to hit records—they had a complete conception of their own talents and what had to be done to become successful. Riley ranks above the likes of Sonny Burgess, Ronnie Dawson, Barbara Pittman, Lew Williams, Art Adams, Larry Donn, and others because his career had much more stylistic depth. His death hasn't changed that. He often verged on greatness—but he couldn't follow through." Burke also noted that in addition to a forthcoming disc of unheard Sun outtakes, much of Riley's archival material (of varying quality) remains unreleased or never reissued, so rockabilly fans can keep looking to the skies for more flying saucers rock 'n' roll.

Interview conducted by John Battles,
Jake Austen, Mike Maltese, Ken Mottet,
and Dan Sorenson (1997)

The Treniers

The Treniers are one of the first self-contained,
bona fide rock 'n' roll groups. They are also
probably the greatest living entertainers in showbiz today. Among some very gifted peers, they
proved to be the only pioneering jump blues styl-
ists that not only survived when the rest of the
world caught up with the rockin' 'n' rollin' they
initiated, but also thrived in the ensuing decades

as a far from sedate lounge act. The group has weathered the ever-changing cycle of disposable pop culture trends thrown their way not in spite of their resistance to change, but because of it. By upholding traditions thought long gone, and by keeping it lively, the Treniers' performances are just as vital and hypnotizing today as they were in the era when they helped to birth the Devil's music. I'd like to think that they've been having too much fun to fully realize just how historical they are.

On July 14, 1919, in Mobile, Alabama, identical twins Claude and Cliff Trenier were born into a musical family (their parents played piano and trumpet, and older brother Buddy was a professional vocalist). In 1939 they began attending Alabama State University (then called State Teacher's College), but studies took a backseat to their love of music. Montgomery, Alabama was then a hotbed of talent, and their school band, the Collegians, was one of the hottest combos in the region. The twins were performing with the likes of trumpeter Joe Newman, pianist Gene Gilbeaux, and saxophonist Don Hill (who still performs with the group today). They left school in 1941, and after the draft board took Claude out of commission briefly, they were at it again. Claude began a stint with the seminal Jimmie Lunceford Orchestra, bringing Cliff in to record the classic 78 rpm side "Buzz Buzz Buzz." The twins honed their performance skills, but after that group disbanded in 1945 Cliff returned home. Claude headed West, where he provided vocals on recordings for several jazz legends, including Charlie Mingus and Barney Bigard, did a lengthy residency at the Melody Club, and replaced the great, foul-mouthed Wynonie Harris at the legendary Club Alabam. The twins, however, were inseparable and they were soon back together, also bringing Gene Gilbeaux, who became the band's arranger, and Don Hill back in the fold.

The act (then called the Trenier Twins and the Gene Gilbeaux Orchestra) was born kicking and screaming as sure as the day the twins actually entered the world. Signing their first recording contract a half century ago with Mercury Records, the Treniers quickly earned a greater reputation for their frantic actions on stage than for their music itself. While Claude and Cliff were undeniably the court jesters, the entire band moved in frantic synchronization. Agile as a snake, wilder than a hyena, the group was a perpetual motion machine. Their seemingly loose, spinning, grooving choreography inspired Cholly Atkins to design a more refined version of those moves for Motown artists in the early '60s. And their manic, staccato "bug dance," which thrilled postwar Los Angeles, must have remained in the Tinseltown ether (smog?) for decades, as it is a clear predecessor to the popping and locking that made '70s *Soul Train* dancers so special.

In the early fifties the Treniers' real heyday began. Joined by older brother Buddy and younger brother Milt, they signed with the legendary Okeh label, producing a remarkable string of killer rock 'n' roll sides. It's been said that the Treniers couldn't capture all the energy of their live act in the confinements of the studio, but what they did come up with are some of the genre's finest recorded moments. "Rockin' Is Our Business," "Rockin' on Saturday Night," and "It Rocks, It Rolls, It Swings!" are all self-explanatory in their rockingness. The drunken revelry of "Hadacol (That's All)," the horniness of "Poon-Tang!" ("Poon is a hug! Tang is a kiss!" Uh, yeah . . .), and the audacious date rape classic "(Uh Oh) Get out of the Car" (covered by Richard "Louie Louie" Berry and Sammy Davis Jr.), were all done strictly in fun, but were the beginnings of a revolution that, fortunately, *was* televised. Though they recorded dozens of records, only one made a dent in the charts ("Go, Go, Go" in 1951) and only one made a dent in the national consciousness (their immortal novelty track "Say Hey," recorded with Willie Mays). Still, their fifties sides were classics. Taking what they learned from artists they'd worked with and admired, like Lunceford, Louis Jordan, Amos Milburn, and Roy Brown, the Treniers added their own inimitable personal touch and took the whole thing into the highest gear imaginable. The phrase "rock 'n' roll" was originally understood as a metaphor for sex, and the Treniers were bringing it to its first climax!

Other artists would soon reap the rewards of the seeds they had sown, but the Treniers found themselves in a very respectable position of visibility by 1956, their departure from Okeh notwithstanding. They were reaching a wider audience through appearances on TV programs like *Ed Sullivan*, *The Jackie Gleason Show*, and *The Colgate Comedy Hour* (in which Jerry Lewis sat in with the band on drums). They also appeared in a number of movies, *Don't Knock the Rock* and *The Girl Can't Help It* being the best known today. In the former the Treniers appeared with Alan Freed (who had been honored by a Treniers original for his theme song) along with Little Richard and Bill Haley (who had switched his band from country to rock after seeing the Treniers perform). In *Don't Knock The Rock*, the Treniers' explosive, boozy, bluesy, hand-clappin,' finger-snappin' performance of "Rockin' on Saturday Night" in a thoroughly white-bread setting is both provocative and surreal. Their clowning on "Out of the Bushes" surpasses it. Alongside pretty-boy Milt's almost robotic primping, Claude and Cliff hold court in bughouse square, each attempting to outdo the other in sheer craziness, even resorting (before even some *parents* of the Lollapalooza Nation were born) to stage diving! The song itself, more or less a word of warning from a stalker ("Something's gonna jump out of the bushes and grab you . . ."), is an outrageous combination of complicated jazzy sequences and the Treniers' brand of contagious humor. It even spawned a purely novelty cover version by Joe Besser–sound-alike Crazy Otto. "It was big in Guam," Claude jokes today.

Their real crowning cinematic moment came in the (hourglass) form of *The Girl Can't Help It*, the greatest rock 'n' roll movie of all time. In gorgeous Technicolor and stereophonic sound, the Treniers performed a beyond crazed "Rockin' Is Our Business," by then their signature song and still their set opener. In such a class-A package, with an all-star lineup that included Little Richard, Julie London, Gene Vincent, Eddie Cochran, Fats Domino, Abbey Lincoln and the Platters, the Treniers still stand out like Jayne Mansfield's Double Ds! Only Little Richard's performance in the film matched them for flamboyance and kick-out-the-jams conviction.

By the late '50s, rock 'n' roll was going out in a blaze not of glory, but of tragedies, scandals, and personal turmoil. Alan Freed was crucified on payola charges. Chuck Berry was prosecuted under the anti-white slavery Mann Act. And the Treniers found themselves on the fateful tour of England with Jerry Lee Lewis where he brought himself down by making public his marriage to his teenage cousin ("That big dummy!" Claude sums up in his best Redd Foxx). Where could the Treniers turn to in the dawning of the era of teen idols who wouldn't know rock if it hit them upside the head? Would you believe Vegas?

Once the smoke had cleared, the Treniers found themselves doing very well on the Vegas / Atlantic City circuit. Milt had left by then to pursue his own solo career, cutting some strong sides in a big, brassy baritone, not unlike Screamin' Jay Hawkins. Nephew Skip, also possessed of a fine set of pipes and enough good looks to keep the ladies coming back, took Milt's place and remains with the group to this day. Rock 'n' roll and Vegas at the time had been strange bedfellows. Even Elvis flopped in Sin City his first time out in 1956. But the Treniers came in anticipating that the patrons not only demanded a show, but the sun, the moon and the stars as well, and the Treniers were there to give that to them. Louis Prima had already proven you could rock the Glitter Gulch and not starve. Though his distant cousins in the Rat Pack (except for Sammy who liked anything hip) dismissed rock 'n' roll as a passing fad, Prima staged his comeback by incorporating its rhythms into his act. With charisma and versatility the Treniers, along with Prima and his hired gun Sam Butera, were the only artists at the time to rock and roll Vegas and Atlantic City with class and without compromise. When other rockers and soul shouters were gaining acceptance in Vegas by the early '70s, the Treniers had already staked their claim. One such figure, Elvis Presley, met up with the Treniers in Vegas and told them that he had learned "Good Rockin' Tonight" from their version. Over the decades the Treniers shared Casino stages with everyone from Sammy to Sinatra to Bill Cosby (who was so fond of Cliff Trenier that he named his sitcom character Heathcliff Huxtable after the lounge star).

In the 1970s Brother Milt opened a most swinging lounge of his own right here in his wife's hometown of Chicago. He booked the band twice a year between engagements in Vegas and Atlantic City, though their visits to the Windy City have become more sporadic as the aura of Atlantic City has dimmed in recent years. Their success in Vegas has been phenomenal and against stiff competition, they've twice won Las Vegas Entertainers of the Year awards.

The group displayed remarkable longevity and seemed indestructible, but sadly, fourteen years ago a reminder of their own humanity fell upon them. In 1983, Cliff Trenier passed away. Claude was faced with a monumental decision: should he retire the group, or should he carry on in Cliff's memory? The showbiz veterans returned to the stage. Skip, the new kid approaching his twenty-fifth year in the group, ably took the dual frontman position with Claude (Buddy has since retired). Don Hill is still lending his distinct sax wizardry to the band, while acting as an affable fall guy to Claude's and Skip's incessant goofing. Dave Akins, also a veteran from years back, keeps the beat steady and smokin,' while more recent additions, bassist Donald Jackson and keyboardist Jack Holland, keep the groove and help things move. Before the band's first set at a recent visit to Milt Trenier's Lounge we sat down with Claude backstage and let the legend hold court as we braced ourselves for the blistering performance we'd soon witness.

To take in the Treniers today is to be transported to an atmosphere and an age that one could be forgiven for thinking we'd never again witness. The friendliness they convey and the obvious love for their work are absolutely genuine. Their kind of one-on-one rapport with an audience I've rarely seen in this era. Most younger performers should live to move like

Claude and Skip do today. Of course, the Treniers would land in the hospi- tal if they were doing all the things they used to do on stage, but then, so would most guys my age if they tried to do what the Treniers still do every night. The Treniers are a live act, best experienced live, always about life, and always lively. LONG LIVE THE TRENIERS!

Roctober: Claude, it's great to speak with you; is it OK to consider you to be sort of the leader of the group?

Claude Trenier: I am, I'm the one that started all this Trenier shit. Me and my twin brother. He was like the comedian and did more of the comedy stuff. Now Skip more or less took over my job and I went into the comedy stuff, but I was the straight man for Cliff.

You started off singing for Jimmie Lunceford.

Actually I started out singing around groups in Mobile, Ala- bama, then I went to Alabama State. Erskine Hawkins and his band just left Alabama State so they were recruit- ing musicians all over from everywhere, and Don *(Hill, saxophonist, still with the group today)* came in from New Orleans and a lot of musicians from Texas came in. They got me from Mobile.

What was the Trenier household in Mobile like growing up? How many of you were there?

Well it was eight boys and two girls. Myself And Cliff, my older brother Denny, our brother Buddy, another brother Maurice, another brother named Edward, then we got our two sisters, Jessica and Antoinette, then Harold, and Milt was the youngest. So like I said, I went to Alabama State College. They had three bands at Alabama State College and a guy by the name of Harley was killed in a bus wreck, and the promoter wanted some- one to take his place and play the job he had booked. So he came by and asked if we wanted to go, so we asked the guys, "What are you gonna do?" "Well I'm gonna be a musician," they would all say, so I said, "We got a chance, lets go." So we took sixteen musicians, had some good guys: Joe Morris, Joe Newman, Matthew Jay. Joe Newman played with Count Basie, and he did a lot of things in Europe. We had some good guys, and some good guys came in after them; we had in our band through the years Sonny Stitt, Lucky Thompson, the Simon Brothers. So we left there with sixteen of them and I wasn't actually the leader; Joe Morris was. But other guys in the band didn't like the way he looked on stage.

Not good looking enough?
Well, he was kind of heavy and looked greasy, so they voted on a new leader, they voted me the leader. 'Cause I was out front anyway.

Did you get paid more for being the leader?
(*Incredulous stare, laughter*) We were lucky to get paid. We were working for so little during that time . . . oh man, we go get four coffee rolls for a nickel. Half a pint of milk for a nickel, you know?

And that was breakfast?
That was breakfast, lunch, and dinner, whatever you're gonna use it for! I remember we went to Mobile once — that's my hometown — we made eight dollars a piece!

What kind of places were you playing when you started? You said you started at the university; were you playing parties?
We played in barns and stuff; you know the South, they play in places like that. They'd get a tobacco barn; they'd clean it up and you'd go in there and play a dance.

Now when you first started the band were you shooting for the whole matching suits, the whole showbiz thing from the start?
No. In fact it just seemed like things evolved. Like how I got into college, there was this woman that had the little school across from the Catholic school I used to go to, and one night the Alabama State Band came to play. I was looking through the window 'cause I couldn't afford to pay to go in, and she said, "Why don't you go up and sing a song with them?" Now, I was a painter, a painter's helper, you know, but I went up there and I did one song, and they said, "Oh you know any more?" I said, "I don't know, whachu got?" And they got a standing ovation. So they said, "Hey, you like

to go to Alabama State?" I said, "Yeah man." I'm not even *thinking* about going to Alabama State; the heck with Alabama State, I'm out there making money as a painter's helper. Then about a week later the same woman that asked me to go up and sing says, "Claude, go home, get your clothes." I said, "Why?" She said, "You're going to Alabama State." I said, "What?!" I had no idea; I hadn't even prepared for this. But I went anyways.

So then you and your brothers all got to go to college?
No I was there first, and then Cliff came up after I was there.

So you're college-educated men?
I didn't graduate; they put us out. This was '41. That's when I left school. We got our first outside job, and the school administration found out we weren't going to play some jobs they had for us that weekend. We all went to a movie, and when we came back they had put all our clothes and luggage and stuff out on the lawn. They took whatever instruments they owned away from us. So we were short of instruments, short a pedal for the drum; we didn't have no sticks. We went to the first job in Columbus, Georgia. I'll never forget as long as I live—we go out there and were playing; we don't have no sticks. We went out on a tree and pulled off some limbs . . . he's beating on the bass drum with a stick. And Joe Newman, he had a trumpet and the valves wouldn't go back up so he played upside down. And the promoter came out and said, "I ain't paying for this shit!" We didn't get paid for that! I said, "Well, great start, great start!"

Did you have moves, choreography from the get-go?
No we just had a band. We played things like "Tuxedo Junction," whatever was popular in those days, and we copied Jimmie Lunceford. We were great Jimmie Lunceford fans in those days—that's why I got the job with him, 'cause I knew all the songs. I was in Pittsburgh at the time I joined Lunceford. See my band had broken up when the war broke and they drafted, in fact they drafted me, and I stayed in about nine months and they let me out.

Before that you had toured backing up Louis Jordan and his people?
That was my Alabama State Band. See Louis Jordan had made a hit—I think it was "Outskirts of Town," or something like that—so they wanted someone to go on tour and play with him. We'd play for dancing, and he'd come out and do a forty-five-minute show. They didn't think a small group could fill these big auditoriums. We'd play through Texas, Oklahoma, Cali-

fornia and we just went out and played; we had a good band, so we got good exposure. Now our manager comes up to us and says, "Now look, I can get a guy called Louis Jordan but we got to guarantee him $500 a night." I said, "You kidding; tell him to guarantee *us* $500 a night!" So he went to make the deal anyway. Louis Jordan must have drawn 10,000 people a night! He made all the money! *(laughter)*

You must have enjoyed the experience. It shows in your music that you obviously picked up a lot from him.
I learned a lot from him. See what we did was we took a little Louis Jordan, with the showmanship and all that, and a little bit of Jimmie Lunceford, see Jimmie Lunceford, everything he played was 2/4. No matter what went around him he was playing 2/4 all the way. So we took his 2/4, a little bit of Louis Jordan, and we added a little bit of the Treniers and that's what we got now.

Were you also working with people like Amos Milburn, Wynonie Harris, Roy Brown?
We worked with Wynonie. In fact I was working at the Club Alabam at the time he was the singer and I was like on production numbers; I used to sing "White Christmas," stuff like that. One night, he got on the oats I guess; anyway he got up on stage and he started calling people a bunch of mothers and stuff so they fired him, and a girl by the name of Norma Miller said, "Why don't you let Claude sing a couple of songs?" So they put me as the featured vocalist. Then I sent for my twin brother, because we had already done the twin act for Jimmie Lunceford. So he come out and we start doing the twin thing; they hadn't seen it. I used to run out one door, he'd come in another, and they'd go, "How did he do that so fast?" I tell you, the first time we pulled that twin thing at the Apollo Theater in Harlem with Lunceford we stopped the show *cold*. They were applauding for a half hour. And after us they put on two other acts. Cliff and I went upstairs and took off our uniforms—we were wearing tuxes—and Lunceford came upstairs, left the band playing, and said, "Put back on your uniforms." We said, "Why?" He said, "They're still screaming for you." We said, "We don't know any other songs, Jimmie." "Do you know 'Stardust?'" We said, "Yeah." He said, "Sing that." We went out and did "Stardust," 'cause they were screaming. That was one of the greatest ovations we ever had except the last time we were in England.

Yeah, you just played to 40,000 people in England!
It was crowded, and they charged $250 a head for the weekend festival. We were not the only group, but we were like the headliners. The promoter said, "You guys are the ones selling those tickets." Well it's funny; they see those movies over there. They've got songs we didn't even know we recorded, 'cause we were drinking a little bit in those days. *(laughter)* Don Hill found out he recorded "Pennies from Heaven"; he doesn't even remember doing that.

Backtracking a half century, after you left Jimmy Lunceford . . .
Well after I left Jimmie Lunceford, well I didn't leave; he fired me. 'Cause, I couldn't read music, and everybody read in his band; that was why it was so tight. He'd write it out and they'd play it. And one day we were recording and I was singing "Sleepy Time Gal," or something like that, and I went *(Claude sings the song with a few odd notes thrown in)*. He said, "Don't you see that note?" I said, "No." He said, "You mean to tell me you can't read?" I said, "No, I can't read." He said, "What!?!" I had a great ear. See, while they were rehearsing the songs I was listening to the melody and reading the words. I got away with that for a long time. One thing was, I knew all the recordings. The first night I sang with Lunceford I remember there was a thing called "Like a Ship at Sea," and I'd have to find the key. The first time I did it, *(sings high)* "I'm like a ship at *(drops low)* sea." Lunceford said, "That's alright, well do it again." It was because the record goes up a little.

After you left Lunceford and played at the Club Alabam, did you work with Johnny Otis?
Yes. Johnny Otis was the band. In fact I was supposed to go on tour with Johnny Otis but we got a job up in Seattle, Cliff and myself and Gene on piano. Jimmie Lunceford came through there and he said, "I wanna see if you'll come back in the band. Everybody's asking for you, wherever we go, 'Where's the twins, where's the twins?'" So I said, "OK," and that night I'm on stage doing the show and a pal says, "Hey did you hear what happened to Lunceford?" And I said no, and he said, "He died." And I said, "Where!" "Somewhere he was signing autographs and just fell out." And I said, "I'll be doggone, he was just talking about us going back with the band." That's the fates. Maybe we wouldn't have what we have now. I really enjoyed my life. I wish we did more that you could look at, but that's why I'm glad we did those movies. They'll be showing them another ten years.

Oh, well after that! What about Milt joining the group?

Milt joined us when he came out of the Army in 1951. We also got Buddy in the group, so we had four Treniers up front singing. In '59 Skip took Milt's place when he went out on his own.

Around 1950 or so you went to Okeh Records, doing the recordings with the scaled-down Treniers as most people know them.

I'll tell you what happened. We were working this after-hours place in Los Angeles and we had to make records, so I got Don, and I had this piano player that was with me in the Alabama State band . . .

Gene Gilbeaux?

Yeah. So he was like our accompanist and he'd write most of the arrangements in those days. And so this club in Los Angeles wanted us to work there so we got a bass player and a drummer. So we went into that club for two weeks . . . we must have played seventy-eight weeks straight! Now we went in there getting $375 a week, which was great money, and we asked him for a raise. We want to get a $25 raise every two weeks. When we left there we were getting $1,200 and something dollars! If we had asked that guy for a $500 raise, he would have threw us out there. How we got the job was some guy used to hang around the bar said, "If you want a get a group that's really good, get them Trenier Twins; they're gonna be good, they're gonna be good." The owner said, "I never heard of the Trenier Twins." "Get 'em; they'll do good for you." So we went in; we did fair. "I thought you said they're gonna do good?" "They are; give 'em two more weeks." So he gave us two more weeks and all of sudden it hit, and people started lining up out there and that more or less made us. Everybody started talking about us; we got on all the TV shows.

This was playing jump blues?

The way we started playing our jump style was I was doing ballads and one night the guys were just applauding for more, and I didn't know anymore. A girl used to sing with Jimmie Lunceford by the name of Tina Dixon; she did a song called "Eee Babaleeba," not "Hey! Ba-Ba-Re-Bop," that Hamp (*Lionel Hampton*) wrote later. I said play me some blues and I started singing it. I did that thing every night. I did it so much I had to get another one. So I got another jump song and another jump song and another. Pretty soon I wasn't doing no ballads. We started adding all that good rockin' kind of stuff and the ballads went out the window.

No, but we would move so much they couldn't get it on the tape. We were moving in the studio like we were on stage. They couldn't get the energy of the live show on the records. Even the guy said, if they ever get on those, what do they call those jukebox things they had with pictures, movies . . .

Scopitones?
Yeah, but we never did one of those.

Did anybody in the band ever get hurt onstage?
Not really.

Nobody ever fell off a piano?
Oh yes! *(laughter)* But we didn't get hurt. I remember one time we were playing—I think it was here in Chicago—we had a drummer by the name of Eddie Burke and Gil said "1–2–3–4 . . . ," and there's no drums. He had fallen off the back of the stage. *(laughter)* He didn't know he was that far back.

Cliff and Claude in action.

Did you and Heathcliff develop the acrobatics between yourselves, or was it just everybody working off each other until you found something that worked?
Well we just did it and people seemed to enjoy it. It was natural; it wasn't rehearsed or nothing; we'd just do things. Like that thing on "Ragmop," where we get into a straight line like that—that wasn't rehearsed. We don't know how we did it, but we just all of a sudden looked up and we were in a line.

Did you ever have a crowd go completely out of control on you?
Well not out of control but we had 'em screaming and yelling. They've done that quite a bit.

What about some of the TV shows you were on?
We were the second black act that Red Skelton had on. And after the first,

one of those guys, Governor Maddox or someone *(to Skip, who is changing for the show)*—do you remember the guy that wrote to Red Skelton and said, "What you doing with those niggers on your show?" Red introduced us and said "Governor Maddox," or whoever, "here's my answer . . . the Treniers!" *(laughter)*

At the time when you started doing all these television appearances, television was a brand-new medium.
Everybody was watching it.

And these variety shows wanted exciting acts, something that was visual, and you had it!
I tell you, the guy used to produce the *Jackie Gleason Show*, a skit wasn't going well, so he said find out where the Treniers are. They found us in Hollywood, California, so he flew us back to New York, got Billie Holiday to work in our place, and we went back there and did *one* number. They said they wanted something to liven it up.

What was Jackie Gleason like to work with?
Oh, nice. I remember the first time he saw us, we were doing a benefit in Miami Beach for one of those Jewish organizations, and we did "Ragmop," and the people were going nuts, and he said, "What's going on out here?"

He heard the people, and he watched us and he said, "You're on my show when you get to New York!"

How did you get to Vegas?
We were hot in L.A. and some people we knew worked at a hot club in Las Vegas and they told the guy, "You have to bring the Treniers." We worked *(to Skip)* what the heck was it called?
Skip: The Domingo Club.
And this guy that used to be on *The Real McCoys*, he was the headliner and they were just laying the foundation for the Sahara.

You were probably the only band that hit the teenage rock 'n' roll audience and the Vegas audience and do so well with all of it. Did it surprise you when the rock 'n' roll thing hit, because you'd been doing it for years?
See it was in the '40s — '46 — and Elvis Presley and all them didn't come on until '56.
Skip: Actually it was a cross between R&B and swing.
What we called rock 'n' roll in those days is nowhere near what they're playing today. They gotta get another name!
Skip: We made one song, really good song, called "Day Old Bread and Canned Beans." Wrote songs like that in those days. We did nine versions of that. We did all kinds of records of it, swing, Latin, even . . . *(sings it in Calypso accent)*
Didn't sell a record yet, we were gonna keep going 'til we do!
Skip: We tried that thing all kind of ways.

While we're running down the list of songs, there's a couple I'd be interested in knowing about. "Crossbone County" . . .
I think an A&R man gave us that song . . . and "Poon Tang."
Skip: I think we learned that one right in the studio.

How did you work them up in the studio with all the funny voices?
We just did what we felt.

Did the people recording the album ask why you making all those noises and why you making all those faces?
No they'd say, "Who did that? Do it again!"

Who did the girl voices?
That was Heathcliff.

What about "Hey Miss Lucy (What Makes Your Lips So Juicy)"—that and "Poon Tang"—how'd you get them past the stations? Did they play that on the radio?
No, they didn't play that. Now they play anything.

What about "Rock-a-Beatin' Boogie?"
That was Bill Haley.

Right, but you put it out before he did.
He was playing across the street from us when he had his country band, and . . .

He asked you what kind of music is that you're playing?
Right. And I said, "I don't know, were just having fun." We didn't have a name for it. I don't like to be categorized. The people, the writers kept saying ". . . this rock 'n' roll group . . ."

You must have started picking up popularity because of all the press.
We got so popular around L.A. that superstar names couldn't follow us. But we wasn't strong enough to headline.
Skip: What did Nat King Cole say?
We were playing the Orpheum Theater with a lot of stars. Nat came down and said, "Oh I've got plenty of time; the Treniers just went on." They said, "No, you go on after them." He said, "No I don't!" *(laughter)* We played with Charlie Ventura, and they couldn't get on. We were rocking and rolling!
Skip: We did the same thing with Dion *(DiMucci, of Dion and the Belmonts fame)*. They had Dion and us together at graduation time in New York City. That's his crowd. We came off and he said, "I'm not gonna follow this tomorrow night. Put me on first and let the Treniers close the show."

Tell the story about going to England with Jerry Lee Lewis on the fateful tour.
Well we went over there, and that dummy, he didn't have to tell the authorities he had married this girl, because her father was playing bass with him. But he goes there and he's talking: "Oh yeah, we got married." "And how old is she?" "Thirteen . . . my cousin." So the next night they put it in the paper, get him out of the country, so he had to leave. They were throwing chairs up there and everything. Then they made us carry the show. They added two more acts. A guy named Terry Wayne and some skiffle band.
(Milt gives his brothers the sign that it's time to start the first set; later John and Mike spoke to Claude between sets)

We used to write a lot. In fact we wrote for Sammy Davis, "Get out of the Car"; he did a version of that. But a lot of songs we had we wrote but we didn't copyright at the time. Like Amos Milburn's "Let Me Go Home Whiskey," I wrote that with another guy but the other guy went and sold it to Modern Records, sold five songs for a hundred dollars. And I asked him — I said, "Hey man, how did they like the songs?" "Oh they said they were alright." "OK, well if they didn't like it, we'll still do it." And I'm down in Florida and all of a sudden a big disc jockey says, "Here's a new one by Amos Milburn, "Let Me Go Home Whiskey." I went through that roof, and you should of seen, this was a big guy, about three hundred pounds, I grabbed that son-of-a . . . "You rotten . . ." I was mad. Now if he had told me he sold them for a hundred, OK, but he said they didn't like 'em. I didn't copyright, so I couldn't get any royalties. I didn't copyright, because I didn't think he sold them, you know.

It's amazing this footage of that TV *show Milt showed the other night; what was that, '54?*
It had to be.

It's amazing! Everybody is moving; I mean Gene playing piano is jumping up nonstop while he's playing.
We had an eight-man line. The only guy sitting down was the drummer. We went back to the Apollo and when we went into that line on "Ragmop," the whole place went ape! And you couldn't really catch that excitement on a record, 'cause when we get in the studio we start jumping and were going, "Go, go, go!" and were not into the mic, so they can't get the full thing.

I notice in the photos in the studio shots you're all going nuts. Of course, the recordings are exciting to listen to today. It seems to me the Treniers are the unifying link between the earlier jump blues and what people later just called rock 'n' roll. You were right in all of it.
That's right. We made the crossover thing. We were playing clubs that black acts didn't really play. We played the Chez Paree here, and one in New York, and no black acts were playing them. In Los Angeles we played Billy Berg's. Lana Turner used to come in there — she drove me nuts — and Ava Gardner took us over to her house one night; we went out there in the swimming pool . . . it's funny, when you get a certain niche in show business you just meet people and some you get to be friends with. We went to her house all

the time. We used to give parties. We believed in parties. We worked the Moulin Rouge in Hollywood, and we used to invite the whole cast over to our house and we'd party two or three days. Nine big statuesque girls, the producers . . . you can't do that nowadays, somebody hears you're having fun they're gonna come in there and break it up.

How do you feel to have basically done everything in entertainment there is to do? You've done it all.

I enjoy it. I love it; that's why I'm still in it. And to me, when I get on stage, that's my altar. I don't want no one to mess up my altar. Take my razor and whack you . . . *(pantomimes the razor shtick from the stage act)* That was Cliff's gimmick; he started that. I kept it in as a way of reminding that Heathcliff is still here. And he is there. He's there every night. It took me a long while after he passed to get used to him not being there. You wait for him to say something; now it ain't there. That's when Cliff started chiming in.

Tell us about the Poontang cans.

We passed them out. A guy in Boston had 'em made up for us. It was called "Extra Fancy Lower Alabama Poontang," by the recipe of Miss Pussy Galore. We'd give away hundreds of those things, but they used to cost us a dollar and eighty cents. I said geez we're gonna go bankrupt handing these out. I used to joke about it and say, "Now if you've had this Poontang more than six months don't open it in the house." *(laughter)* "It might spoil."

Some of these jokes in the act, you say them night after night, but you always tell it like it's the first time and you really get the audience reaction.

You always got to do it like it's the first time. Some I got from Redd Foxx; some I made up myself. You never know where you're gonna get a joke. I'll never forget when they first got integration at the Sahara; this waitress came up to me and said, "My kid told me this joke. These kids, they were

Famous Trenier Twins *alike in everything* except in their *choice of bourbon*

Claude always asks for   Cliff insists on famous

EARLY TIMES   **OLD FORESTER**

Every ounce a <u>man's</u> whisky!   "...Nothing better in the market"

in school, and it was the teacher's birthday, so they all decided to give the teacher gifts. Someone brought apples, some brought other stuff, but the black kids didn't have much money so they got together and made a cake. They baked it and decorated and brought it in and set it on the teacher's desk. So she came in and said, "Oh children how you doing?" and they said, "Happy Birthday Teacher!" So she looked down at the cake and written on it says, "Happy Birthday Teach F-U-C-K," and she says, "Who decorated this cake!" and Little Willie says, "I did, Teach!" She says, "Little Willie, do you know what F-U-C-K means?" So he said, "Yeah Teach, it means From Us Colored Kids."

Update

Our celebration of the last living jump blues / rock 'n' roll originals now stands as a time capsule, as mortality began to set in not long after this interview. The first to depart was the hallowed site of the conversation, as within the year Milt Trenier's lounge ended its twenty-year run, closing an important chapter of Chicago entertainment history (in addition to hosting annual Treniers' visits, the club helped develop the careers of jazz vocalist Kurt Elling and comedian Bernie Mac). In 1999 Buddy, the long-retired brother, passed away. And in 2003 the magnificent showbiz career of Claude Trenier came to an end when he succumbed to bladder cancer in Las Vegas at the age of eighty-four, joining his twin brother in rock 'n' roll heaven. Skip and Don Hill retired, remaining in Vegas, occasionally taking a stage if the situation warrants it. The youngest Trenier brother, Milt, doesn't know the meaning of the word *retire*. He is currently playing a few fantastic gigs a month, ushering in a seventh decade of family stage magic. Long live the Treniers, indeed!

Sam the Sham

y favorite garage-rock band, bar none, has
always been Sam the Sham & the Pharaohs.
They hit their commercial stride in the post-
Beatles era, invading the Top 40 with the likes of
"Little Red Riding Hood," "Ring Dang Doo," "Ju
Ju Hand," and their all-time monster from 1965,
"Wooly Bully." Sam was part of what he called
"the American Retaliation" (in response to the

British Invasion), which included not only the Byrds and Bob Dylan, but also less canonized talents like the Bobby Fuller Four, the Sir Douglas Quintet, and Paul Revere & the Raiders. What was great about Domingo "Sam" Samudio was that he actually remembered life before the Beatles. His blues credentials were in good order; he hung out with Freddie King and John Lee Hooker, played rough Texas joints, and covered songs like Johnny "Guitar" Watson's "Gangster of Love." Sam and his Pharaohs also led a one-band rockabilly revival, with tracks like "Ain't Gonna Move," the flipside of "Wooly Bully," and "I Wish It Were Me." Plain and simple, Sam and company got over the hump playing greaser music when almost every-body else left it for dead. Although he stresses that he has nothing against the Beatles and their kind; nonetheless, Samudio makes clear, "I didn't sit in the back of the bus for nobody. When the Beatles hit, everybody was goin' British — except Sam. I was holdin' what I had."

Sam provided an unexpected TV treat in 1992 on *The Desi Awards*, a syndicated celebration of Latino achievements. Receiving a special merit award, the turbaned icon came out, guitar slung over his shoulder, and did a slammin' version of "Wooly Bully." Although emcee Paul Rodriguez joked, "I thought he was Egyptian," Sam is pure Tex-Mex. If any phrase belongs in the Spanglish Hall of Fame it is his signature song's killer count-off, "Uno, dos, one, two, TRES, QUATRO!" Born and bred in rural Texas (where his tight family taught him to love music, work hard, and wrestle goats), Sa-mudio enlisted in the Navy at age seventeen, and upon his honorable dis-charge in 1959 set off for college, where he studied classical voice. The lure of nightclub rocking derailed him from the opera track, and for the last half century Sam the Sham has been the king of garage rock. Despite never abdicating that particular throne, over the decades Samudio has demon-strated impressive range. In 1971 he recorded a straightforward blues rock LP for Atlantic with Duane Allman. (He won a Grammy for that LP's biker-poetry liner notes in which he thanks his deceased pet monkey Squeeky, the nuns for teaching him "there are no NIGGERS and no MESKINS," and "the towns I was run out of; for they ran me to better places.") In 1982 he contributed beautiful Spanish ballads to Ry Cooder's revered soundtrack for the Jack Nicholson film *The Border*. And in the nineties he turned his attention toward the Lord, entertaining prisoners in Tennessee jails and recording sacred music that recalls the gospel-blues of Rev. Gary Davis and Pops Staples. Not long after we spoke, he sent me a couple of homemade

tapes of his then-current music (sez Sam, "you heard of unplugged? This is disconnected!"). The title of one of them sums up his current state perfectly: "Wired, Fired, and Inspired."

Prior to this interview most of the reference material I had seen on Sam concentrated on the Arabian get-ups the band wore, the hearse they drove to gigs ("it was the BV era," he explains, "before vans"), and the novelty songs like "Little Red Riding Hood." But listening to the early albums you hear that though some songs are humorous, very few were out-and-out nutty—this was a howling Tex-Mex bar band slightly tamed for public consumption. After "Little Red Riding Hood," the label played up the cartoon angle, to the point where Sam was reduced to doing dreadfully unfunny numbers like "Old McDonald Had a Boogaloo Farm." I've got nothing against performers who play up the shuck-and-jive vibe, but to label Sam as a straight-up novelty/parody singer is to criminally sell the man short. Hopefully this interview can set the record straight.

James Porter: *Tell us how you got started in the music business?*
Sam the Sham: After getting out of the Navy in 1959 I worked construction for a while to save up money and go to school. I went to Arlington, which is

Texas State University at Arlington now. I ran out of money so I was studying classical music during the day (*laughs*), and rocking and rolling at night
till about four in the morning, and that's where it began.

Were you playing all your life, or did you just start when you got to college?
No, I had been around music . . . my father used to sing and pick a little
bit. And down in Texas when I was growing up, there was a man that used
to live where we lived and he used to sing, Webfoot, they used to call him.
I just grew up around it. I liked music, I had a good range, and everybody
sang in my family, around the house, so that's where it began.

So how did you get started with the Sam the Sham persona?
We formed a group called the Pharaohs and that was composed of Omar
Lopez, Carl Medke, Russell Fowler, and Vincent Lopez, and we played
around . . . really rotten joints, I mean five-dollars-a-man-type stuff. We
played at a place called the Maverick that was in downtown Dallas, the
good-paying jobs were Guthrie's—that was classy. After the guys would get
off at Guthrie's, sometimes they'd come down to where we were. We didn't
have a lot of class, or whatever, but what we had, we had pretty tight. It
was two guitars, actually three guitars, but one of 'em was a Fender of some
kind, and he'd turn all the treble off and he'd play the bassline, and I played
harmonica . . . we played John Lee Hooker, Elmore James, that kinda stuff.
Played a lot of Jimmy Reed . . . there was a lotta blues comin' out of there,
a lotta blues comin' through there. So, my band broke up, the Pharaohs,
'cause I just refused to work for five dollars a night any longer. Our agreement was with any club owner, he'd tell us what he'd pay us and I'd say,
"fine." But after we packed the joint, we'd want a raise. We had a following,
we'd pack it and they'd try to get funny with the money (*both laugh*), so I'd
just pack up and leave, and we'd hold out, but my band just didn't wanna
hold out. I knew there had to be somethin' better, so I was unemployed at
the time. I got a job at the Texas State Fair . . .

You were a carny, right?
(*Laughs*) Yeah! Sellin' garbage, pushin' garbage . . .

Like on some medicine-show-type thing?
No, we were sellin' hot dogs and French fries, Jack's French fries . . . Jack
Pyland was his name and our French fry stand was right next to the Cotton Bowl revue. I met some carnies, learned a bunch of tricks, how they
worked the skin, the live cushion bands (*laughs*), all that stuff, how to make

change and how to skim, how to scam . . . I didn't learn it to practice it; I learned it to be aware of it. The guy that I worked for was a carny; when the Texas State Fair was over, around Thanksgiving, he'd head to New Mexico and buy Christmas trees, bring 'em back to Dallas, flock 'em, put stands on 'em, and sell 'em, and when that was over, he'd start planting grass for the spring. In other words, I learned from him that if you're not too proud you can always make a living. Well after that job I was looking for another job, and organ was really a great sound, the way it was played in Dallas . . .

It was really big then, 'cause you had, like, Jimmy Smith and all those guys . . .
They played real jazz, but see, I didn't know anything; I'd used it as a percussion instrument and as a rhythm instrument. I couldn't read music, but I'd learned triads and chord structures, so it would put that body in it, that wall of sound under everything else that was playing, and it was good for dancing 'cause nobody ever had to look for the beat.

So if the bassist was slackin' off, there you were with that organ, huh?
So, this guy David Martin and I had gone to the same high school and we had known each other; he was a bass player in Tommy and the Tom-Toms, they backed up the Drifters on tours, Chuck Berry on his first run, Lightnin' Hopkins, Muddy Waters, Freddie King, all those guys; they'd be the touring band, so he knew the structure, and how they did it. He'd been in Memphis when a group came in, Booker T. and the MG's, just real excited about a song they had cut. Well, when he got back to Texas, the song that this band had been raggin' about when they were in Memphis—"Green Onions"—it became a hit, and it just really grieved him that he had gone back to Texas, and he was tryin' to get back to Memphis. So he left his band and went to Louisiana with a group called Andy and the Nightriders. Their organ player was leaving and at that particular time I didn't play anything but the harmonica and shammed . . . I just cut up in front of the band, emceed and kept everything going, I was the frontman. I bought an organ, 'cause you were always runnin' into organ players but they never owned their own instrument. I had the organ three days and David and them had heard that I purchased an organ and came up to talk to me and asked me if I wanted a job and I told them I don't know how to play; I just bought this thing three days ago. They said, "Well, we have a tape of all our songs; you willin' to try out? You'll have to learn on your own time." So they came back to Dallas and picked me up—this is Andy and the Nightriders, David was with them, and Vincent the drummer from my original group, the

Pharaohs, was workin' with 'em—so they came up and got me; we went down to Leesville, Louisiana, and spent some time there, workin,' workin,' workin.' I was just glad not to be workin' construction, because by then I'd run out of money and dropped out of college. David and I were roommates and we'd work every night at a roadhouse called the Congo Club on Highway 171, and I mean, it was rockin'. The band was good! Andy Anderson was way ahead of his time. He was Anglo and spoke Spanish, and was tall and thin; he could play like you wouldn't believe. He'd been on stage with Freddie King and B. B. King and those folks, when they backed 'em up, and he was into electronics so he'd get these Gibson Tweed amps and he'd take the speakers out of 'em and would put jukebox speakers in 'em, overdrive 'em.

It must have sounded really bassy?

A lotta guts, man, those fifteen-inch speakers and one of those little amps—I got one in my studio now. So, I had the organ, and all of us sang, so four men, man, we were cookin,' and every time I'd come in—I mean, I was in hog heaven, wearin' a clean shirt every day to work, didn't have to sweat or anything, so I came to our efficiency apartment that David and I slept in and every night—I'd come in he'd be sittin' in the dark, smokin,' and you could always see that little flame—every musician at one time or another spent time in a joint like that, with a bare bulb in a little hallway that went to the shower. Where I was sittin' at the table, the light was on me, but it wasn't on him, and I saw it flicker and I was eatin' a baloney sandwich. I said to David, *(rough voice)*, "What're you thinkin,' David? What do you think about every night?" So he got outta bed and came over to where I was and leaned across the table and got right in my face and he says, "Do you know that while we sit here in this joint eatin' baloney sandwiches, there's folks out there makin' thousands of dollars a night and not even half as good as we are?" Heh heh heh . . . I thought he was about to go off! *(Both of us laugh)* I looked at him and I says, "Well, what does it take?" And he told me—he says to me—"ONE GOLD RECORD." And I says, "Let's go get one." And he looked at me—he said, "I'M NOT PLAYING, SAM." I says, "Man, I'm not playing either." So David and I made an agreement that night. So we got our band tight and we headed for Memphis, and in a week we had a job. But Andy had started getting homesick for Louisiana. He'd met a girl down there and he wanted to go back and after about a month or two, we were renegotiating with a club owner and Andy said, "Well,

man, I'm goin' back . . . I-I-I just cain't help it, I'm h-h-homesick and I got
to go." And I was willin' to go back, 'cause you know there's some people
you can't stand offstage—you don't get along that well offstage—but the
music, when you work together, man, there are times where if you'd died
after the song was over, you'd felt that you'd lived a full life, you know what
I'm saying? *(laughs)* With writers, sometimes you write a piece, you look at
it, man, sayin', "If I fell over right now, I think I've done somethin'!"

Your legacy!

So I was ready to go back to Louisiana, 'cause they was rough down there,
man . . . I mean, the sheriff had asked us to leave town! *(laughs)* And I told
Andy, "I'll go with ya." And David said, "Sam, c'mere . . . are you goin' back?
You remember what we said?" I said, "Yeah, man, but that's our partner—
where we gonna find a guitar player like that?" He says, "We'll find one." I
says, "Who's gonna lead the band?" He says, "You should lead the band." I
says, "How can I lead the band? I can't even play any organ." He says, "You
take care of the frontin' and all o' that, and I'll take care of the music." So I
stayed, and we found Jerry Patterson and Ray Stinnet and we renamed the
group the Pharaohs. But by this time, folks had been callin' me "the Sham,"
Sam the Sham. To musicians it was like an inside joke. "He didn't know
how to play it, so he's shammin'," and shammin', y'know, when you jump
around and cut up, you're the Sham. So, folks'd come up to me and see me
playin' the organ and say, "Aw, man, how 'bout some Jimmy McGriff?" I
say, "Man, I can't play Jimmy." "Aw, how 'bout some Witherspoon?" *(Probably referring to Jimmy Witherspoon, a jazz-blues vocalist who had organists
like Richard "Groove" Holmes backing him up from time to time)* "Man, I can't
play the organ!" "Aw, you just jivin', you just . . ." *(both of us laugh)* We
pooled our money together and recorded an old Chuck Willis tune called
"Betty and Dupree." We had a little label, Tupelo Records.

Did that come out?

Yeah, it was on a pink label and we distributed it, but at the same time,
a musician in the same town had asked me for the words to "Betty and
Dupree." I'd given 'em to him, and he went down to Sun, Sam Phillips's
studio, and released it on Sun Records.

*This wasn't Billy Lee Riley, was it? (Riley did a version of that song himself for
Sun, although it wasn't released until the seventies.)*

No, that was Billy somebody else . . . he never did anything . . .

Oh, Billy Adams?

Yeah, Billy Adams! Where'd you get that name? You got your act together, huh? Well, at the same time, we had the rural blues version of "Betty and Dupree" and on the flip side of "Betty and Dupree" we put a song called "Manchild," which is a Delta-type shuffle. We'd pool our money and have our records pressed down in Coldwater, Mississippi, and by this time we had a hearse. We were playin' a six-hour gig at the Diplomat where we'd get off at four in the morning on Sunday, we'd have a load of records in the back, and we'd drive to wherever we're going. One person would sleep in the back while the other one drove. We'd try to get somebody to distribute it. Man, when we'd get to these different distributors, man, pick of the week was Billy Adams . . . I mean, 'cause Sam Phillips had just picked up the phone, man . . .

He was Sam Phillips, so he must have had a lot of pull in those days.

One of those trips, man, I had an accident, fell out of the hearse, 'bout sixty-three miles an hour. That was disheartening, seein' how someone can shut you down like that, so we recouped and regrouped and then we pooled our money together and went in and recorded "Haunted House."

Was this before or after Jumpin' Gene Simmons? (NOTE: this Gene Simmons isn't the guy from KISS, but rather a Memphis rockabilly cat who dented the Top 20 with his version of "Haunted House" in 1964.)

Before! Do you know, that was originally on Johnny Fuller, in the late fifties on Specialty label, and he wrote it. *(NOTE: sometimes the credit for writing this song goes to Bob Geddins, an Oakland-based record producer who worked with Fuller and other Bay Area R&B musicians.)* Gene Simmons didn't get the whole market—we got the Texas-Oklahoma southwest market—and we got the Atlanta market. But what was disheartening was that Gene Simmons was a featured vocalist in the clubs where we were workin', at the Diplomat and Quentin's. So we got on television, local television, and we were cuttin' up and man, everybody started calling and asking for that record. Joe Cuoghi, who owned Hi Records where Simmons was always hanging around, also owned Pop Tunes *(Poplar Tunes)* here in town and along the Delta where all the rack jobbers came, and he sent Simmons to say they wanted to talk to me, see if we could recut it with their men in the studio . . . and I told them I'd think about it, 'cause I had been in their studio prior to that and they had told me they didn't need anything. *(laughs)* Gene Simmons went back and says, "He doesn't wanna do it. I know the song 'cause I work with him; I'll do it." So the devil musta gotten into his ear on the way back, *(laughs)* and he did it, and you can compare the two. That was disheartening, man, takes the wind out of your sail.

Yeah, but the real big one was right around the corner!
Yeah, somebody says the people from XL Records sent word from the label owner Stan Kesler that he'd like to talk to us. When you've been down the alley and back, you're cautious! *(Laughs)* They told me what they could do and I said, for what? I'm sure it's not out of just concern. Well, they said, this is business, and we want part of this and part of that and we tried—we released one called "Signifying Monkey." Have you ever heard that song?

Uh, by other people, yeah! Whole buncha different versions of that.
Well, it's sort of hokey, the way they had us play the rhythm. We were primarily a blues band. We'd sing things like Otis Rush and Elmore James "The Sky Is Crying," "Double Trouble"; we used to bring the house down with that. *(Recites lyrics to Rush's tune)* "Lay awake at night because of love, I'm just so troubled. Hard to keep a job, got laid off, have double trouble, hey hey." And you remember Gene Allison's "You Can Make It If You Try?"

Yeah!
When I sang it, after bein' whipped all over . . . *(laughs)*, nobody had to tell me that you had to try. We brought that up here with us some Cajun songs, some Louisiana songs—"Whispering Winds," and of course "Mathilda." We came up loaded; we had a purpose! We released "Signifying Monkey," and

they said, "Give us another one; give us somethin'!" So we had a rhythm that we played, and we just played the rhythm and made up lyrics . . . our repertoire consisted of over 300 songs . . . six hours without repeating a song. And sometimes just to break the monotony, I'd tell 'em to kick off a rhythm whether it was a shuffle or a rock and roll rhythm or a blues rhythm and I'd just make lyrics as I went along, and that's another reason they called me the Sham. So, he said, "Well, do you have lyrics?" I says, "Well, not really; I could make some up" I told 'em to kick it off, and we recorded it—it was on a three-track, we recorded it three times, had three different versions . . .

This was "Wooly Bully," right?
Yeah, I didn't intend for them to leave the count on there—I counted it off in Tex-Mex! We'd do that just to keep our sanity, just goof. I didn't allow my band to drink onstage . . .

That turned out to be the big hook line of the song!
Stan Kesler argued, "You got to leave that on!" I says, "Naw, man, don't leave that on, man." He says, "Yeah, you got to, man." It's an argument that turned out to be a good one to have yielded to, and it hooked 'em. It's exciting. We used to goof like that in clubs and folks'd tear that floor up. Our music was primarily dance music. David used to say, "Make it so easy that the fumble-fistedest individual out there can dance, and they won't have to be lookin' for a beat." It worked out, next thing is history. I felt awful when the Beatles made it. We went to New York one time—I think it was LaGuardia *(airport)*, they were pickin' us up in a hearse on the tarmac, and of course the media was there, and they asked me, "Do you submit to the Beatles?" And I said, no, of course not. And folks thought I was crazy. My own band said, "Man, are you nuts?" I don't care who they are, man—I know where they got their music and their influence.

And they know, and you can still hold your own!
That's it . . . hah! I didn't come to follow the trend, I came to set it!

At least you let folks know from the gitgo that you were American, despite the Egyptian garb. Some U.S. groups, like the Beau Brummels and the Sir Douglas Quintet, were passing for British bands! And you had hits!
I think "Wooly Bully" was the first American-produced record that sold a certified million during the onslaught of the British invasion.

David Crosby, from the Byrds, once said that your "Wooly Bully" outsold their "Mr. Tambourine Man" two to one for 1965. You guys were doing alright.

We had the books audited, and it was certified three and a half million. *Billboard* didn't recognize that until a couple of years ago, and they went back and corrected their records. They had been calling "Wooly Bully" the number-2 record of 1965. They went back and changed it . . . it's the first record they ever done that with. But the thing is, I was all business. I didn't shuck and jive with the club owners. We were playin' six hours a night, my band used to say, "Man, how come you don't ever hang out?" They're havin' a jam session over at this club after hours and all." I said, "Man, we got a six-hour gig here. Now if you wanna hang out, drink, you go ahead. If you wanna jam, I didn't come to this town to jam." Freddie King, a friend of mine now gone, used to say, "I came to play, not to stay" *(laughs)*, and to that I added, "I came to play, not to stay; I'm gonna do my bit, then I'm on my way." I didn't want my band table hoppin'. You find you a table and keep to yourself! I wouldn't let 'em drink on a tab; every band in the world knows that trick bag! *(laughs)* Man, I said, "If you wanna buy somethin' at the bar, you pay for it! Ain't nobody takin' a tab!" At the end of the whole thing, one thing that would get me is folks, or my band, would say, "D'ya think you're too good, man?" I says, "Naw . . . I don't think I'm too good but if you wanna hang out, man, you come back ten years later . . . the same dudes that've been hangin' out'll still be hangin' out."

. . . or dead.

. . . and I'm on my way. If you wanna come, come on. Like the song by John Lee Hooker *(sings)*, "come onnnnn, if you wanna go!" *(both laugh)*

It amazes me how you were doing basically rockabilly and Louisiana R&B in '65 and '66 and getting away with it. Jerry Lee Lewis, on the other hand, was doing the same type of material at the same time and couldn't buy a hit! You did a Johnny "Guitar" Watson song on the first album ("Gangster of Love") . . .

Oh man . . .

. . . and you had, like Little Willie John's "Big Blue Diamonds" on the third album . . .

Beautiful song, beautiful song, man.

And you must have got "Red Hot" from Billy Lee Riley . . .

Billy Lee Riley. *(sings)* "My gal is red hot . . ."

"Your gal ain't doodledy squat!"
And then that song, "Every Woman I Know" . . .

". . . crazy 'bout an automobile!"
Heh heh heh! See, we weren't followin' the Beatles!

See, that's the good thing about you guys! The average band of that time . . .
. . . IS OLD and BITTER!

*Well, not only that, but most American bands then, with the exception of the
Byrds and a few others, filled their LPs with obvious cover versions, like "In the
Midnight Hour" and "Like a Rolling Stone." You didn't; you reached into that
Tex-Mex trick bag and kept everybody guessing! And you were getting over like
a big fat rat!*
That's it. Just keep your eye on the cat! *(both laugh)*

At one point you toured with your MGM labelmate, Hank Williams Jr.
Uh-huh. I remember that.

*Hank says that the two of you used to sit in the back of the tour bus and
complain about what a lame company MGM was! (After their regional hit with
XL, the Pharaohs signed with MGM Records.)*
(laughs) Well, we didn't understand corporate. *(laughs)* I'm glad that I was
there, 'cause you know, I look at it now, man, and you talk about MGM, you
talk about *Gone With the Wind*! You're talkin' about people that really did
some classic stuff and back then I liked the way that lion roared! We had a
great time . . . you know, I did a tour with James Brown!

I believe it!
Did some dates with James Brown, uh, Pasadena and Oakland . . . I don't
think people knew where to put us, and it really didn't matter . . . we were
always doin' different things . . . I wore a turban and they wore sheets and
we just . . . showed up. Now I wore a beard and I don't know of any other
who wore an earring. Back then, if you wore an earring, you better be bad
enough to keep it in your ear. The Beatles started wearin' beards and earrings and now they got 'em in their nose and bellybuttons and everywhere.
I dunno, King Solomon said, "All is vanity." You gotta be careful you don't
start believin' your own promo!

*There weren't too many people with mustaches, let alone goatees . . . you shaved
off the beard for the* On Tour *album.*
We almost got hooked into that . . . you come to New York, "Let us fix

your image." Somebody told me once, "Be yourself and you'll never be by yourself." We went to Europe on the tour without the beard . . . man the folks freaked! But once they heard the music they knew it was us! At the Star Club in Hamburg, Germany, we were playin' there and we kicked off "Wooly Bully" and the joint went nuts! Beer bottles started goin' straight up in the air . . . beer bottles were breakin', "Hold it, wait a minute, Jack!" I recognized this from Louisiana, so I started easin' off to the side . . . the stage manager said, "That's what they do when they really like you."

I guess you guys did a lot of TV. Did you do American Bandstand *at all?*
I think so . . . no, *Where the Action Is. Hullabaloo*, the Supremes were on there, but I had the flu, and my voice broke when I went for the high note. Man, I had a hundred and somethin' temperature that night, couldn't quit 'cause it was your big shot. We couldn't get on the *Ed Sullivan Show* for a long time 'cause he thought we were Arabs. We just heard it rumored . . . we were doin' benefits for St. Jude Hospital, and we got to meet Danny Thomas, and somebody made the remark, "They won't let 'em on the *Ed Sullivan Show* 'cause he thinks they're Arabs!" Thomas said, "What?" And you know, Danny Thomas is Lebanese! For whatever reason, next thing you know, we get contacted to get on the *Ed Sullivan Show*, and he screwed that up: "And now Sam the Sham and the Pharaohs with 'Hully Gully.'" *(Both laugh)* Aw, man, wake up Eddie! When we were on that show, there was a troupe of forty Fiji Islanders wearin' grass skirts, carryin' spears or somethin'. We're all standin' backstage when their interpreter asks us, "What'll you do?" "Wooly Bully." That went like a current through the dancers. It was like a Tarzan movie — "WOOLYBULLY! WOOLYBULLY!" *(both laugh)*

Tell me about when you switched up and got the new lineup of Pharaohs?
David came to me and says, "I think I'm gonna go, Sam; we'd like to try it ourselves. Do you mind us usin' the name so we can . . ." I said, "Not at all." They got a release on MGM as the Pharaohs, and it didn't do much. But when they made their decision, I made mine; I flew the next day to New York and had another band. Of course, everybody thought, "Well, they was a spoof, because it was such a monster hit; he'll never do it again."

And that's when you came up with "Little Red Riding Hood"?
Yeah, so we recorded "Little Red Riding Hood." That was Frank Carabetta, Billy Bennett, Tony Gerace, and a guy by the name of Hahu *(Andy Kuha)*.

MGM tried to mold you into a novelty act after "Little Red Riding Hood."
That wasn't me. MGM misunderstood "Wooly Bully." After that we had

the Sam the Sham Revue *(with the female backups the Shamettes)*, and then things started waning . . . we had a little revue rollin'. Jimmy Page was with us when we did the Dick Clark tour with the Yardbirds, and he rode all over the country with us on a bus. After that, I backed off, man; I just needed a rest, went to acting school for a while. Then I was in England . . . I was over there by myself with an English band and Freddie King was there, John Lee Hooker was there, and we were in a pub and we were just hangin' out and we were all stayin' at the same hotel. Somebody walked up and said, "Sam! Sam the Sham!" I said yeah? He says, "Ahmet Ertegun with Atlantic

Records. What are you doin'?" I says, "I'm just . . . here." He says, "When you get back to New York, gimme a call." So when I got back, Jerry Wexler and Ahmet Ertegun took an interest and that's when I rode down to Miami to record . . .

On that motorcycle you're sitting on, on the cover?
Yeah, that was taken on the side of the highway with a Pentax. We put 500 miles on that baby that day. So, I got down there and they had some good pickers—the Dixie Flyers, Tommy McClure, Charlie Freeman, who's now dead, and the organ player Mike Utley, and the drummer *(Sammy)* Creason, they were the rhythm section. We recorded "Sam, Hard and Heavy." I wasn't implying that I was hard and heavy; we were gon' hit it hard and heavy.

You were billed as Sam Samudio. Were you, or Atlantic, trying to hide the fact that you were Sam the Sham?
I don't know; I just thought I'd do it under my own name. In other words, I'm not shammin' now. This is where I've been at. There was just an initial issue of that . . . the contract wasn't picked up; we couldn't agree.

Are you doing any of the lead guitar solos on that LP? (Sam is credited with playing guitar.)
Duane Allman and Charlie Freeman. Duane Allman was playin' on "Relativity," he really stretched out on that . . .

And there were those Grammy-winning liner notes that explained where you'd been.

I didn't do it to get an award or anything, you know? I'se just reevaluating a lot of things and I can't be angry at anybody. If nothin' else, I oughta thank 'em, even the folks that ran me outta town. If they hadn't run me outta town, I'd probably still be there! *(laughs)*

And you wouldn't be at the Grammy Awards, hangin' with Roger Miller and Neil Diamond in the lobby, jivin' around, when they called your name and said you won!

I had just had a tax problem there, I believe. I had just been notified and that tied up everything. My brother had sent me the money for me to rent a tuxedo . . . sure enough, I won. I'd been nominated before, twice . . .

. . . and you lost out to the Beatles and Herman's Hermits, I believe?

But the liner notes, I was in competition with Miles Davis, who had written his own liner notes, so I wasn't in light company.

So after '72, did you do the rock revival circuit?

I never did. It's okay, if somebody else wants to do 'em, but revive is when you die. I ain't dead. As a writer, I've yet my best song to write. As a singer, I've yet to sing my best song.

If memories were all you sang, you'd rather drive a truck, huh?

I recorded some dynamite *(unreleased)* stuff with Zappa's musicians, John Sebastian's musicians. It was real intense music. I remember walkin' into a record company president's chamber and I played this, he said, "No, no Sam. Bring me another 'Wooly Bully,' another 'Little Red Riding Hood.'"

I heard you were supposed to play at Max's Kansas City in the late seventies, but something happened . . .

That was at the last minute . . . there was no airfare, no nothin,' you know. That was supposed to be taken care of, and I know better than to get out on the road on a promise. I mean, I learned that from Chuck *(Berry)!* *(both laugh)* When I come in, that's a grand. When I open my box and start playin,' the price goes up!

What about the soundtrack to The Border, *that you did a couple of songs for, with Ry Cooder?*

Jim Dickinson was doin' a lot of work with him, as a player, and I was out on the water, I was workin' on a boat. They called my house, my wife at that time was a singer, Brenda Patterson. She had a great voice but people kept tryin' to make a Janis Joplin out of her. They wanted her to sing "Building Fires" on the soundtrack. Ry Cooder found out we were married; he says, "Man! Tell him to call me!" I had a song that I had written in Spanish *("No Quiero")* . . . he said, "Send me a copy." He told me what the story was, and I came home, sat down, and wrote "Palomita."

So how did you find God?

Well, I just got tired. I had it all together, but I couldn't remember where I left it! *(laughs)* I don't know, a lot of people have problems with the name Jesus . . . I had tried voodoo, candle burning; I studied sorcery with a Haitian woman, hand analysis, palm reading. I was all stretched out on that mess! I even had an alligator claw in my pocket! One day it just dawned on me, man, this ain't no lucky piece! The alligator had twenty of 'em and he didn't make it! *(both laugh)* One's not gonna do the trick! It just didn't quite make it. I decided, why ride second class? And I broke down and did it again, man—I was in a heap on the floor. I thought I was clean of coke; I said, "Lord, let me up." I said, "Forgive me, you gave me a talent, look what I've done, I've blown it, I just need help, forgive me." I felt such a peace come over me. A lot of my friends are still watchin' me; they say, "Sam is on a super scam 'cause he's cuttin' somethin' up!" *(both laugh)* You look around, you know there's somethin' fixin' to happen! The scripture speaks of it! Earthquakes in diverse places—look at Cobain. Catastrophes, calamities—look at the West Coast. Look at the East Coast. Look at wars and rumors of wars. It ain't gonna last. Why isn't it gonna last? The Scripture says it's not gonna last. I don't know about theology or all of that stuff, but I do know that this dope addict had a habit. When it got too thick, everybody thinned out. All I had to do was say, "Lord help me, I blew it, forgive me." Since that time in my life, I haven't done a toot, an ounce, a line, a gram, nothin'. At one time or another, everybody says, "God, if you're up there, help me out of this one, and I promise I'll do this and I'll do that," and then you get out there and forget about what you promised. But God doesn't forget.

Update

In the decade and a half since this interview Mr. Samudio has continued with his mission as a minister, but also has found time to play secular concerts (with a little gospel thrown in) on the nostalgia, blues, and even hipster circuits (he performed at the South by Southwest music conference in 2007). He has continued to write songs and record music in his Memphis home studio, self-releasing three CDs (of gospel, ballads, and country). A CD reissue of *Pharaohization!* (a best-of, beefed up with extra cuts that spotlight Sam as an all-around rocker and not a shallow court jester) garnered raves from *Living Blues* and *Blues Revue*, and he subsequently was hired to host *Beale St. Blues Caravan*, a syndicated radio show showcasing live concerts. In 2004 he was chosen to represent Memphis as a musical ambassador as part of their "50 Years of Rock 'n' Roll" ceremonies, and he has served as both a Grand Marshal and a pace car rider at Memphis NASCAR events. He is available for motivational speaking should you need it.

Interview conducted by
Jake Austen, Jacqueline Stewart,
and Ben Austen (2001)

The Good Rats

To the non–New Yorker, "Long Island" brings to mind images of extravagant Great Gatsby parties and "Jewish American Princesses" with nose jobs. But those moneyed masses come from Long Island's North Shore, and there is plenty of real estate with far lower property values elsewhere on the isle. For example, you certainly won't experience a country club atmosphere in Seaford when you're drinking drafts with biker chicks at the High Noon Saloon.

I'd long been a casual fan of Long Island's legendary rude rockers the Good Rats, and fate would turn that interest into a visit to the High Noon. Being familiar with the Rats' recording history (a stellar garage rock LP from the late '60s and a half dozen absurdly decadent '70s rock albums), I was surprised to find out from their website that they were still active. When I called their hotline and heard not only listings for countless upcoming live shows (including something called "Ratstock III") but also an unyielding rant in a heavy "New Yawk" accent against certain Rats fans for not being loyal enough, I was hooked. A New York visit the next week coincided with the High Noon hosting a series of Good Rats shows, so I made it my mission to get a grasp on what this band was all about.

Over the course of their career the Good Rats have been compared in print to Kiss, the Grateful Dead, the Music Machine, Journey, Cole Porter, Queen, Leatherwolf, the Turtles, Chuck Berry, Steely Dan, Frank Zappa, Blue Cheer, Rod Stewart, The Jimmy Castor Bunch, Van Halen, Extreme, and the 1959 B-horror flick, "The Killer Shrews." What's amazing is that *all* of these comparisons make perfect sense once you've listened to their albums. They've probably played as many shows as any rock band in history, they've released numerous albums, usually to positive critical response, and they shared stages with some of the biggest bands of the '70s. Yet the Good Rats remain virtually unknown outside of their tiny but intense cult following. "If the rest of the country was Long Island," Rats' drummer Joe Franco once lamented, "we'd be The Beatles."

Well, I doubt even if you scaled the Beatles down to Good Rats level that Ringo and his son would be rocking England's equivalent of the High Noon in 2001, but that's London's loss. Because the Rats (original songwriter/singer Peppi Marchello, joined by his sons Gene on guitar and Stefan "The Weasel" on drums, with nonrelative Denis Perry on bass) *rawked* the house. Mind you, the house being rawked was a tiny bar with a "stage" only big enough for a drum kit, and rawking consisted of Peppi standing in the middle of the floor looking less like a rock star and more like a well-fed Teamster in shorts, a T-shirt, and huge sunglasses ("I'm not wearing these because I think I'm cool; it's my allergies . . . it's like a million spiders going up my nose . . ."). Ignoring the venue's shortcomings, the shoulder-to-shoulder crowd responded with the kind of fervor usually reserved for a stadium concert. Every classic Good Rats song was seemingly their favorite, and every new tune was given full respect.

Though Peppi describes Good Rats fans as "everyone from bikers to dentists, captains of industries to the guys in jail for rape and murder," the High Noon looked like it was short on CEOs that night. The crowd of a 150 rabid "Rat-Heads" consisted mostly of the Harley-riding variety, but that doesn't mean they didn't have sophisticated tastes. Despite Peppi's rough edges it's very easy to see, even in a dark bar, that he's an unusual talent, gifted with the intangible magnetism most classic frontmen possess, and also with an excellent gravelly voice perfect for expressing a full range of sincere, soulful sentiments. It's also clear that his songwriting is beyond what you expect from a bar band. Even if you don't love the tunes, it's hard to deny that the craftsmanship is equal to or better than commercially successful radio songs.

It's sometimes difficult to notice how good the songs are because of Peppi's oversized personality. His stage persona is that of a smart-mouthed, neighborhood tough guy (a writer once described him as "SOOO Italian, you want to just puke spaghetti!" and pointed out that the band sold shirts saying "Music so loud, it gives you *Agita*"). But the fans see beyond his hooligan exterior. When Peppi went into his dramatic ballad "Man on a Fish" the crowd was completely entranced, with one behemoth of a biker—not a weekend warrior, this was a six-foot-five-inch hairy beast—literally weeping. But even if you happened to miss those tears of a goon you wouldn't have been allowed to not know the score, because after the song Peppi declared, "See, not only am I the greatest rock 'n' roll singer . . . *but I am also the world's greatest balladeer!*" Obviously this was a very special man. We were more than honored to sit down over pizza slices and hear him tell his story.

Born in Brooklyn into a working-class, first-generation Italian American family (his grandparents came from Sicily), Peppi moved to the island when he was seven. His parent's American Dream of upward mobility was seemingly furthered when Peppi became a college boy, going to St. John's on a baseball scholarship. A bout of rheumatic fever at age thirteen had wiped out hopes of a pro ball career, but he enjoyed playing and it kept him in school, which made his folks happy, even if his heart wasn't in his studies.

When the Beatles hit, and guys started playing guitars in the cafeteria, Peppi, who previously was into swing music, decided to give rock 'n' roll a

chance. "Did you ever see when the Beatles came into Idlewild *(airport, now named JFK)*? I was one of those guys yelling 'Get a haircut!' But I was kidding around; I really liked them. We started a little band at school. The guitarist was this guy Eric, very handsome; all the girls loved him. Someone came up and said, 'You guys want to play in our church?' We said, 'Sure.' We must have been terrible, playing Beatles songs mostly, maybe one or two originals. We were called the U-Men, for University Men. And the response was so tremendous; the girls were yelling and screaming. We thought we were talented guys, but it was because this guy Eric was so handsome. Well nonetheless, from then on I said, this is what I want to do, go into music. At St. John's I was a biology major. My parents thought I was going to go on to become a doctor."

Eric became the first pothead Marchello ever met and quickly stopped showing up for practice, so Peppi recruited his little brother Mickey to take over guitar duty. "My brother was five years younger than me, fifteen years old, he knew the songs. At that time you needed a cabaret license and had to be eighteen to play in bars, so I forged his birth certificate and driver's license. My mother thought as long as he was with me it was all right; I was not a crazy kid, you know. So we were playing all the bars, and then I informed my parents that medical school was not for me. I'm not even going to classes anymore, I'm hiding out upstairs where they have pianos at the

different music departments, learning how to play and write songs. When I told my parents I didn't want to go to medical school my father freaked out and knocked me into every closet; it could have been a scene in any Italian movie. My father was a little guy, looked like the guy on *Taxi*. My mother was going 'You're going to give me a heart attack.' So anyways, as soon as he got tired of hitting me he said, 'So you're going to finish up school and go to medical school, right?' I said, 'What was this all about?'"

This was 1966. Soon after Marchello quit school, the U-Men's lead singer was drafted into Vietnam, and Peppi became the frontman. "Before that he was the lead singer; I was the guy with the Italian voice to fill in the ballads. When I became lead I'd scream in a towel to try to get a raspier voice. I started writing some songs; they were awful. By then I was running into the city all the time, with whatever demo we could make, knocking on doors. Finally found two guys who were interested in the songs. They got us a record deal, and they proceeded to take everything."

Rob Haffkine and Barry Oslander were producers who possibly saw in the Good Rats a chance to establish themselves as superproducers, in the Phil Spector, Don Kirshner, or Kasenetz-Katz mold. Open up the gatefold sleeve of *The Good Rats* (1969), and you'll see two huge portraits of Ron and Barry and a third one of them in action, talking on the phone, and "producing." Tiny pictures of the band appear hanging off the tail of the giant rat gracing the cover. The words "A Ron Haffkine and Barry Oslander Production" appear in boldface bigger than the song titles. The band members' names do not appear.

An action shot of Haffkine and Oslander producing from the Good Rats gatefold.

"Ever see the cover where they're giant and we're tiny? That kind of represents the way they thought the money situation should be, too. We didn't get anything for that record. We were the band, writing stuff, but they have the publishing, and they have their pictures on the album cover. They ought to be embarrassed about it because to this day I've never seen producers pictured on an album, let alone that big."

The band was still called The U-Men when they were signed. But at that point to have a college dropout and his fake-ID-bearing brother in a band called the University Men mocked the Marchello parents' aspirations, so perhaps it was a good thing when the producers insisted on a name change. "There was the Animals, the Byrds, the Yardbirds, the Beatles . . . we wanted to be an animal like everyone else, so since we're from New York we decided we'll be Rats." Not quite comfortable with the rodent connotations H & O convinced the boys to add the "Good," but Peppi stood his ground when the producers insisted "Rats" should be spelled "Ratz." The producers had the last laugh, though, as the band logo on the album cover was a hand-scrawled graffiti job, with the *S* backward, making it essentially a *Z*.

When they began recording the album, Peppi was enchanted with the Animals and his songwriting was heavily influenced by Eric Burdon's blues-style tales of adversity. As on all subsequent Good Rats LPs, Peppi wrote all the songs, with the one exception on the debut being a song he cowrote with his new bride ("She never got a royalty either, but we're still together

. . . when you think about it she's the real producer of the new band—I'm playing with two sons"). Peppi had been married shortly before the photos for the album cover were shot, and if you look closely at his tiny picture you'll see he's wearing pasted-on fake sideburns ("I had to be cleanshaven for the wedding; I looked like *Dustin Hoffman!*"). What also felt fake to him were the arrangements of his songs. To Peppi's dismay the producers had the entire album orchestrated with strings and horns galore. "This was not as heavy as the band was playing."

Despite Peppi's misgivings *The Good Rats* is a phenomenal LP. Though many Rats fanatics ignore this album, considering the vastly different lineup that recorded *Tasty* four years later the real Good Rats, a comparable number of psychedelic/garage collectors only recognize this LP and forego listening to the slicker '70s stuff. Whatever the case, one would be hard-pressed to not love an album that starts off with a theme song that explains that despite rats being a "symbol of hate since the beginning of time," *these guys* are the *good* rats. Combining heavy, weird sludge rock with cartoon soundtrack music and a Dixieland break, the originality of this declaration of rattiness is undeniable. As the song ends with motorcycle sound effects and *Pong*-like electronic noises, it segues into arguably the Rats finest tune ever.

"Joey Ferrari," based on a neighborhood character, is one of the best rock 'n' roll ballads of all time. By ballad I don't mean love song, but rather *ballad* in the traditional Middle Ages / folk song sense, where the epic story of a hero or god is told in verse. What differentiates a true rock 'n' roll ballad from an old-timey one is the lack of action. Because the foolish immediacy of youth and the importance of *right now* are key elements of rock 'n' roll, instead of do (as in *do* great things) the subject of the rock 'n' roll ballad merely has to be (as in *be* cool as hell). Chuck Berry's hero "Johnny B. Goode" or Bikini Kill's heroine "Rebel Girl" may eventually do something in the future ("*maybe someday* your name will be in lights") but they aren't being celebrated in song for their accomplishments, but rather for their awesome presence.

"Joey Ferrari was a guy that worked in a gas station next to a bar that we played and rehearsed at. Just a greasy kind of an Italian kid, a mechanic, nice guy, heart of gold. I told him, 'I'm going to write a song about you.'" The "heart of gold" aspect didn't make it into the final mix. With "a chip on his shoulder bringing him down" Joey was "raising hell all over town" and "looking for trouble wherever he goes *(in)* black shiny shoes and secondhand clothes." Peppi warns him that "the world's gonna wipe off that smile." Overall the lyrics achieve an amazing balance of sounding tough and dumb while actually painting a three-dimensional portrait of a not-so-simple character. But even if the lyrics had been gibberish, this hard-rocking, up-tempo (faster than you expect from anything this heavy) punk rock battle cry would still whoop ass like a bike chain in a rumble. Peppi's singing takes it to another level, showcasing one of the Good Rat's greatest strengths: a juxtaposition of comic book absurdity and completely sincere delivery.

Despite the rough-hewn portrait being painted of him, the real Ferrari loved the song and bought ten copies of the album. Peppi himself still recognizes the greatness of the tune, having recently recut it with his sons.

The rest of the LP also holds up well. "The Hobo" is an interesting post–Summer of Love tune, a working-class outsider's take on Hippie values ("I'm a Hobo, no account, living free"). Peppi's love of the Animals shines through on some Burden-esque tunes, including "My Back Is Achin' (And My Mind Is No Better)." And the most dramatic tune is certainly "For the Sake of Anyone," where Peppi relates in dire tones that "He was a good father to me even though he was dirt poor. I never once heard him complain . . . his whole life was my mother; he could never satisfy her . . ." As the melodramatic song climaxes, tragedy and suicide and revenge all build to an explosive boil, ending with the singer's howling return home to his evil mother.

"I guess I was very much like the black guys today who come from suburbia but act like they have a chip on their shoulder. That song about the guy whose mother cheated on her husband and the husband killed himself . . . my mom and dad are both alive and they're very good people. This is just what you write about."

The Good Rats in many ways wasn't as different from later Rats' work as it seems. Though Peppi believes the orchestral flourishes mar his vision, the excessive, schizophrenic blending of styles and genres achieved by the strings and horns here would be a recurring theme on most of the band's best work to come.

The album did nothing professionally for the boys, resulting in empty pockets, no tour, and a cloud of disappointment that caused all the non-Marchello members to leave the band. However the Kapp LP definitely made a couple of notable impressions. Most importantly the press the band got legitimized the pursuit of rock 'n' roll in their mother's eyes (crucial for a band living at home and practicing in the basement). On the more ridiculous tip, a billboard of the cover art, with the boys hanging off the tail of a huge rat, appeared around New York, and had to quickly be removed because neighbors complained about the unpleasant presence of a fifty-foot rodent.

Mickey and Peppi (referred to in the 'hood as Heckle and Jeckle for their jet black, straightened hair) went through numerous Rats over the next few years, trying to assemble a group with some chemistry. Eventually they met bass player Lenny Kotke, who brought with him a great guitar player, Mike Raff, and a college boy drummer, Joe Franco. Though Raff was a strong guitarist who drew positive attention to the band, Peppi recalls, "He just didn't have any brains in his head. My brother eventually had to beat him up and send him on his way.

"Mike Raff just had to go; this guy was unbelievable. On the hottest day of the year we were waiting in my basement for practice, and he never showed up, never called. Finally we got him on the phone, he said, 'It's really hot today—I went out to get an air conditioner.' 'I know it's hot, we're down here for five hours, it's a hundred degrees, you couldn't call and say I can't make it?' You know this guy thought he was a real tough guy from Brooklyn. Mickey beat the hell out of him and the guy was crying."

The apparently not-so-tough Raff was soon replaced by John "the Cat" Gatto, "this perfect guitar player, real good guy," and the lineup for the rest of the decade was in place. The Rats began gigging constantly, developing a huge fan base and honing their skills considerably. Soon the Rat style was established. What differentiates them from many of their '70s contemporaries is that at the heart of everything they did, no matter how poetic or self-important it might get, the Rats were regular guys. Their shows didn't climax with lasers and explosions but with Peppi emptying a garbage can of rubber rats into the crowd. These were guys you would drink a beer and watch a game with (Peppi tossing an oversized football around the stage, or swinging—and air-guitaring—a baseball bat play on this sports fan theme). They earned a rep for jamming onstage, but not in artistic or trippy ways; they kept it playful and lively for the blue-collar rock fan.

Most importantly, they were never pretty boys; the Good Rats wallowed in their ugliness, playing in street clothes, with beards and long hair . . . but never looking like hippies. Peppi wore his unkempt mane at every length imaginable over the years, sometimes topped by a wool cap with the words "Rat On!" Most memorably, Mickey grew his beard as long and bushy as a mountain man while keeping his hair short. Though their music often related to the grandness of the glam stadium acts, if you even suggested these guys wear makeup or tights you'd likely face the fate of "tough guy" Mike and his air conditioner. The ugliness was driven home by Peppi's signature stage shtick——he'd yell at and abuse the audience viciously, to their undying delight.

Their antics, look, and sound drew attention. "Eventually we ran into a guy who was working at a radio station and selling drugs. He knew people at Warner Brothers and then, believe it or not, Warner Brothers records signed us and we did the *Tasty* record."

Their great fortune was hard for the boys to believe, and they were sure they were on easy street from then on. "Warner Brothers records? Bugs Bunny? That was the most impressive thing to me about Warner Brothers. They had drawn this great-looking rat and put him next to Bugs Bunny. What kid wouldn't think he'd arrived. Bugs Bunny and Good Rats together on a T-shirt?"

Nineteen-seventy-four's *Tasty* had sleeve art featuring that rat, a grotesque cartoon rodent bloated on delicious garbage. Despite the comical cover, this was a very serious endeavor for the boys, one that Peppi and his Rat brethren still consider their crowning glory. Moving away from the raw garage foundation of their debut, the Rats were now a bizarre combination of prog, boogie, jazz fusion, uptown, big band, and bar rock. Having honed their skills with nonstop gigging they were supertight, with Mickey and "The Cat" playing twin leads. Peppi still kept it dumb at times, but most of the album featured poetic, literate lyrics, the best poetry being about rock 'n' roll itself (including "Songwriter," a tearjerker where Peppi tells it like it is about telling it like it is). In addition to his writing skills, this album also demonstrates what's great about Peppi's voice. It sounds rough and gruff like a been-there/done-that bluesman (or the English equivalent thereof) but it also has a cleanness and sensitivity that infuses even the rockers with the heart-tugging power of a love song. The best tune on the album, "Fireball Express" could have easily been a coarse, thundering metal monolith if Bruce Dickinson or Rob Halford sang it. But with Peppi's voice it maintains that urgency and power while keeping a patina of class. Mind you, this isn't fundamentally an album about classiness; it's about nastiness . . . but it's about nastiness with class! *Rolling Stone* praised them as "musicians in a time when non-musicians (The Dolls) are thought of as brilliant." Of course, Robot Hull in *Creem* said pretty much the opposite, but the way *Creem* reviews were written he probably never took the shrink wrap off the record.

Unfortunately the tenure at Warners was brief. After a short West Coast tour (where they met and jammed a version of Billy Cobham's "Stratus" with Tommy Bolin, as heard on *The Tommy Bolin Archives: Bottom Shelf, Vol. 1*), they returned home to find that they had been dropped. "We had the reputation of being either the East Coast Doobie Brothers or the New York's Grateful Dead because of the loyalty of our fans. *Tasty* got tremendous reviews and was starting to catch on; then they just said, 'This is under a certain amount of sales,' and dropped us. So we were devastated. That was the first time I was devastated, finding out we were dropped by a label. I've been devastated many times since.

"People think when they get a record deal they have it made; you haven't made it until the check has cleared and people all over recognize you. We eventually got the rights back to *Tasty* and reissued it many, many times, and *Tasty* always does great for us."

Unlike the aftermath of their previous disappointing record label experience, this time the Rats were stronger and more united, and committed themselves to a "Do-It-Yourself" attitude. This was fueled by rocking huge crowds every night of the week, as locally they played clubs like My Father's Place, the 2,000 capacity Hammerheads, CBGB's, and the Bottom Line. There were countless other places to rock in New York State, Jersey, and Connecticut, at the time. To a band today it's hard to believe that an unsigned act could play to a thousand people regularly and be considered a bar band, but the 1970s were a magical age. "You see it was a different world physically. There were a lot more people at the age of partying. There are many more Baby Boomers than there are Generation X-ers. Number 1, we were dealing with baby boomers. Number 2, the drinking age was eighteen; now it's twenty-one. Number 3, the cops used to look the other way, and now they're looking for you. This was a time when everybody was partying. We were working six or seven nights a week, primarily in the tri-state area. This is the most populated area in the country, and any direction four hours from where we live, we could still get home that night and not run up big bills. You know I have a family and I wanted to come home at night and sleep in my own bed with my wife. So we were able to do very, very well, play bigger clubs, and we played every night."

In '75 they started looking around again and got the attention of Danny Goldberg, "the big muckety-muck" who was also working with Led Zeppelin, and would go on to manage Nirvana and start Artemis Records, home of "Who Let the Dogs Out." The Rats also eventually became involved with David Sonenberg, Meatloaf's manager. Their new high-profile management couldn't drum up any interest from the major labels, but encouraged the band to start their own. Ratcity Records became viable when Peppi's soulful voice helped them land a distribution deal with All Platinum, Sylvia Robinson's R&B label, that had scored with Shirley and Company's disco hit "Shame, Shame, Shame."

"They had a fight with Shirley and brought me in to sing on the follow-up, 'I Like to Dance.' Topless dancers used to come up to me and say, 'Oh yeah, we dance to that all the time.'" Peppi's foray into disco / lap dance music helped get their third album heard when Ratcity/Platinum's *Ratcity In Blue* was released in 1976.

The album opens with the mighty "Does It Make You Feel Good," a rocker that brings to mind the best Peter and Ace KISS material. Peppi's raspy, soulful vocals complement the heavy pop grooves, and as a bonus he rhymes "cigarette wrapper" with "Venus Flytrapper." The rest of the album is a bizarre collage that goes from "Boardwalk Slasher," which sounds like a Journey song about a serial killer, to the title track, which sounds like a Manhattan Transfer tune about heroin. At points the album can be accurately described as "boogie prog." The ballads, the tributes to high and low culture (Bach, Bowie, and Bogart are all name checked) and the hooks are all on point. "Writing the Pages" is a three-minute tune about Hitler's inner dialogue during the one second between the bullet entering his head and death. Not exactly average bar band subject material. The cover art featured a classy rat in top hat and tails against the NYC skyline, and the dust sleeve featured a pizza with the Good Rats' ugly mugs as pepperonis.

The Rats toured the US supporting the album, and their skills and management's clout eventually scored a deal with Passport Records, which was distributed by Arista. For their next album they even had name producers, Mark Volman and Howard Kaylan a.k.a. Flo & Eddie.

The association with Flo & Eddie was a natural one; both acts dealt with absurdity while fully respecting the sanctity of rock 'n' roll, and both acts could really sing harmonies. It also represented a potential breakthrough for the Rats. Though Flo and Eddie, like the Rats, were not in possession of Teen Idol prettiness, they had conquered two arenas that Marchello and Co. hungered for. As the Turtles they achieved legitimate chart success, with the perpetual royalties that go along with it. Working with Frank Zappa they also knew the ins and outs of international, sustained cult appeal, something that exists a few rungs above being able to pack tri-state-area showcase rooms. While that circuit provided good short-term money (Flo and Eddie were surprised to see the Rats pulling in more dough then they were), it was definitely time to take it to another level. They hoped 1978's optimistically titled *From Rats to Riches* was going to do just that.

While Peppi stands behind *Tasty*, I have to back *Rats to Riches* as the classic lineup's finest recorded moment. The Flo and Eddie production must have provided a little something extra, as this is a superfun, ridiculous slab of rock 'n' roll voodoo. The sweet-sounding "Just Found Me a Lady" and the rockin' rollercoaster "Mr. Mechanic" (both released as singles) are two of their best tunes ever. "Taking It to Detroit" is a postmodern reconfiguration of "Detroit Rock City" (that actually mentions KISS's tune in the lyrics). "Victory in Space" manages to work in references to both Great Neck and Entenmann's baked goods.

The two most powerful songs lyrically have pretty good narratives behind them. "Don't Hate the Ones That Bring You Rock & Roll" was actually written for another "Winning Ugly" New York–area club act, Twisted Sister. The song is a plea to hecklers to appreciate the truly important folks. "Hate your mommies, hate your daddies . . . hate the rich oil companies . . . but don't hate the ones who bring you rock & roll!" The verses feature epithets hurled at the band by player hater "fans," including lyrics like, "Son of a bitch . . . prancing around like a goddam faggot." Twisted guitarist Jay Jay French was uncomfortable with the harsh language, so the tune, which actually works the words "twisted sisters" into the lyrics, ended up staying with the Rats.

"I said to them, 'You guys are the bad boys of rock 'n' roll and you're afraid to sing these lyrics?'" Peppi chuckles recalling the incident. "Dee Snider was watching us for nine years before he started yelling and cursing at the people like I was."

The other interesting song on *Rats to Riches* is "Dear Sir." The distribution deal they signed had Arista handling the album, and Peppi knew from the start that Clive Davis didn't know what the hell to do with the Good Rats. "We were never an Arista band. Who was the Michael Bolton before there was a Michael Bolton? Barry Manilow! Clive Davis knew *that* kind of stuff. He didn't know our songs, and we weren't about to change." "Dear Sir" is a musical open letter to Davis ("I'd rather clean the cages at the zoo than change my songs for you").

The Rats were soon enjoying a tremendous industry buzz, and more great reviews, but again nothing happened. Maybe Davis did drop the ball, mishandling the band's career, releasing the wrong singles, mucking up the promotions. But perhaps they were the victims of a self-fulfilling prophecy . . . what do you expect a man to do when you call him out on your record?

When the nutty approach didn't make them superstars, the decision was made to go serious. Peppi had been working on a play about a counselor in an old-age home who begins to resent the old people he fears becoming and his children who he can't be. The Rats' management decided to morph the material into a concept album about the different stages of life. Goldberg and Sonenberg listened to over 100 Peppi-penned tunes and handpicked what they felt were the top 10. Sonenberg arranged for the Rats to open for Meatloaf at Hammersmith in England and then do some recording for the new album at the Who's Rampart Studios. With the lavish production and tasteful material combined with good management, promotion, booking, and distribution, the new album represented the Rats best chance yet.

Unlike previous albums, *Birth Comes to Us All* (Passport, 1978) features cover art that is subdued and "classy," with a painting of a newborn baby's foot on the front and photos of the Rats as Greek busts matched with their pastel-tinted baby pictures on the back. The dust sleeve features a photo of Peppi's young child, Rat-to-Be Gene Marchello. Not the strongest Rats album, *Birth* nonetheless has its highlights, including the Queen-like "Juvenile Song," the upbeat "School Days" and "Man on a Fish," the tune that still makes Harley riders weep. But overall the package removed from the Rats what made them Rats; tastelessness, crudeness, and ugliness. This was a band that insulted the audiences while throwing rubber rats . . . all of a sudden they were sensitive? While Peppi had always mixed in literate songwriting with the goofiness, this swung the scales way too far toward maturity.

Though they performed the material to a crowd of 3,000-plus at a triumphant charity concert at the Palladium (in which little Gene made his stage debut), *Birth* would, again, not be the breakthrough they waited for. Some critics praised it, but the *Village Voice*'s lambasting (calling it "fatally tasteful" while hoping the Rats "don't piss away the emotional credibility they earned" as never-say-die bar rockers) may have been closer to the opinion of many Rats fans. Needless to say the record didn't deliver the Rats to the mainstream, and soon after its release the Rats were once again divorced from a record label.

Their last big shot blown the Rats were on their own again and they went to where they were loved . . . the clubs. For evidence of their rock prowess, check out the self-released *Live at Last* (Ratcity, 1980), a double LP recorded at My Father's Place in Roslyn, a showcase room where Bruce Springsteen, U2, and the Police played to modest crowds on the way up. "It was the type of place where you see a band and six months later you see them at the Coliseum . . . unless they were the Good Rats. The Ramones opened up for us, Blondie, the Talking Heads. Cyndi Lauper, the Cars. There was a time that everyone that opened up for us became big stars within a year. We tried to figure out how we could open up for ourselves." The way this confident album sounds, it's hard to believe the band had such self-doubts. Recorded raw enough to capture the live energy but slick enough to showcase the tight harmonies, this is a good document of the crowd-pleasing live madness. It was also the end of an era as the "original" Rat lineup decided to call it quits, and Peppi and Mickey had to draw from the locals to fill out the Rat lineup for the first time since the early '70s.

In 1981 they released what would be their last LP of the twentieth century, *Great American Music*. Though the classic lineup is gone, Bruce Kulick (who later played with Michael Bolton and then spent over fifteen years in KISS) on guitar and Skyler Deal on bass replaced Lenny and John, and provided a lot of *oomph*. *Rolling Stone* gave *Great American Music* a glowing review, saying they finally captured their live energy in the studio. Peppi's songwriting is solid on this, and rather than going the concept album route this LP is an exercise in writing what you know. "Great American Music Halls," "Audience," and "Rock and Roll Point of View" are all rock *about* rock (*Village Voice* once derisively said that Peppi's most moving works deal, "with his anger that nobody's buying his records").

Of course the band was still playing out constantly, but the chemistry wasn't there. Kulick's heart wasn't in it (he later complained he felt like a hired hand with little creative input, a role he played without complaints, but with a lot more compensation, with KISS) and the band took its biggest blow when Mickey decided he had enough.

And here is where the story gets "Twisted." The early '80s saw one of the Good Rats' contemporaries, Twisted Sister, get a break after a decade of toiling in the same tri-state bar circuit. They became multiplatinum sellers, partially with the help of Peppi's obnoxious influence on Dee, and it was time for the bands to help each other out again. The Good Rats came to Twisted's rescue by providing a new drummer, former Good Rat Joe Franco. Twisted's helping hand to Peppi would be much more profound.

Record exec Jason Flom championed Twisted Sister and became influential at Atlantic for it (he later made it back to the top with Lava Records and Kid Rock). Jason asked Twisted Sister if they knew anybody that wrote great songs, and Twisted recommended Peppi. Jason loved what he heard, and Peppi remarkably ended up getting his own solo record deal without auditioning on the strength of the songs.

Peppi hit the studio recording his album and also was put to work writing and producing Atlantic's recent signing, lite-metal chick Fiona's 1985 debut album *Fiona* (the girl must have had a rodent fetish, because her next producer was Ratt's Beau Hill). After the Fiona record was released to moderate success, Atlantic president Doug Morris took Peppi in his office and praised his work, played him some unreleased tracks by new signee Julian Lennon (dating Fiona at the time), and acted like Peppi had the keys to the castle.

"I told my wife, 'I'm in!' I couldn't even dream of getting a guy like Morris, the president of Atlantic, on the phone, and now he's calling up my house—this is amazing." But it wasn't amazing for long. Morris ultimately decided Peppi was too old and his look wouldn't cut it.

The record was never released, but somehow the tapes went over to CBS. Someone at Epic called Peppi and revealed that he was a Good Rat fan. He set up a showcase. Peppi wasn't gigging with the Good Rats at the time, so the showcase couldn't feature the Rats. However, he performed every now and then under a different moniker that would lead to the next bizarre chapter in Ratstory.

"What happened was we did a thing called Pop's a Rocker with me and Gene." Gene Marchello, last seen as a bowl-cut-coifed adolescent on the *Birth* dust sleeve, was now a hot lickin' axeman in his own right. His Van Halen / Randy Rhodes–influenced chops were a marvel to behold, and the novelty of the father/son act was a good one, especially considering the regular guy / family man foundation that much of Peppi's work is based upon. When the Epic bigwig came to see Peppi's album performed live, Pop's a Rocker was the band he saw.

"The Rat fan from Epic brought down his boss, who looked at me and said the guy's an old guy but the kid's a great-looking kid, so he ended up giving Gene the record deal. Had it been a stranger, I woulda been like so jealous. I just shrugged my shoulder and said, 'It's my son!'"

Since the Good Rats should be considered fundamentally the work of songwriter Peppi, had his solo album come out it would have essentially been a Good Rats record. But now the exact set of songs he recorded for Atlantic was being rerecorded by Gene with some '80s heavy metal polish on it, and production by Peppi. The band's name was Marchello, but it's not a stretch to call 1989's *Destiny* a Good Rats album.

Destiny featured arguably the last great Metal album cover; a painting/collage of a half rock-slut / half demon standing on a pedestal in a postapocalyptic landscape. The only thing missing was an ornate logo, as sadly "Marchello" was spelled out in plain white type. The album was light if you think of it as metal, but fairly heavy for a Rats record. Though some absurdity survived ("Heavyweight Champion of Love," "Rock 'n' Roll Rumble") for the most part this is played straight, delivering a solid slab of rock for the kids. The album was well received by Metal fans who didn't mind some Journey with their Yngwie. "First Love" was the MTV video (and a grass-roots hit), and the band got to open for Ozzy, Extreme, and others during their run. Though Peppi had pretty much completely crafted the album, Gene was heavily involved in writing the follow-up when the grunge ax fell.

As the '90s bloomed, all label rosters had the hair bands replaced with Seattle moaners. Gene got dropped the night the US invaded Iraq. "The second Marchello record we did with Sony, I wrote half, Gene wrote the other half, and they got the guy who did Firehouse to produce it. They spent like $300,000 dollars on it, and then they bring in a new guy named Griffith to the Epic side and he dropped Gene and twenty-five other artists. We worked three years of our life on that record; we got a shot with the biggest record company in the world and they rip your soul out, your heart out. It's the nature of the business."

"I just had one of those careers; I'm looking forward to the second half . . ."

The second half may be well under way as the last few years have been pretty active for the Rats, with none of the Marchello boys needing day jobs. "After the Epic deal I said to Gene, 'Why don't you come and play with me again?' We've been playing ever since, and then Stefan joined the band a number of years ago playing drums. They both lived through the Mickey syndrome. In other words, Mickey was playing with me when he was fifteen years old, Gene was playing with me when he was fourteen, and Stefan joined when he was fifteen. So it was always my underage brother, underage sons playing with me."

The most significant Rat development since the reformation was the recording and self-releasing of a new album, *Tasty Seconds* (Uncle Rat Music, 1996). The CD is a great showcase for the talents of Peppi and Gene, and the disc is rounded out with a guest appearance by Bruce "no hard feelings" Kulick. "Cover of the Night" is a mighty rock anthem, "Football Madness" is absurd Jock Rock, and "Major Minor Chord" delivers like one of the old-time complex Rat-sterpieces. Throughout the album Peppi's rough-hewn vocals and (theoretically) commercial songwriting shine.

In 1998 the "original" lineup (Peppi, Mickey, Kotke, Franco, and "The Cat") reunited in a Rochester biker bar for a (roughly) Twenty-Fifth Anniversary show. As the new century dawned, they kept busy with new recordings and some serious touring.

"We're the hardest-working band. You saw that beat-up van out there; we drove nineteen hours straight to Nashville, played two shows, somebody says we want you to play; if we can work it out well, work it out. We play prisons in Pennsylvania; we did eighteen in twenty-two days. You go in there and most of these guys haven't seen a rock 'n' roll band in a long time. It's a tough, tough gig. We're not going to do a lot of Good Rats stuff; we'll do Sabbath—that's what some of them want—but primarily the prisoners are black, so you're playing for guys that don't like rock 'n' roll to begin with. We were walking through a cellblock; it looked like the TV show

Oz, and a guy came up to me and said, 'You got nerve coming in here without any women in the band,' because what do you think they're going to be doing that night? We played a girl's prison, and I said to the guys, 'How do you like it; you're going to be in their sexual thoughts tonight.' Only the Good Rats would do gigs like this. It's pretty hard for the band members to bitch and moan, though, because two of the guys are still living under my roof."

Even more ambitious than their Lockdown Tour is Ratstock. "Because so many of our fans have been around so many years, they have children of all ages. Guys have been married three times; they have two-year-old sons and thirty-year-old sons. And they all tell me they play our music and their kids all sing the songs 'hate your mommies, hate you daddies,' 'Coo Coo Coo Blues,' goofy stuff like that. They'd like to bring the kids to see us but the shows are always in beat-up bars, so we decided to do Ratstock, a campsite thing with two days of rock 'n' roll. People show up with their families; we had fifteen or sixteen that came from Michigan last year. For me it's like being a guru; all the kids run up and say, 'There's Peppi, there's Peppi!' because they know my songs. It's a great feeling. Each year it gets bigger and better . . . this year is Ratstock III. Ratstock is the only place where parents allow their children to sing a song like 'Mean Motherfucker.' I tell the kids, 'You guys watch the WWF . . . come up on stage and when I say *Mean Motherfucker*, you guys pose like your favorite wrestler.' It's the only time the parents say, 'Go crazy—have a good time.' This might be the last Ratstock, though, if this new album takes off."

Which brings us back to the High Noon Saloon. In addition to fresh material they've recorded for their new CD, they've also been in the studio rerecording some old hard-rocking tracks, so Peppi has the band "debut" the song "Joey Ferrari" to the crowd. As they rip through the raucous punk portrait, I'm overwhelmed with excitement . . . *I can't believe I'm hearing the Good Rats play "Joey Ferrari!"* In the afterglow of the song I hear the biker who welled up during "Man on a Fish" explain to the next barstool that the song came from their rare first LP, and I can't help but hope against hope that somehow the new album, or something down the pike, works out for the Good Rats. Sure Peppi's fifteen years older than the last time they told him he was too old, sure Gene may not be over his major label snubbing, sure contemporary radio rock is miles away from anything the Rats do, but it sure would be nice if something worked out. Then again, there's something nice about what they're doing right now. I see a hundred rock shows a year and this is one of the best I've attended, and the reaction from the Rat faithful to the Marchellos is REAL! No matter what happens next and no matter what happened during the last thirty-five years, when you see the loyalty and love and joy the fans bring to the Good Rats it's hard to conclude that their tale is anything but a rock 'n' roll success story.

Update

Not long after this article's publication, the Good Rats made another stab at mainstream success by changing their name to Dum and promoting a novelty drinking song (with a video and CD art that obscured Peppi's involvement, focusing on his young, telegenic sons). After that fizzled, the band had another setback in 2003, when Peppi had to spend long months off the bar circuit as he recuperated from open-heart surgery. But the Good Rats are now back on the tri-state scene, playing up to a hundred shows a year at joints like Joey D's, Orphan Annie's, and the Nutty Irishman. The roster has now morphed, as Gene left his father's band to become Bono in the tribute band 2U, "The World's 2nd Best U2 Show." Though Peppi is saddened that the gig does not allow Gene to play guitar, he's  proud of his son's success (in 2011 Disney booked 2U to play a week at EPCOT Center). In 2008 the Good Rats, along with Blue Öyster Cult and Beverly Sills, were inducted into the Long Island Music Hall of Fame. In 2010 the Rats rocked the Catskills for Ratstock XII, continuing a tradition of turning beautiful campsites into dingy Long Island bars, and in 2008 the band started a new tradition, as the classic 1970s Good Rats lineup rocked a packed house for the first of the now annual reunion shows at B. B. King in Manhattan.

Zolar X

I believe aliens *have* landed on earth. Like Roswell and all that crap. I saw a show about it on TV. But what I can't understand is *Why? Why* this particular pile of dirt? Why *Earth*?

Take Superman, as one fictional (?) example. He's this amazing superbeing from a very advanced race. You'd think he'd have the pick of all the planets out there, but he winds up on our dump heap where everyone is always getting into trouble, and where the two most significant native intelligences are both gunning for him. I refer to Lex Luthor, and the true criminal mastermind of our lousy race: *Lois Lane*. At the end of the day, I bet Kal-El felt pretty screwed over.

Likewise for Zory Zenith. He came to Earth on a peaceful mission of hope and love, and look where he ended up!? In *prison*, with prostate cancer, depressed out of his mechanical mind. Even though his first CD was recently released and got great reviews, you can understand him feeling bad about being here.

Any alien would!!!

But I need to back up, as not everyone is familiar with this particular space saga. I myself heard about it a year (or so) ago, while I was researching the biography of another alien glam singer (Jobriath) who played a concert at L.A.'s Troubadour club in August 1974. The opening band, I found out, was Zolar X. They were a rock band in L.A. and wore spacey costumes and antennae and stuff. *They dressed like aliens all the time.* They were incredibly weird, basically, and had never been released on CD, which was sad.

I was fascinated! They'd self-released one LP in 1982. I hunted around for a copy. Lisa Fancher at Frontier Records laughed at me, saying it was "beyond rare" but that *she had a copy!* She said it was good, or actually, "REALLY good. Every time someone new hears their record, they go insane!"

I wanted to believe!!!

Later I found out there was talk of her releasing Zolar X's first CD reissue. That honor went to Jello Biafra's Alternative Tentacles label, which is more of a punk/political/whatever type of label, but they liked Zolar X for some reason. So *Timeless* hit the shelves last October. At the very least you'd have to be *amused* at the idea of an incredibly bizarre rock band not getting signed for the 7-plus years of its existence (1974 to 1981), so they disbanded, went their separate ways, until *twenty years later* the tapes are released and music rags across the planet say it's great!

My own response was beyond amusement. I put my finger on the play button and got an *electric* shock—not from the stereo, but from the sound! This bizarre alien voice was suddenly speaking in . . . *Alien*. I had no idea what he was saying. Then the band kicked in for song after song, the rest unfortunately in English, but all very weird and fun.

The CD was great, but *that* voice entranced me. It was androgynous and

energetic, aggressive actually—a sound like you don't hear too often. In the CD liner notes you see him, the band's lead singer, Zory Zenith, looking like a boy Joan Crawford in blonde alien drag; a rather amazing presence, highly alert and funny.

Suddenly, I had his address! In the course of Jobriath research I discovered that the former lead singer of Zolar X was living four hours away from me (by human car; by spaceship it'd be much faster). *Zory was in an Oregon state prison!!!*

Instantly I sat down to write, pausing only as I wasn't sure how to address him. He had lots of names (in true glam style), and a virtual whirlwind of personalities. His "real" name was George William Myers.

I finally settled on, "Dear Zory."

He wrote back!!!

I prize this letter very highly. If I woke up and saw the house burning down around me, I'd run over and grab it. Glam is so depressing, this endless alien tragedy. Jobriath is dead; Bowie is a shadow of himself. But Zory is *here*, a lingering member of that race of strange, beautiful beings who touched down on this awful planet in the early 1970s. *And they did it to save us!* The mission of a glam singer is always to save the planet from approaching apocalypse. I had so many questions for Zory. One of them was: Why bother? From what I can see, humanity isn't worth saving. My only problem with the apocalypse is that it's overdue.

"I *just* received your letter," Zory replies, in his all-caps lettering on lined notebook paper. "Delighted to hear from you! I'm thrilled you are enjoying the new Zolar X CD. Unfortunately I cannot share in your enthusiasm as —"

He goes on for two pages about not having signed contracts or anything for the new CD. He asks me to contact the record label and relay his concerns.

"Compliance is NOT OPTIONAL!"

But then his mind spins around, shooting back into the early '70s like a time machine. His memories seem to glitter on the very page. "Those *magical* years after David Bowie first came to L.A. as Ziggy at the Santa Monica Civic in '72 were a dreamy hopeful time," he sighs. "A new dawn of Sci-Fi color after the explosive yet *pathetic* 60s." He goes on for five pages. Everything is so great. Zolar X's concert with Jobriath was their first major gig. "We knew our 'compositions' were excellent," he says, "but our live shows were still 'sticky' with the acoustic, crap p.a.'s, our *beautiful* yet highly impractical costumes and moving props."

Some people say glam ended with Bowie's live album in July '74. But for me, it was weeks later, in L.A., at the Troubadour, when Jobriath was dying and Zolar X was born.

"I did ask Jo," Zory recalls. "Where do you think glam is going?"

Jobriath replied, "Back into the woodwork where all true art goes, probably."

"He was *right*," Zory confirms. "Late 1975–76 that trash scum ball punk rock stole our hair color, added leather instead of lurex, celebrated drugs and degeneracy, and *destroyed all of the 'sophisto' religious Sci-Fi that the earth so desperately needed!"*

The thing to know about Zory is that he utterly loathes punk. Humanity *needed* glam! By the early '70s the planet had been rocked by war after war. The Vietnam War had just died down, so everyone was eagerly waiting for the next one to start. But *then* . . . Ziggy Stardust and a host of gleaming, glamorous aliens appeared on earth, prophesying the imminent end of the world, and preaching the one possible cure.

Zory capitalizes, underlines, and highlights it:

"SPACE AGE LUV!!"

Then punk came and spoiled everything. That, and KISS — a band that Zory hates, if possible, even more. Zolar X hung out with KISS in 1974, and did not come away unscathed. "Ace took his tufted silver lamé accessories from *us*," Zory fumes. KISS was a direct affront to his greatest ideal—the beautiful space alien *vilified* and *demonized*.

"Kids in Satan's Service," he huffs.

After glam, it's like humans *wanted* to be humans again. The lower they could go, the better. Zolar X was cast into the dustbin of pop, until found by . . . Jello Biafra?

"It's a sick irony to me," Zory fumes, "that a former *punk* would release our songs."

He ends with news. He has cancer but it's in remission. He's writing his memoirs. He's become a serious Christian, sings in prison chapel, and gives sermons. He mentions the cause of his imprisonment ("my best friend, a drunken brawl, he got nothing, I got 10"). He signs the letter "The Capt." because he's *Captain Zory Zenith!!!*

I have my orders! I send Zory's address to Alternative Tentacles, who thank me as they didn't have it. Suddenly I'm in touch with Ygarr Ygarrist, the Zolar X lead guitarist! He seems a lot more normal than Zory. Maybe it works for him, I don't know. Anyway, I find more vintage photos of Zory. His look was so fascinating. Not male, not female, but not faggy. A difficult balance. It's like he was . . . *on a mission?*

I admire that a lot.

There's praises for the CD in mags from *Classic Rock* to *Uncut* to *Mojo*. It's showing up on year-end "best of" lists, and Steve Jones (former Sex Pistol) plays it on his L.A. radio show. Only *one* review I find isn't that positive, and it's by a woman. I clip them and mail them off.

"I'm close to tears," Zory replies. "But one can never quite decide which emotion is appropriate twenty-plus years late!"

The question of "emotion" is tricky for him. He can't decide which one to have, *since he doesn't have emotions.* I learn in this letter that Zory Zenith is not exactly biological. He is—a phrase he uses a lot—"the Zorian Zormar Mediator Model 11000."

He is an ANDROID.

"And," he concludes, "an android has little programming for emotions."

He lists all the things that he is, in order. "1. *Android*. Rock music's first 'robot' rockstar. 2. *Superhero*. The raygun, ballet leaps in the air, alien Peter Pan, etc. 3. Zolar X's *Vocal Emissary*."

I'd asked Zory for a brief history of Zolar X, especially on points where the CD liner notes were sketchy. If they were aliens from outer space, for instance, what planet were they from, and why did they ever come *here*? I felt sure Zory would know, and he did.

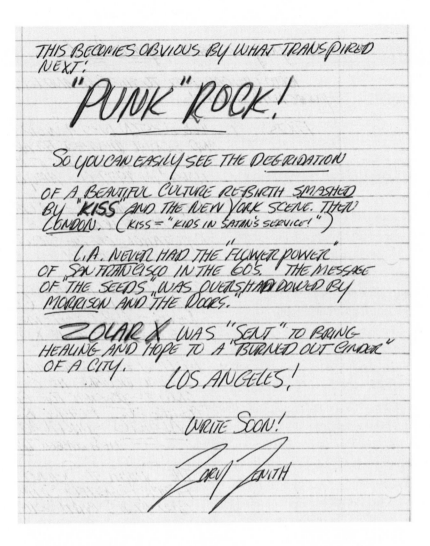

THIS BECOMES OBVIOUS BY WHAT TRANSPIRED NEXT!

"PUNK" ROCK!

SO YOU CAN EASILY SEE THE DEGRIDATION

OF A "BEAUTIFUL CULTURE REBIRTH SMASHED BY "KISS" AND THE NEW YORK SCENE. THEN LONDON. (KISS = "KIDS IN SATAN'S SERVICE!")

L.A. NEVER HAD THE "FLOWER POWER" OF SAN FRANCISCO IN THE 60'S. THE MESSAGE OF "THE SEEDS" WAS OVERSHADOWED BY MORRISON AND THE DOORS.

ZOLAR X WAS "SENT" TO BRING HEALING AND HOPE TO A "BURNED OUT CINDER" OF A CITY. LOS ANGELES!

WRITE SOON!

Zarv Zenith

"Ygarr, Zany, Rojan, Eon, Ufoian, Romni, etc., were the alien biological beings from *Plutonia*," he replies. Their mission was *"to warn Earth of its future cataclysmic doom."* And also to announce "the soon universal return of the Son of God, Jesus Christ."

"Zolar X was not a glam rock band!" he exclaims.

He highlights the letters in green magic marker, to drive the point home. "It was an alien peace emissary unit who developed a communications for human youth called 'Rocket Roll.' The purpose being 'Space Age Luv.' Zolar X was 'sent' to bring healing and hope to a 'burned out cinder' of a city. LOS ANGELES!"

He sighs. The subject is so complex.

"It will take the book I'm writing to sort truth from fiction," he says. He'd entered prison intending to begin his memoirs immediately. Titled *The Greatest Show Never Played*, it was envisioned as a down and dirty tell-all, a sequel to Marc Spitz and Brendan Mullen's book *We've Got the Neutron Bomb*, a history of punk rock in L.A. that opens with Zolar X. But Zory then realized this was "Satan's design." The book took on a more redeeming tone. Now it's called *Chained to the World: An Underground Rock Star's Crawl From Bondage*.

A really good title, I think.

He's cowriting with a pastor friend, but they haven't gotten much done. "I'm too depressed," Zory says. "I need vitamins. I stay in bed a lot."

The answer hits me like a comet.

I can do a *profile* on him! Maybe a website. Get the ball rolling. This is a major *alien crash landing* on the level of Roswell! Zory's referred to a lot of unpublished photos and music. Someone needs to go through the wreckage, maybe with a toothbrush.

Zory agrees.

Or in his words, "REALLY? REALLY?"

He's excited. The story of his life, what he calls "my tragedy," is his last gift to the planet. "We will *milk* the publicity the Devil is giving me back for the glory of Christ!" he exclaims. "Amen!"

He gives me my own Zolarian name, *Zaanan Zelek*, and we get to work!!!

Zory was born (on Earth, alas) on May 18, 1952. His father was a coal miner. "I was a hillbilly kid," he says, which is somehow amazing to me. He was an only child, which he credits as inspiring his amazing imagination.

When he was little his family moved to Kentucky, a time marked in his memory by three events. First, his parents started to drink. Second, he started going to church and singing in the choir ("a soprano," he always notes). Third, he went to the movies with a babysitter he had a crush on. She ditched him for her boyfriend, and he was left with the movie, *Girls! Girls! Girls!* . . . and its star, the great inspiration of his life, the reigning alien of Pop Culture:

ELVIS.

Zory's dad was laid off and the family moved to L.A. "It was a run for my life every day to keep from being beaten up and robbed," he says. His dad became a security guard and both his parents became, not just drunks, but angry drunks. "The violence was over the top," he recalls. "Knives, skillets, you name it. Dad would take a lot of verbal abuse from Mom. She was obnoxious! Knowing full well that eventually he'd get up from his easy chair and wreak destruction!"

By 1965 they'd moved to a nicer neighborhood, but Zory's childhood was at that point totally screwed over. He was a "lousy student" who got by on comedy, dancing, mime, and *music*. He got a drum set and piddled around in a few bands, and with his girlfriend ("my first true love and sex queen") saw all the major bands that blew through town, from the Who to an earthshaking concert by the Beatles, where the screams of girls were like "roaring jets."

By eleventh grade Zory's attendance at school was a series of cameos. They told him he was being sent back to tenth grade. Zory told them where to go, and left. (He's working on his GED now.) His real future was apparent. He was a rock star.

Zory's everyday human name is "Billy," since his father was also named George. At age eighteen, he pulled his first self-promotional stunt. Following the "Paul is Dead" hoax that made everyone think Paul McCartney was dead, he "conned" his dad into letting him change his last name to McCartney. He then printed up flyers with the question *"Who is Billy McCartney?"* and posted them up and down Sunset Boulevard. He tells the story with relish. Without even having to lie, he says, he was accepted as Paul's cousin, and rubbed shoulders with famous folk in the L.A. club scene.

But he wanted to be an artist, not a con artist. He needed a band, and in 1971, he got one. Having kept up his drumming, he was accepted into Shady Lady, a proto-glam band whose members did lipstick, platform boots, and satin pants way before all the other guys.

"Women loved us; guys hated us," Billy gloats. "The press called us a 'shitty litter' of young punks!" Musically they were akin to the Rolling Stones, and anticipated the New York Dolls. They recorded an LP, but their label dropped them before it was released, and a band member stole all their equipment to support his drug habit. Shady Lady was over.

Billy wasn't the least bit phased. He'd seen the future: Ziggy Stardust at the Santa Monica Civic.

"I was stunned for days!" he exclaims. "That hair! Those wedgie boots and space suit! The 'Martian Elvis!' I was in love. I saw him up close again in 1973 at the Hollywood Palladium. To me, the sci-fi god was collecting his chosen few. I took the flight!"

Launching into orbit, he dyed his hair red and began dreaming of a four-piece band of blonde aliens with pointed bangs, to be called Zory

Glory and the Seattle Satellites. (He liked Seattle, for the Space Needle.) He began writing space songs, and with his new girlfriend Kitty Wayne (a.k.a. "Veonity" or "Ve") he began making and wearing outrageous space-age costumes. (Ve—as Ve Neill—later became a major Hollywood makeup artist, winning three Oscars, including one for *Mrs. Doubtfire*. Does the male makeover go back to Zory??)

"I *became* Zory," he says. He drew comic book pictures of himself as a superhero and again plastered them across Sunset Blvd. Then one night in 1973 he went to Rodney Bingenheimer's English Disco, the famous club, and saw two guys with silver-blonde hair and pointed bangs, *looking like they'd stepped out of his sketches!*

"It was eerie!" he exclaims.

"What kind of music do you play?" Ygarr asked him.

"Rock 'n' roll," answered Zory.

Hmmf! "We play *Space Symphony*," Ygarr shot back.

That's how Zolar X was formed.

They wanted him to play drums.

"I told them, *nope*," Zory says. "Zory is a singer and an android! I'm looking to *front* a band, not sit behind one."

Together in Laurel Canyon, the protoaliens listened to a heady brew of tunes, from Bowie to Beethoven, colliding in the cauldron of pop. They honed two songs, "Space Age Love" and "Parallel Galaxies." Zory knew his singing voice needed work. ("Lots of work!") But his mission was before him, for the first time in his life. He'd have a staggeringly successful rock band, and *save the world*.

Zory and I write a lot, not just about the past, but about the *future*. In the wake of the CD release, Ygarr is working to reform Zolar X and play some gigs. The problem of the missing frontman weighs heavily on Zory's mind. But he comes up with the answer. There will be a *new* lead singer, a GIRL ANDROID, to be named Zana Zormarr, model number 10036. (Note: she's more advanced.) Zory sends me a magazine clip-out of a space-age babe in a skin-tight silver suit. With a magic marker he's colored in a new blonde hairdo for her, and two antennae.

Otherwise, his mind rockets around, sometimes manic, sometimes depressed, sometimes in the same sentence. "The doctors think I'm bipolar," he reports. "I told them that in my mom and dad's day it was called GENIUS!"

The doctors, he says, "just looked at me."

He was on medication but is off it, alluding vaguely to side effects. He struggles for clarity. "I'm in a transitional state mentally," he says.

Zory can always be divided into several parts. One of them longs to be part of Zolar X, another longs to be free of it. Upon his arrest in 2002, after a lifetime spent flirting with faith, he became a Christian. In his letters he frequently rises up to sermonize against the entire entertainment establishment. This is "Bible Bill," or "the evangelist Billy Myers."

"God has his own realm," he says. "He doesn't want or need the Devil's art, music, prose, or clothes."

With a clean sweep Bible Bill dismisses all the prior characters in Zory's mental theater. "Billy McCartney is *irrelevant*. Zory Glory is *irrelevant*. Billy Bo Day *(his rockabilly persona)* is *irrelevant*."

But strangely enough, Zory Zenith—*Captain* Zory Zenith, of Zolar X—remains *highly* relevant.

"Well bless our hearts," he says. "What are model 11000 androids FOR right?!! (the 'black box' keepers). I managed, co-produced, designed, sang, danced, promoted and composed that band into its very EXISTENCE. I've seen the captain's seat often. That's why around 1975, I added the designation of 'CAPT.' upon myself!!!"

Typical Zory talk. The hillbilly preacher and the alien wrestle in the prison cell of his thoughts. This is not an "identity crisis" per se. *For the glam singer, identity itself is a crisis.*

He is also, I should add, increasingly obsessed with getting out of jail. He now says he was railroaded into his ten-year sentence. A witness lied, the D.A. had no interest in the truth, and his public defender lawyer was a wuss. The altercation for which he was convicted Zory now describes as "mutual combat" or "self-defense." He's intent on raising money for a federal appeal based, he says, on a recent Supreme Court case governing sentencing in jury trials, except he didn't have a jury trial.

I don't know quite what to say.

He's whipped up a minihistory of his life for me, and suggests other contacts. And to keep up morale he sends autographed pix of Zolar X, where he sits among his alien bandmates, staring at the camera cool and austere, *commanding*—lip slightly snarled. Even on photocopied paper colored with magic marker, he has it: the X factor of Zolar X.

In 1973, the band was off to a rocky start. Zory (now Zory Glory), Ygarr, founding bassist Zany Zatovian, and keyboardist Ed Dorn (Rojan) could not find a drummer. Broke, they were evicted from the house they shared in Laurel Canyon, and regrouped in the Bay Area. By October they'd found drummer Eon Flash, rehearsed intensely, and in November were ready to rock. Zolar X amazed local audiences with laser blasts of alien energy. They were booked at L.A.'s new Starwood club for a two-week run beginning on New Year's Eve.

Zory rarely gets into specifics, but prefers to think back with fond vagueness. "We wore our togs 24/7," he sighs. "We made up our own language. We wrote symphonies and pop hits for another planet! We schmoozed with English and American pop stars and rock legends. We were never out of character so we were the darlings of the Hollywood scene. All except for the cigar-chomping pot-bellied record execs." ·

Zolar X just could not score a record deal. But then, I am still not sure how well regarded they were at the time.

I ask around.

"I saw them play maybe six, seven times over the years," replies Dennis Cooper, the novelist. "You know, they weren't so great, in memory at least. They weren't well respected in either the glam or punk scenes. They were very marginal. Sonically, I remember them sounding a bit like early Tubeway Army, though not anywhere as good."

Lisa Fancher saw them at the Troubadour, but mostly recalls the spacemen on the streets of L.A. "They were always dressed to the nines in their get-ups no matter how much shit they caught from the locals," she says. "And it's not easy to stand out on Hollywood Blvd., let me tell ya!"

I believe her. Zolar X's major studio recordings were years away. Until then, they *stood out* on this rock spinning in space—beautiful freaks!!

Zory, for sure, was a star on the rise who never quite rose. But he *was* a star. He posed for Norman Seeff, the famous rock photographer, who included him in his 1974 book, *Hot Shots*. There we find Zory nestled between snaps of Mick Jagger, Carly Simon and co.—an alien boy lying on his bed in full face paint, a perverse smile on his face as his hands creep near his crotch. I can see it in his eyes. No human would do for him. His affair is with the camera itself.

"I considered myself 'sexless,'" he writes. "I was an android and often passed on one-night stands. I was more into the mind. The soul. Art. Music. Poetry. Theater. Sex was actually superficial to me compared to these 'higher' pursuits.'" He counts up all his sexual partners. There's forty-seven. Unlike Jobriath, Zory is "exclusively heterosexual"—he was an alien, but not *that* alien. It's like he put all his energies into being himself. I get a snippet of video footage from the Troubadour show, taken from the audience. Zory *was* funny. He does a little alien dance and moves weirdly so it looks like he's floating. (Jobriath, by contrast, looks like a demon in hell.)

Zolar X could never quite be a joke band, as they were carried forward into a weird seriousness by Zory's presence. He brings something odd and hypnotic to anything he does. In 1974, Zolar X recorded two songs, including "Space Age Love"—a different pressing than what appears on the CD. The original is peculiar, for sure. Zory's voice is high and clipped, like a mutant child. As always with Zolar X music the primary impression is *enraged fun*. It got some radio play but they were still an unsigned band—aliens wandering the streets, talking to themselves in a language nobody else could understand.

With a shifting lineup (Ed Dorn was fired) they continued to play the L.A. area. In December 1974 they were at a rock festival at the Palladium, rubbing shoulders with the Stooges, the Dolls, etc.

From a review: "Zolar X is considered pretty much a joke around Hollywood. Their gimmick is space-suit costumes with tendrils and a singer who sounds like he's on helium. The band features a guitarist who knows a few notes which he repeats in monotonous cascades, and a drummer who continually loses his 4/4 beat. As somebody remarked, 'without their echoplex, they'd be out of business.' They created a lot of noise, earned a few titters and scattered applause, and floated off."

They had their fans.

An L.A. cartoonist named Armando Norte *heard* about them and was naturally very excited. He showed up at the Troubadour concert, and met them backstage. Over the next years he drew cartoons for their publicity and lyrics: superheroes and sci-fi visions (some are in the CD packaging). Ygarr doesn't know where he is but I locate . . . *Etron!*

"Their look was *so* unique," he tells me. "It wasn't what Bowie was doing, or the other glitter bands. It wasn't glam rock. It was a new flavor. I always felt it's gonna take awhile before people catch up. They were seen more as an oddity."

He admits that Zolar X was, in fact, odd.

"Sometimes they'd walk around talking in an alien language. They'd be somewhere, and doing their own speech. It just made the whole experience that much stranger."

He laughs. He notes, as many do, that Ygarr was the musical force. ("He could go on and on. It was like opening black holes.") But Zory was the theater! I ask for description.

"Somewhat *androidian?*" he says. "He could turn it off so quick and become very . . . robotic. He could stare and hold a pose, and not move, and he knew everybody was watching him."

Etron warms up.

"He'd walk down Hollywood Blvd., and everyone would *stop*. He could walk into a building and *everybody* would turn. Once we went to the Rainbow Room. He was wearing a bright yellow body stocking, and it only had a little silver pocket right at the crotch, like V-shaped, it was metallic, and he had little silver shoes, soft and slip on. And those donut rings around his wrists. His makeup was always *perfect*. The girls were mesmerized. He was perfect on stage. He could have become an excellent actor. He could switch it on and off. I never saw him lose his temper or anything. He seemed gentle, like a gentle person."

For him, Zolar X's story from 1975 to 1977 was of a band staging amazing concerts but slowly falling apart. Their concerts, at the Starwood or Rodney's (where they were a house band for awhile), were sci-fi extravaganzas with silver sets, neon and glitter, lasers, and the rocking, dancing aliens. But Zolar X could not get signed, even when *Star Wars* was huge. "The whole science fiction thing was just in air," Etron sighs. "It was the right time for them, but it just never happened."

The band had a number of offers. The CD liner notes mention that a TV producer had wanted to make Zolar X into a television show, like *The Monkees*. Zory was in favor of the idea!

The Captain was outvoted.

Etron last saw Zory around 1980, when Zolar X was disbanding, unable to get new bookings. But he'd get updates on the former frontman.

"A lot of bad things happened after he left," he says, hesitatingly.

This is exactly how it happened. Shortly after talking to Etron I heard back from Zory's daughter, whom he'd asked me to contact. He hadn't heard from her in months, and was worried.

I stare at her note.

"There's just so many things about him that are evil that I'm kinda reluctant to have anything to do with him. He's an extremely talented con-artist and I don't want to be the one that falls for it."

I write back, feebly. Are we talking about *the same Zory Zenith??*

"OK, first of all please don't act like you know my father better than I do," she replies.

She's really angry.

"If you don't think he's a con, then it *worked* and he conned you into believing that he's a decent person. He had no chance of being one with his upbringing. Did you know he has *beaten* every woman he's ever been with? He beat my mother so severely when I was three and my sister was one that her eyes were swollen shut when she showed up at my grandma's house with myself and my handicapped sister in her arms barely able to stand?"

"Did you know that I would have had an older brother or sister by my mom if Billy hadn't beat it out of her and caused her to lose it?"

"Did you know that before I was born, one night he was drinking again, got pissed at my mother, picked up her cat, broke its neck and threw it out the window? Hmmm, did ya know that great piece of info? Did you know he was beating my mom one night, and my now-stepfather came to help her and Billy pushed him down a flight of stairs and both his knees have been screwed his entire life and he just had a total knee replacement?"

She's almost finished.

"Billy is an *entertainer*. He may be one of the most charismatic people you could meet and people always like him. He cons you into believing that he's just a great guy. And don't tell me he's not a con because I got that gene; I could make you believe anything I wanted to. I am A LOT like Billy and there is an anger inside that is uncontrollable. Don't tell me it's alcohol . . . this was in him from the *beginning*."

I'm very upset and re-read Zory's notes over and over. The peaceful alien, the mission to humanity, all that crap is going up in smoke. I suddenly wonder if there's a devious mind at work, not sweetly kooky but crazy and conniving. *Not* alien. Vintage *human*. I write him but prison mail can take two weeks or more. I'm left with his past, trying to understand it.

The time: 1975.

Zory is growing desperate. The apocalypse is drawing nearer, and he's done nothing to prevent it. "I read Hal Lindsay's *The Late Great Planet Earth*," he writes. "I took LSD. One night I flipped out and ran down Hollywood Blvd. in an orange lurex space suit screaming the world was coming to an end!"

He was arrested and thrown in the drunk tank.

Next: out driving on a desolate highway with his future first wife Karen, he got in a horrible car wreck. "We were ejected from the vehicle as it flipped over three times. The auto landed on its roof and was crushed down to the seats!"

Suddenly a mysterious woman was at his side. "You're all right," she said. "Help is coming."

An ambulance arrived moments later. Zory believed she was an angel. *"This began my quest for God."*

He and Karen were seriously injured, but recovered and married soon afterward. "Unfortunately," Zory continues, "I continued to drink and smoke dope."

And beat her?

During this time, Zory was in and out of Zolar X. He alludes to being kicked out of the band several times, but never says why. The CD liner notes (by Chuck Nolan) say his behavior was "erratic." I ask Ygarr.

There's been a change.

Ygarr replies that he'd rather not answer, for fear of affecting Zory's legal appeals. "I could fill a chapter for you, but I want him out of prison first."

My impression is that Zory's "erratic" behavior undid many of Zolar X's commercial prospects. I'm told Ygarr was urged to go solo. I write him

again.

He replies.

"I never really kicked him out, our managers did. I liked him up front. His act and his designs were needed, and he kept getting to be a better singer, plus I loved him like a brother! I feared him at times but that feeling never lasted."

In 1978, kicked out of the band, Zory moved to the Bay Area. He was twenty-six. Newly married, with a family on the way, his rock career seemed behind him. He went to beauty school and did "promotional pantomime" on the side. He and his wife began attending church. But, as he says, "I would not repent of being a rock star, groupie-lovin' drunk! Only I was losing control. I was becoming early last-stage alcoholic. Violent. Crazy. Wild."

Other replies come in.

The "Billy McCartney" hoax was more elaborate than he'd let on. On the basis of his changed name and a forged photo (showing him and Paul McCartney with their arms around each other), Billy had gotten an endorsement deal, which was later revoked.

Violent scenes. Around 1975 Billy sat in as a drummer with former members of Shady Lady. Karen was present. She left the room and came back. On her return Billy got up and began beating her savagely. The other players had to pull him off her and chew him out.

Billy and Karen divorced. They were to have three children. The first, I've come to believe, was aborted by a beating; the second was the daughter I'd written, whom he saw infrequently—forgetting, or too drunk for the visitations. His *third* daughter with Karen is severely mentally disabled, which may be attributable to Billy beating his pregnant wife again. I'm told he refused all contact with the girl and claimed he could not have produced such a defective child. He's told me that he's paid a total of $18,000 in child support and is delinquent $18,000. I know in my bones he intended to pay for only one of the girls.

Ed Dorn, the original member of Zolar X, gives me more early history of the band. In the early '70s, he and Ygarr were in a house band at a strip club in the Bay Area. They decided they'd better launch something big, and seized on the alien stuff.

I ask how much they *believed* in it.

"It kind of evolved," he replies. "We were looking for a shtick, I guess you would call it. Seemed like the thing to do."

They met Zory in L.A., and against Ed's wishes, accepted him as frontman. Ed thought Zory was a drummer.

"He'd sit down and, 'It goes like this'—bang it right off. I was going 'Why are we looking for a drummer? We've already got one. What we need to find is a better *singer*.'"

Ed never cared for Zory's voice.

"Too affected," he says. "In a way that was not his true voice. It was like something he'd put on."

Also, Ed thought they should only wear their costumes in concert. Zory wouldn't have it. Tensions escalated and their manager ("a doorman at the Starwood") threw Ed out.

Fast forward: 1978.

Ed answered the phone.

"*Owwww*, like what's *happening?*" the caller howled.

It was Zory! The two made up, and within a week had a new project: a new wave sci-fi band called the Aurora Pushups. With a home recorder they did two songs, Zory's "Angels on Runway 1," about an elite group of astronauts, and Ed's "Victims of Terrorism," which lately sounds rather spooky. ("Someday we all will be . . . victims of terrorism.")

They pressed 1,000 45s and almost sold out in the local market. I get a copy. These should have been Zolar X songs. The sound is very poppy and fun, albeit lo-fi. Zory sings lead on both tracks, but his voice is rawer than on the CD . . . *hesitant?*

"Suddenly we're getting all this airplay," Ed continues. "We're selling records. So, we better get a band! We assembled players and started rehearsing. But he wouldn't show up to rehearsals. His problem is he was drinking. It was a problem for a long time."

Ed returned the old favor. He fired Zory.

I ask if booze was really the problem, or if there was a deeper one.

"It was there without the drinking," Ed sighs. "The drinking allows it to come to the fore. He has demons he can't seem to exorcise. What they are, I don't know."

I also get through to Stefen Shady, the lead singer of Shady Lady.

He thought Billy had the potential to be one of the great drummers—on the level of Keith Moon. They worked with him a lot. Later, he saw Zolar X up close. "I thought it was developing," he says. "It was going to take a lot of money. And, this was the part I don't know if they could've handled: It was going to take direction from outside. Somebody they believed in, who had the power to mold them."

As we continue talking, I get a surprise. After Billy and Karen divorced, Karen and Stefen (not friendly until then) had married. *Stefen Shady* was the stepfather of Billy's daughters.

Relating these facts, his voice is calm, modest . . . fatherly.

"I don't know that I really succeeded in being a good father, or stepfather," he says. "But I had to be better than having no father."

Or, I add . . . having Zory.

The alien mystique withers in my mind, as I'm left with the pathetically human truth.

Who wants an alien as a dad?

I suddenly see in the E.T. fiction something I'd never seen—a hostility to earth, to fellow men, and women.

I probe Stefen about the scene Billy's daughter had mentioned—pushing her stepfather down the stairs.

Stefen is defensive.

"Physically I could *beat* his butt," he replies. "I *never* felt fear of Billy. I'll tell you what happened to me. I just had one of my knees operated on. A total knee replacement. I'm having the other one done. The reason my knees are this way is because he was drunk, he broke a bottle and put it to my throat, slipped around behind me and put it to my neck, opened the door, and kicked me from behind down some steps. When I landed, my knees were totally blown out. I had no insurance, I had no money to get an operation. Finally they did scope my knees to take everything out, but it was bone against bone for years.

"I didn't even charge him. The police came. His ex-wife, because he hit her, split her head open or something, she brought charges. I didn't bring charges. Of course I didn't know how much damage he'd done to me. And you know what? He never apologized. He doesn't acknowledge the shit that he does. I don't hate him for it. I didn't kill him. I didn't cripple *him*."

Billy careened from one career to the next. While drinking, doing drugs, cutting hair at a posh salon, and beating his wife, he started up a new career as a Christian evangelist. "I preached on the streets in San Francisco with a bullhorn. The very heart of Sin City. Too bad my own heart wasn't in it."

Ed Dorn recalls the period.

"He used *religion* as a means of absolving himself from some of the things he'd done. I don't want to badmouth him, but he was in relationships with women in which he was abusing them, and then he'd go to church on Sunday and absolve his guilt."

The main name I have for this period is the pastor of Billy's Protestant church—who, Billy says, is cowriting *Chained to the World*.

I call him up.

Something is clearly wrong.

"What am I to talk about?" he says.

I don't quite know what to say. I ask if they were friends.

"Well, he came and preached in our church and I knew him, you see, but I would not characterize him as a friend. His mother was a member of our church. I *wouldn't* characterize him as a friend."

(pause)

"Why is this of interest?"

Well, I say, Billy was a in a rock band.

"Yes," he replies.

They recently released their first CD.

"Without him, of course."

"Well," I say, "they had these recordings which they'd been sitting on for twenty years . . ."

"Amazing."

He's not amazed.

"Yeah," I say. "I don't know if you knew this but for many years, Billy dressed like an alien."

(silence)

"You maybe *didn't* know that."

"No."

(silence)

"As an *alien?*"

"Yeah," I reply. "An alien"—suddenly realizing how odd that is.

I ask for a description of Billy's preaching. He suggests I ask Billy. I ask again, nicely.

"I would say . . ." he begins. "Who is that comedian—Robin Williams. He reminded me of Robin Williams preaching. You can imagine that could be quite entertaining, wouldn't it? But not preaching *wrong*. Preaching what I would consider to be the truth, but with different impersonations, a little Elvis, Groucho Marx, that sort of thing, thrown into one sermon. Which was quite . . . unique."

He warms up.

"I think that having failed at the entertainment industry, or not accomplishing what he wanted, he was now trying to do it in preaching. But he fuzzed out, back into drugs and all that, and was incarcerated and then rethinks it, and then it comes back together for him. That would be my guess."

"Were you aware," I ask, "of the situation with Billy's wives?"

"He was divorced," the pastor replies. "No, he was married when I met him."

"He was beating them."

"He was *what?*"

I feel suddenly embarrassed, or ashamed, that I've had anything to do with a man who seems clearly crazy and criminal, that I would ask *anyone* about him, think anything of him, tell anyone.

"He was beating them, pretty badly."

"He was *beating* them."

"Yeah."

(pause)

"Well," the pastor says on a note of conclusion, "Billy Myers is an interesting and a strange person."

"For sure."

"Is there anything else I can help you with?"

He wishes to get off the phone, but I ask about a few items in Billy's letters. He says the pastor was writing and guiding him throughout the years.

Now I've done it.

The pastor starts to talk.

"You understand that I didn't hear from this man for a long time, from the middle '80s to the early 2000s. I didn't hear from him for sixteen, seventeen years. All of a sudden he writes me from prison. He writes me *long* letters, because I think he's lonely and has few people to talk to, that sort of thing. I don't have *time* to answer him at length. I've sent him some of my books and I have acknowledged the fact that I have received his letters. I write *short* replies. And that's about it."

(silence)

"This is his last straw, so to speak."

I feel the same way.

Somewhere in various boxes in closets across the country, there's the remaining evidence of the later music of Zory Zenith. He calls it his "back catalogue." To anyone else it'd look like a bunch of dusty old tapes. Ed Dorn has some, including demos he's fond of. There's a song, he says, called "Gibraltar Rock." Zory gave him a demo tape called *Future Shock in France*. Zory mentions a major work in the late '70s: a seventeen-minute, four-part "pop epic" called "Judgment of Man." He says it should have been a major hit.

(He says that about all his stuff.)

Then there was the *surfer* Billy Myers. Pushing thirty and gaining weight, he took up surfing, and with collaborator Joel Veach did an album of "futuristic surf music" under the moniker the Freaking Tikis. (In 1994, surfer documentarian Bud Browne used one track, "The Green Room," in his movie *Surfing the '50s*.)

And Billy remarried, a woman named Mary. The word is he didn't beat her much. "She would've kicked his ass," Stefen thinks. "Billy's *not* a tough guy. He's only tough to people who are weak, or he's a sneak attacker."

But despite relative career stability, fun on the waves, and marital happiness . . . *artistically*, Zory Zenith was adrift.

He focused for his next act, however, on August 16, 1977.

Elvis Presley died.

I notice that Zory is very drawn to the deaths of superstars . . . after which he steps into their place? He began studying *rockabilly*. He calls himself a "time traveler," moving not into the future, but the past. He latched onto Elvis's early Sun recordings and the next year emerged with his next major alter ego: *Billy Bo Day and the Howlers*. I call up a source Zory suggested for the period: Lloyd Pratt, the Billy Bo Day "official photographer."

Lloyd is shocked.

"In PRISON??"

He laughs, and eases into his favorite Billy Bo Day stories.

"I remember one time I went over to his apartment. He'd built a little shrine to himself. He had a special little table, with a photo album of all the pictures I took. Then he had three 8 x 10s framed on the wall in a little triangle shape. He was a great customer. When you took pictures of him, he'd buy every other shot. Then when he got more money, he'd try to fill in every other one he didn't have. He loved pictures of himself."

Lloyd recalls a brief phase before Billy Bo Day, a Sci-Fi band where Billy and band were dressed in "these matching PVC outfits that made them look like space-age gas station attendants." They played a local club. In the middle of sets, Billy would pull out his Bible and read to the audience.

Zory as Billy Bo Day.

"He loved being on stage," Lloyd says. "I remember those rockabilly gigs. He'd always throw in something weird. They did 'Boogie Disease' and right in the middle, he started shaking. He'd go, 'I got the boogie, I got the boogie disease,' then shake, and then fall on the floor. He'd shake on the floor, then get back up. Hopping around. Little hops."

At one concert, Lloyd went backstage to Billy's dressing room to find Mary sitting alone crying.

"She was all pissed off because Billy was saying he wanted to keep their marriage a secret, because he thought he was going to be a big rock star, and he thought this would damage his attraction for women. I was like, 'Oh my god.'"

In a bid to make her husband jealous, Mary grabbed a male coworker of Billy's, a hairdresser who was effeminately gay, and made him out as her new love interest.

"It was a real scene," Lloyd laughs. "And then Billy went out onstage and got the boogie disease."

Ygarr remained in L.A., continuing on as a power trio called the Spacerz, with Zolar X members Eon Flash and Ufoian Ufar. I hear from a guy who caught one of their party gigs. "They played a hard, fairly complex, flashy space metal with probable nods to Bowie," he recalls. Their desire to release an album as Zolar X remained alive. In 1976 they did a major recording session in Memphis, to which Zory was not invited—until the last minute, when he was. In 1979, Ygarr did another Zolar X recording session in L.A., in which Zory was not involved. The sound of these sessions is a driving, hectoring alien sound without a lot of emotional variation or personality.

Meanwhile, Billy Bo Day was busy with his latest bid for superstardom. Having played locally, he was ready for the big time.

VEGAS.

"I became the toast of the rockabilly West Coast!" he exclaims in one letter. Or, "the West Coast's premiere rockabilly star," he says in the biography from his defunct website.

I ask Lloyd Pratt.

"It was a cheesy little lounge act in a place called the New Frontier, down at the end of the old strip," he says. "They made him turn down the volume since they didn't want to distract from the gambling."

Billy Bo Day was active, I guess, for seven years, during which Zory drank and did drugs, had lots of affairs and fell away from his unheartfelt religion. It was a fairly standard genre performance, albeit with Zory's odd alien voice. It wasn't greatness, for which he had only one opportunity in the course of his musical life. It came in 1980, when Ygarr had a final change of heart, firing Zolar X's manager in order to take Zory back. They regrouped for a final recording session in San Francisco. These six songs, four with Zory on lead, are the backbone of the CD, praised most often in reviews. It was alien rock, weird, fast, funny, and always a strangely violent wall of sound. In Zory's voice, the hesitation and mimicry was gone. He was, however briefly, himself. A star.

Finally I get Zory's delayed response to his daughter's charges. "I must say, I'm in a bit of shock," he begins. He hems and haws self-defensively. He regrets all his marriages. ("I should never have married any of them!") He moans. "I don't really deserve any of you to love me." He despairs. "I have been a fool. Drunken. Violent. Evil. Wicked. An adulterer. A liar. *But so has everybody else!*"

The punch line: "The events she related were true but with a one-sided 'relish' obviously from her mother."

His next flurry of letters have a new tone. He's very busy with his plans for new Zolar X products. The *Timeless* CD is selling well. Zory plans to gather his scattered "past catalogue" and package it as a CD. He fiddles with titles, settling on *Zory Zenith: Singles*. He's set a release date of May 2006, undiscouraged by the current lack of tapes, a record contract, etc. He

also lays the groundwork for a future CD, his longtime dream of recording
a souped-up, hi-fi album of rocked-up classic hymns, for which, naturally,
he'll tour.

"Pray, and *advertise*," he says.

But there is an undertone of suspicion, building into a paranoia at my
research. "You can feed me all the DIRT on me floating out there," he says.
"I'll be glad to answer all of it. *In my book.*" He writes dirt in return about
those he suspects are informing on him. He speaks increasingly of his
book—now retitled back to *The Greatest Performance Never Played*. It will
expose his enemies. It will lay them flat. It will be the vessel for all the rage
and bitterness of his life.

When addressing his letters now, I am no longer "Zaanan." He questions my profile of him. Friends, and bandmates, do not "turn tale" on each
other, he says. He worries, not for his sake, but the band's! Ygarr's reunion
tour could be harmed. "The more negative publicity about *me*," he whispers,
"the more uphill it gets for *them*."

He's now on a series of medications with huge names, which he reports matter-of-factly, as his tone shifts more wildly than before—from
a hushed, almost childlike wish to please me to an angry attack mode, enraged rivers of words directed at me and nobody. "So hate me, vilify me,
crucify me in print! Do whatever suits your tainted imagination folks! Every
true rock 'n' roller *lives* it. So they're either dead, dying, or *in prison!!!* Wake
up fools! The music you claim to 'love' only proves what true *hypocrites* you
really are!"

He then changes pens, calls me "beloved," and explains that I'd just been
hearing "Zory" talk.

"If you want to focus on *him*, I can give you all you can take."

Zolar X was over in 1981. Live gigs had dried up. Zory returned to Billy
Bo Day. I get a videotape of a 1985 concert. It's surreal seeing the alien in
Elvis drag—a black-haired, squatty, hip-shaking, sweating hillbilly with
pale skin and weirdly intense eyes. He introduces his band by name, and
then himself.

"I'm whoever you want me to be."

The bass player in the Howlers was Alan Barrentine. Weirdly, he's now
big in Christian prison ministries. He sighs at the news of Billy's current
residence.

"I told him one of these days, that's what's going to happen. The drugs,
the alcohol. He always had alcohol problems. I took him to detox twice."

He thinks over Billy's career.

"He always *believed* he should have been David Bowie. He believed he should have been a major star. And as much as a lot of his stuff was good . . . the people who make it are good businesspeople. Billy was not."

The end of the classic Howlers lineup came when Barrentine financed a recording session for an album. He had a studio lined up, and backup players flown into town. The day they were to start, Billy arrived, he says, "very drunk," and proceeded to make havoc—damaging microphones and throwing a guitar at the drummer.

Barrentine quit, and moved away. He kept up with Billy as a friend. "He called me from California saying he was so drunk he thought he was going to die," he recalls. Flying down from Seattle, Barrentine drove Billy back to his home. Shortly afterward, Billy headed back south, and resumed drinking.

His wife Mary left him for another man. I talk with Scott Noel, or Qazar, an erstwhile member of Zolar X, who roomed with Billy in San Francisco in the early '80s. Naturally, they decided to form a band. Assembling the players, Qazar booked studio time to record a demo.

"The rehearsal the night before went solid as a rock," he says. "Everyone was in top form. Zory had been growing his hair back out to its original Zolar X platinum point. It was gorgeous! He shows up at the studio the next day in a pair of white stretch pants, mime slippers, a red-and-white-striped T-shirt, and black beret. His hair was cut, creased back and dyed chocolate brown and he even drew a pencil-thin mustache above his lip. The whole session went right in the shitter!"

Just when one character seemed to be gelling into place, Zory would whirl into the next one. "I never saw Billy Bo Day," says Qazar, "but I saw a shitload of other characters come out of him in his quest to find the right performance vehicle."

Qazar pauses.

"I recall these stories with a fair amount of mixed emotion," he says. "Especially now, knowing the result. But at the time, it was just another day in rock 'n' roll."

But then . . . the music stopped.

There were no more bands. Billy moved to Half Moon Bay, and married a secretary. "Deliciously sexy, smart and beautiful," he says. He beat her and she fled to her parents near Eugene, Oregon.

He followed.

The final act for the artist formerly known as Zory Zenith begins in 1991, when he arrived in Oregon to find out, very weirdly, that his third ex-wife did not wish to reconcile. ("We were better off as friends," he says.) He continued in Eugene, living in an RV behind a Baptist church, cutting hair at a mall salon, and drinking. "I stayed alone for two years," he says. "Heartbroken. Lonely. Suicidal."

Then he met the *third* greatest love of his life, after alcohol and Jesus. "She was a female composite of me," he says, his tone quickening in excitement. "A drinker. A drugger. A rock 'n' roller. A party animal. And she was *violent*. Two inches taller than me with a mean right cross."

It was like Romeo and Juliet, with booze, illegal drugs, animal sex, domestic violence, cops, three stepchildren, and regular visits to prison and church. He beat her. She beat him! They were in love. Her name was Cindy.

His music was reawoken.

Billy worked at a salon, owned by the wife of Gary Hill, who owned a recording studio in Eugene. It wasn't long before the two teamed up to record the first Billy Bo Day solo CD.

Gary Hill's voice is old like a mountain, and calm. He tells me about his long history in music, working for Jerry Lee Lewis and the King Family. Members of the Grateful Dead live nearby and play at his birthday parties.

He liked Billy's music. He enjoys talking about Billy in general.

"Definitely unique. He still wears the white suede shoes and the hair combed back, the collar turned up. He *lives* that part. It's not just a part that he plays; it's a part that he lives. He *is* rockabilly. You see him walking down the street, you'd think it's still 1950-something."

He laughs, and describes how their music started. "He'd come over, do a little recording here and there. We have enough songs for an album."

It's titled *Blonde With Legs*. Billy plays almost all the instruments himself, from guitar to drums, and vocals. It's mostly rockabilly. There's one gospel number, for which Gary plans to add in a female singer to make it a duet. But most of it was nearly finished when Billy was thrown in prison.

Gary has the Zolar X CD, and is amused by it. "It's better than I expected it to be," he says. "You hear Billy. But it's such a different kind of music. It's been quite an evolution."

He sighs.

"If he can get away from the alcohol. That's the main thing right there. And he needs to stay away from his wife. Those two are poison to each other. About the only reason he married her in the first place is because she looks like the twin sister of his other wife. He wants all his wives to look alike."

"Blonde?" I ask.

"Yeah," Gary replies. "And they aren't even real blondes. But this alcoholism is the thing that's really got him."

The time: early 2002.

Billy's marriage was spinning out of control. "It was a blur of parties, work, kids, soccer, school events, jail, beach trips, kids, cops, parties, jail and probation, and more jail!" he says. "Cindy and I split up to appease everyone else."

A court-ordered separation was also there in the mix.

Zory's mug shot.

Billy lived in his van and at friends' houses, notably his best friend, Bob, who lived several houses down from Cindy's house. The three fell in together. Zory would sneak to be with Cindy, and Cindy would sneak to be with Bob. One night when she and a drunk Billy were alone, she taunted him with the affair.

Billy attacked her.

In county prison, he says he became a Christian. He was sentenced to fifteen years. It was reduced down to thirty-six months' probation and a fine.

He was released. "I was sick. A walking talking rock 'n' rollin' DEAD MAN."

Two days later he showed up at Bob's to find Cindy there.

The two men fought. Zory smashed a bottle over Bob's head.

Here is where he is pinning his legal hopes. He says it was self-defense. I consider researching more, calling Bob and Cindy, but the motivation is gone. All I can say is that, in the moment of fighting like an animal with another man over a female, the alien Zory Zenith became, for the first time, completely, 100 percent *human*.

June 18, 2005: Zolar X has just given its first reunion concert, in San Jose to a large, enthusiastic audience. Ygarr sang lead, with Eon Flash and a new guy named Jett Starr. There's blog reviews: "They came out in new costumes, nothing really special, black tights with glittery rings around the arms, legs and waist and the name, ZOLAR X, embroidered across the front," says one.

"Who knows if they will ever be heard from again, but I now can say I got to see this band before they left again for their home planet!"

Memories of the original band continue to filter in. I hear from Danny Wilde, formerly of the Quick and the Rembrandts.

"Are you kidding?" he exclaims in his California surfer's voice. "*Yeah!* We used to see them at the Starwood all the time. They tripped me out. They had *full-on* production. For a kid from the valley to go in and see these guys with a light show, and god, all those crazy-looking guitars and weird chrome outfits. It was *awesome*, like pre-KISS, you know what I mean?"

I do.

Then Jenny Lens, the L.A. photographer who shot Zolar X in concert, and let them practice in a house she owned.

"They did not impress me," she says. "I was not into their music at all — or them. There just wasn't anything for me to relate to on a human or musical level."

Once they were rehearsing so loud, the neighbors called the cops.

I keep hoping to find women who like Zory's music. I play it for a girl at work who likes classic rock. She flips through the CD liner notes and turns away dismissively.

"They look like *wimmin*."

Zory doesn't, anymore. I get his latest prison mug shot. Heavyset and pale, with facial hair, the alien is gone. If his cancer stays in remission, he'll get out on May 20, 2012. Under Oregon's strict sentencing, there is no chance for early release.

Our letters have ceased. I flip through them, hoping for some alien intelligence to break through and say it was all worthwhile. It's so easy to get sick of humanity, that anything alien — anything at all — is a relief. I went to see the new *War of the Worlds* movie, but I just found myself rooting for the Martians. Except they die of earth's diseases before they have a chance to wipe out humanity. I guess that's what our planet has going for it. We have the best bugs.

I end up putting aside all the other papers, and thinking about a piece of paper I haven't mentioned yet. It was an answer Zory sent me to one of the first questions I asked him. His reply was one of the most bizarre things I'd ever seen in my life, so I'd really wanted to include it.

He'd written my question at the top of the page. "*Does Zory want to experience human emotions?*"

"DOES ZORY WANT TO EXPERIENCE HUMAN EMOTIONS?"

THE "BETA-NEURON PIECE"   © ZORY ZENITH 2005

THE ZORION ZORMAR MEDIATOR MODEL 11000 SERIES IS BY FAR THE CREME DELLA CRETE' OF DELIAR SPACER TECHNOLOGY. ALL HUMANOID FACTORS ARE ON AN INSERTABLE-REMOVAL CHIP KNOWN AS THE BETA NEURON PIECE. THE INITIAL MODEL, "CAPT. ZORY ZENITH," COMMUNICATIONS AND EMMISSARY OFFICER FOR ZOLAR X IS, UNFORTUNATELY, OUR FIRST SUCCESS AND EMBARRASSMENT.

TIME "RELOCATED" TO EARTH 1973 A.D., OUR POLITICAL SITUATION ON PLUTONIA WAS SUCH AS TO FORCE A PREMATURE INTRODUCTION OF THE ZENITH MODEL. THE NEURON PIECE WAS APPROXIMATELY 3RD ON THE PRODUCTION LINE, PLUTONIA WAS IN WARFARE WITH THE KRELL. THE ZENITH MODEL WAS RUSHED INTO SERVICE AS A PILOT. THE PROCESSOR UNIT INSTALLED WAS FAULTY. THE CHIP, NEW AND UNTRIED.

PROCESSOR CANALS WORE THIN OVER 3 DECADES IN THE EARTH ATMOSPHERE. IN 2002 THE ZENITH MODEL EXPERIENCED "DATA DISTURBANCE" DOWNLOADING. THE HUMANOID FACTORS OVER RODE THE POSITRONIC CAPITULATOR JOINTS. THE MODEL BEGAN TO EXPERIENCE EMOTIONAL DIFFICULTY AND TO OUR CURRENT ASSESSMENT, LITERALLY FRIED 3 CHANNELS OF SKILL LEVEL.

THE CHIPS ARE NOW, TO OUR KNOWLEGE, DUE FOR REPLACEMENT EVERY 10 YEARS - EARTH TIME. HUMAN AUTHORITIES CAPTURED THE ZENITH UNIT AND HAVE PLACED IN CUSTODY AT T.O.R.C. "TIME/ORDINANCE RECLAMATION CENTER" AKA T.R.C.I. UMATILLA OREGON - EARTH 2005 A.D. SECURITY MESSURE: DELTA-FI-DA CONDRAX 777

The answer is a memo, titled "The Beta-Neuron Piece," supposedly written by the scientists of planet Plutonia. They describe the creation of the Zorion Zormar Mediator model 11000 as "our first success and embarrassment."

They were forced to release him too early. Plutonia was at war with "the

Krell." They had no choice. They rushed him into service, and sent him off to earth, even though they knew his "beta neuron chip" was faulty. This was the chip that allowed him to feel.

So they watched, and still watch their creation from afar in space, noting that in the year 2002 his "positronic capitulator joints" began to fail. "The model began to experience emotional difficulty." His mechanical brain began to fry as he was flooded with feelings he couldn't control. He was an android.

There's lots of details. Zory really is kind of crazy. But it's all there, really.

He emerged from two races at war—men, and women.

His ability to feel was damaged. He functioned best when he had no feeling at all, and when he was making rock music, as rock is the music we love the best, as it's the density of the earth and of the human heart. *To be unfeeling and to channel the savage powers of the cosmos*: Zory Zenith: rock star.

In jail, when he was left alone with himself, Billy Myers, he had a breakdown, as anyone does, when they're alone.

He says that's when he accepted Jesus. I believe him. I can't see what Jesus would want with any of us, but maybe He does. It's not like aliens want us. They don't even bother to attack. Sometimes, maybe, they show up here and there for a split second, and then they're gone. They came all this way, millions of miles, and when they get here they're embarrassed to be seen. But you can't blame them. It's not like there's intelligent life on this planet. We kill our own aliens. We're aliens to ourselves.

If I were them, I'd cruise right along to the next world. I hope they do.

Update

Upon receiving this article in prison Zory was pleased to be flourishing in the "underground press." The author and subject discussed whether or not the handicaps of his second daughter could have been caused by prenatal injury. Zory insisted they could not have been, Poletti sent him information to the contrary, and Zenith cut off their correspondence. That particular speculation, and the alleged forced miscarriage stated as fact by Poletti in his text, were the most troubling aspects of this article to Zolar X's historian/liner note author/documentarian Chuck Nolan. Nolan was nonetheless impressed by the scope of the article, despite historically being skeptical and critical of Poletti's motivations and practices (as the article makes clear, the author can be difficult and obsessive at times). Nolan's long-in-the-works Zolar X film hit a few meteors when he had a falling out with the woman who came aboard as producer (and subsequently began dressing like an alien, married Ygarr, and joined the band under the name Raidia Visual-X). Everything has since been worked out, and postproduction was being completed at this writing, including prison-recorded Zenith voiceovers. The Zenith-free Zolar X reformed, toured and recorded, releasing two albums of new material that made limited impact. Their big break fizzled when a much-touted appearance on *The Next Great American Band*, a rock band competition reality show from the producers of *American Idol*, was less than stellar. Though Zolar X appeared in all promotional material for the show, they were used as a punch line in the premiere episode, playing less than a minute before Simon Cowell–wannabe judges began insulting them. Undeterred, Ygarr is looking toward the future. On the band's MySpace page, he has a note reading "Upon his release from the Capian Zell *(prison)* in 2012, the Mechanical Mediator Model 12000 will take center stage."

Suggested Listening, Viewing, Surfing

Though we hope *Roctober* readers get their fingers dirty at used record shops, thrift stores, garage sales (and, in moderation, eBay) making terms such as *out of print* and *reissue* meaningless, for those of you with actual lives here is a guide to relatively easy-to-find examples of the work discussed in these pages.

Oscar Brown Jr.

Unjustly, but fortunately for you, Mr. Brown's LPs do not command collector's prices, and can be obtained quite easily, but for the digitally minded there have been CD reissues of most of his work, including a series of discs from the Collectables reissue label (www.oldies.com). His collaboration with Max Roach, *We Insist! Freedom Now Suite*, has been reissued a few times in Europe over the last decade on CD and vinyl. Collections of his *Jazz Scene USA* TV program on DVD are currently out of print, but the finest document on Mr. Brown's life, donnie l. betts's documentary, is available on DVD directly from the filmmaker at www.musicismylife .info.

Guy Chookoorian

Though his classic 78s and 45s sometimes appear on eBay, the best way to find Chookoorian's work is on CDBaby.com, where you can purchase compilations of classic tracks, issued on his own Lightning Records, as well as CDs by his son Arshag.

David Allan Coe

For Coe virgins, Sony's *The Essential David Allan Coe* is as good as any starting point. Virtually all his recordings, including his rare early LPs and self-issued "underground" albums, are on CD (some as "official bootlegs," whatever that means) or available for download. His website is www .officialdavidallancoe.com (www.davidallancoe.com, is not associated with the artist, and is a bit too white power–friendly for most tastes), but the way to get the best, rarest, weirdest books, CDs, shirts, audiobooks, and knickknacks is at the merch table of the perennially touring troubadour.

Sugar Pie DeSanto

Although her Chess singles were spectacular, we would not recommend paying sky-high collector prices for her ultrarare Chess LP, as it is more subdued and romantic than her ass-kicking signature songs, which have been collected on a number of great compilations, including *Go Go Power — The Complete Chess Singles 1961–1966* (Kent, 2009). Her recent recordings are all available at her label's website, www.jasmanrecords.com. For a real treat check out the *American Folk-Blues Festival: The British Tours 1963–1966* DVD (Hip-O, 2007), featuring live performances by Sugar on a legendary tour with Chess Records all-stars.

The Fast

The Best of the Fast on the Canadian power pop label Bullseye is still available on Amazon. Although the great 1995 CD compilation *Male Stripper: The Best of Man 2 Man*, appears to be out of print (one online buyer complains that the copy he recently ordered was a CD-R), the spectacular two-disc remastered *Male Stripper: Hits and Rarities* (Sanctuary Records, 2007) is available as an import. Paul Zone has also made most of the band's recordings, including his brother Armand's incredibly rare Ozone LP, available on iTunes. In 2009 After Hours Cinema (www.AfterHoursCinema.com) released *Grindhouse Double Feature: Punk Rock/Pleasure Palace*, a DVD featuring a 1977 hard-boiled detective-themed porn film that was retooled as a (theoretically) more mainstream exploitation film in 1978 by having the hard-core sex scenes removed (though the film still features more flaccid and semierect penises than any detective movie in cinema history) and adding a subplot in which the detective meets informants at Max's Kansas City. At the legendary club, live songs are performed by the Fast, the Squirrels, Spicy Bits, and the Stilettos. The Fast performances are breathtaking, and the band's songs are also used as incidental music throughout the film. A lo-rez version of their only official video is included as a DVD bonus.

The Good Rats

Peppi Marchello has acquired the rights to all of the band's releases, and CD versions of every album go in and out of print (check the band's website for availability, www.goodrats.com). Of course, if you have a record (or 8-track) player, eBay usually has all their original releases, other than the debut, for $3–$12 each (the '60s LP may run you $20). The band's website also features info on the Ratstock campsite festival, a list of cover songs they perform (including songs by the White Stripes, Weezer, and Journey), and a template of a letter for you to send to your local bar so they will book the Good Rats.

Billy Lee Riley

Billy has a number of relatively recent CDs of new and classic material, and most are worth hearing. Undoubtedly, www.rockabilly.net is the best source for info on where to get his "swag," and it features extensive excerpts from his proposed autobiography. But if money is no object, rockabilly fans are always wise to consider Bear Family (www.bear-family.de), the German reissue label that has some great Riley compilations, including *Classic Recordings 1956–1960*, and also a series of CD box sets reissuing the entire Sun singles collection.

Sam the Sham

Samudio has his own website, www.samthesham.com, where he sells his self-released albums from the last two decades, as well as photos and embroidered Sam the Sham berets. Probably your best bet for a retrospective CD is Collectables' *Wooly Bully / Lil' Red Riding Hood*, reissuing the first two LPs. Unfortunately, Rhino's excellent *Pharaohization* is out of print, and Island Records' *20th Century Masters* CD skews toward novelty songs. However, a very nice tribute to the breadth and flavor of Sam's music is Norton's excellent album *Turban Renewal*, featuring Sam the Sham cover versions by Hasil Adkins, Ben Vaughn, Untamed Youth, the Lyres, and many more.

The Treniers

In 2010 Germany's Bear Family label (www.bear-family.de) released a fine compilation, *Rock*, and the excellent out-of-print Treniers CD compilation *They Rock! They Roll! They Swing!* has been reissued by Collectables with much uglier artwork, but nine great bonus tracks. Two of their classic sixties live albums (sold mostly at shows) have been reissued on CD under the title *The Hoss Allen Sessions* (Night Train, 2005). On video their classic appearance in *The Girl Can't Help It* is available in the box set *The Jayne Mansfield Collection* (Fox, 2006), and *Don't Knock the Rock* was issued on DVD by Sony in 2007. Passport Video released a collection of the Dean Martin and Jerry Lewis *Colgate Comedy Hour* episodes, including the stunning Treniers' performance, but considering the limitations of the kinescope master version, you are not missing much watching this on YouTube.

Zolar X

Though the stardate for the documentary *Starmen on Sunset* release has not been set, both their compilation reissue CD and comeback album are still available on vinyl and CD (www.alternativetentacles.com). The official band website is www.zolarx.com. Their next scheduled release is their frontman . . . from prison.

Steve Albini is a recording engineer and music fan from Chicago, Illinois.

Ben Austen is a contributing editor to *Harper's Magazine*, a contributor to the *Wall Street Journal* and the *Atlantic*, and a White Sox fan.

Jake Austen is the editor of *Roctober* magazine, produces the cable-access children's television show *Chic-A-Go-Go*, and has written for such monosyllabic-titled magazines as *Heeb*, *Vice*, *Spin*, and *Zisk*. He is the author of *TV-a-Go-Go* (Chicago Review Press) and the coauthor of the forthcoming *Darkest America* (Norton).

John Battles is a writer, musician, and artist based in Chicago. He has been with *Roctober* for over fifteen years, and has written for *Bad Trip*, *Psychotronic Video*, *Cool and Strange Music*, *Black to Comm*, and others.

Bosco is a sleaze merchant of the highest (lowest?) caliber who spends most of his life drinking rum, smoking cigars, and tracking down pornography of the most perverse sorts to disperse to the masses.

Ken Burke is the author of *Country Music Changed My Life* and the coauthor of *The Blue Moon Boys: The Story of Elvis Presley's Band* (Chicago Review Press). Besides *Roctober*, Burke's credits include

Blue Suede News, Brutarian, Country Standard Time, Goldmine, the *Contemporary Musicians* series of books, and the *Encyclopedia of World Biography* series.

Mike Maltese is part of the band Fortune & Maltese (and the Phabulous Pallbearers). He currently resides in Detroit as a photographer, art director, and basement musician.

Ken Mottet is jokingly known as the mayor of Chicago rockabilly. He has emceed the city's Big C Jamboree since its inception, as well as other music events throughout the Midwest. He is the host of *The Otherside*, Chicago cable's long-running music video show. And he loves his wife and his art deco house very much.

King Merinuk is the only underground cartoonist to emerge to date from the backwoods hamlet of Lundar, Manitoba. He has designed more than one hundred LP/CD/7" sleeves for primitive noisy combos from around the world. Also to his dubious credit are innumerable gig posters and illustrations for oddball publications worldwide. He wishes he had more time for painting and drawing comics. He likes rock 'n' roll, monster movies, and nice cold beer. Enjoy his virtual museum at http://intherubberroom .blogspot.com.

Jonathan Poletti is a poet and independent scholar, living in Winston-Salem, North Carolina, USA, Planet Earth (regrettably). He enjoys gardening and nervous collapses.

James Porter is a Chicago-based writer who has written about roots-music legends for *Roctober, Blues Revue, Time Out Chicago, New City,* and *Blender*. Alongside John Ciba he DJs old soul 45s in clubs as the East of Edens Soul Express. He is currently working on a book about obscure African American rock 'n' rollers.

"Colonel" Dan Sorenson first hit the big time when his picture ran in *Famous Monsters of Filmland* magazine. His work as a promoter and band manager in Chicago has put him in the good graces of many true music legends.

Jacqueline Stewart is an associate professor of radio/television/film at Northwestern University, and the author of *Migrating to the Movies* (University of California Press). She coproduces and directs *Chic-A-Go-Go* and runs the South Side Home Movie Project archive.

Jake Austen is an independent music writer and the editor of *Roctober* magazine. He is the author of *TV-a-Go-Go: Rock on TV from American Bandstand to American Idol* (2005) and the editor of *A Friendly Game of Poker: 52 Takes on the Neighborhood Game* (2003).

Library of Congress Cataloging-in-Publication Data

Flying saucers rock 'n' roll : conversations with unjustly obscure rock 'n' soul eccentrics / Jake Austen, editor.
p. cm. — (Refiguring American music)
Includes bibliographical references and index.
ISBN 978-0-8223-4837-5 (cloth : alk. paper)
ISBN 978-0-8223-4849-8 (pbk. : alk. paper)
1. Rock music—United States—History and criticism.
2. Rock musicians—United States—Interviews.
3. Popular culture—United States—History—20th century.
I. Austen, Jake.
II. Series: Refiguring American music.
ML3534.3.F595 2011
781.6609—dc22
2011006305